Through the Lens
of the Reader

SUNY SERIES, THE MARGINS OF LITERATURE

MIHAI I. SPARIOSU, EDITOR

Through the Lens of the Reader

Explorations of European Narrative

Lilian R. Furst

State University of New York Press

Published by
State University of New York Press, Albany

For information, address State University of New York
Press, State University Plaza, Albany, N.Y. 12246

Production by Diane Ganeles
Marketing by Dana Yanulavich

Library of Congress Cataloging-in-Publication Data

Furst, Lilian R.
    Through the lens of the reader : explorations of European
narrative / Lilian R. Furst.
        p.   cm. — (SUNY series, the margins of literature)
    Includes bibliographical references (p.   ) and index.
    ISBN 0-7914-0807-8 (CH : acid-free). — ISBN 0-7914-0808-6 (PB :
acid-free)
        1. European fiction—History and criticism. 2. Narration
(Rhetoric) 3. Reader-response criticism. 4. Books and reading.
I. Title. II. Series: SUNY series, margins of literature.
PN3491.F87   1991
809.3'0094—dc20   90-19546
                                                           CIP

10   9   8   7   6   5   4   3   2   1

But in reading great literature I become a thousand men and yet remain myself. Like a night sky in the Greek poem, I see with a myriad eyes, but it is still I who see.

—C. S. Lewis

Contents

vii

viii   *Contents*

Acknowledgments

Earlier versions of some of the chapters have appeared elsewhere, and I acknowledge with gratitude permissions to reprint as follows:

"Goethe's *Italienische Reise* in its European Context" in *Goethe in Italy, 1786–1986*. Ed. Gerhart Hoffmeister. Amsterdam: Editions Rodopi, 1988.

"'Paris Change!': Perception and Narration" in *Essays in European Literature, for Walter Strauss*. Ed. Alice Benston and Marshall C. Olds. Studies in Twentieth Century Literature Monographs, Manhattan, KS, 1990.

"Reading 'Nasty' Great Books" in *The Hospitable Canon*. Ed. Virgil P. Nemoianu and Robert Royal. Amsterdam: Benjamins, 1991.

"Reading Kleist and Kafka" in *Journal of English and Germanic Philology* 84, 3 (1985).

"Realism and its 'code of accreditation'" in *Comparative Literature Studies* 25, 2 (1988).

In Lieu of a Theory

The chapters in this book are to some extent conjoined by their common generic and temporal parameters. They all focus on major European narratives from the late eighteenth to the early twentieth centuries. The authors analyzed include Goethe, Chateaubriand, Stendhal, Smollett, Hazlitt, Kleist, Balzac, Flaubert, Zola, George Eliot, Henry James, Thomas Mann, Rilke, and Kafka. This is a large spectrum, and it also comprises different kinds of writing: travel descriptions, the singular stories of Kleist and Kafka, and the great central nineteenth century tradition of realism.

Beyond this admittedly rather capacious commonality of genre and period, the chapters share something ultimately of greater importance: a style of reading. I use the word 'style' deliberately for I would not wish to lay claim to anything as definitive — or as rigid — as a theory or method. My emphasis is, on the contrary, on flexibility of approach, on the essential need for readers to heed and to adapt to the demands projected by each text in all its individuality. At times, as in the case of Kleist and Kafka, the signals may be mixed or contradictory, but that in itself is a vital guide to the appropriate reading strategies. To follow the promptings of the text does not entail a neatly homologous set of readings, where everything is made to fit into a pattern, as was the ideal of the New Criticism. Where harmony predominates, as in Goethe's travel writing, it should be recognized. On the other hand, where dissonances and conflicts are latent, as in many of the texts I work with, they have to be openly confronted as such and their purpose in the disposition of the work as well as their implications for our readings taken into account. To do so is not only to read according to the text's own projections, but also to respect its integrity as an aesthetic artifact.

For my title I have chosen the image of the lens. The lens is, literally, an essential part of a creature's means for perceiving and forming intelli-

1

gible images. Manufactured, it is, according to the *Oxford English Dictionary*, "a piece of glass or crystal cut or ground so as to affect in various ways the rays of light and modify vision." A precisely ground or molded piece of glass or plastic, or other transparent material, a lens has opposite surfaces, either or both of which are curved, by means of which light rays are refracted so that they converge or diverge to form an image. The dual, but not antagonistic qualities of a lens are its simultaneous transparency and capacity to effect modification of the image. In this twofold action it has a metaphorical application to the process of reading.

The transparency of the lens suggests readers' endeavors to understand the text by seeing into its workings. Its internal laws, patterns, and connections must be uncovered in an act of vision willing to steep itself in the medium, the words, allusions, configurations, and forms that animate the text. This attempt to identify the means used by the text and to grasp their intrinsic function within its economy is the readers' central responsibility. Yet they can only embark on this task through their own lens, which is bound to have certain peculiarities since we each bring different backgrounds of experience and associations to bear on the text under scrutiny. So each reader's lens is liable to make modifications, as they lie in its nature, but such modifications must not be allowed to assume the proportions of encroachments or distortions imposed by the lens on the text.

Such a conception of reading as a pragmatic procedure envisages the readers' lens as a filter through which the text is constructed. That is the purport of my epigraph: "But in reading great literature, I become a thousand men and yet remain myself. Like a night sky in the Greek poem, I see with a myriad eyes, but it is still I who see."[1] The text is indeed, as Wolfgang Iser insists,[2] given actuality by readers; however, that must be done not by an imperious reader asserting power over the text, but by a considerate reader inclined to submit to the signals emitted by the text and prepared to pay scrupulous attention to its linguistic and narrational characteristics. This constitutes, therefore, a model of co-operation between text and readers, in which the text retains its primacy as the given postulate while readers are the agents of its realization.

This is not to deny the individuality of readings, much less the possibility of multiple readings, all of which may be granted validity. But it is to limit the range of acceptable readings, or at least to draw a distinction between those that are purely personal, stemming from quirks in a particular reader's lens, and those that command a wider consensus. One way to draw such a distinction is to clarify the difference between public and private associations to words. The public ones devolve from domains accessible and available to all readers; they may be as varied as the Bible, mythology, other literary or artistic texts, and popular culture.

Apple, for instance, may conjure up a computer to many nowadays; or it may suggest health through the resonance of the proverb, "An apple a day keeps the doctor away"; alternatively, it may bring temptation to mind through recall of the Biblical story of Adam and Eve. To me apple denotes, curiously, security and prosperity. During my childhood days as an impoverished and endangered illegal refugee in Belgium, I so longed for apples, an expensive luxury in our marginal situation, that my parents feared I would push in the storefront through the intensity of my gaze, my head pressed to the window. That signification still has so much force for me today that I have a compulsion always to keep an ample stock of apples in my house, and to carry some whenever I travel, heavy though they are. But as a reader I have the obligation to discriminate between a purely personal mythology such as mine in regard to apples, and the public ones shared by the vast majority of readers and ready to be mobilized consensually in the construction of a text. My personal associations to apples can certainly not be dismissed as 'wrong.' On the other hand, they are not likely to be comprehensible to other readers without categoric explanations. It is therefore important to recognize that in reading "apple" as emblematic of prosperity and security I am drawing on a specialized private order of associations, legitimate for myself, but wholly devoid of that meaning for other readers. Insofar as they reach beyond the norms common to our culture, idiosyncratic readings must be avowed as deviant, although that term should not be taken as having judgmental connotations.

To differentiate consciously between private and public associations also affords the possibility of steering through the by now traditional polarity between objective and subjective criticism. The New Criticism, in its quest for rigor and a quasi-scientific exactitude, posited objectivity as its cardinal rule. In reaction against the loosely effusive commentaries of some of their predecessors, the New Critics demanded attention to the nature of the object rather than to its effects on the subject. In many respects their close scrutiny of the text itself was salutary, although it could not in the long run avoid the danger of a repetitive schematization bordering on rigidity.

The formalism of New Criticism found its rebuttal in the more recent school of subjective criticism, which places reader response at the fulcrum of the interpretive enterprise. Norman Holland in *Five Readers Reading* provides the experimental basis for the subjective approach, while David Bleich in *Subjective Criticism* offers a more theoretical rationale. Holland's five readers are described as "good-natured, easygoing, dapper Sam," "Saul, a scholarly type, ... circumspect," "Shep, a rebel and a radical," "Sebastian, sophisticated, sardonic, somewhat cynical, a lapsed Catholic with aspirations toward aristocracy," and "Sandra, a tall, very attractive woman, gentle and subdued in her manner."[3] As seen through the lens of these untrained, undisciplined, free associating readers: "The text almost vanishes in the astonishing variability of different readers' re-creation of it," becoming instead "a pre-text for readers' creativity."[4] Therein precisely lies the objection to criticism subjective to this degree: the text vanishes. The fact that a figure in the story reminds a reader of his or her aunt Julia, or that another reader strongly identifies with or recoils from a certain protagonist may be of some interest for the psychology of those readers, but as far as the construction of the text goes, it holds absolutely nothing.

Even in Bleich's more cerebral version, the aesthetic dimension of the text is lost when, to take his example, Michaelangelo's *Moses* is seen as "no longer a block of stone in the shape of a seated man, but ... a symbolic representation of something."[5] If "the block of stone" is the objective perception, and the "symbolic representation" the subjective one, where is the space necessary to discern the patterns and shapes governing the sculpture's aesthetic configuration? And it is its aesthetic configuration, not its material substance ("a block of stone") nor even its message as interpreted by viewers ("symbolic representation") that makes it a work of art of unending fascination.

Only by keeping the focus sharply on the text as a work of art can justice be done to its special qualities and role in the world. Of course it can be seen only through the lens of the reader, and of course each reader modifies to some degree. The particularity of each lens cannot, indeed should not be eliminated, yet it must remain subservient to the directives of the text. Readers will naturally each have their private associations, but such musings are irrelevant to the central concern of literary criticism, which is to attain a deeper understanding of the aesthetic disposition of the text—what in fact makes it a work of art that rewards rereading and rereading.

Reading of this kind is essentially a comparative act. Texts may be reread from a variety of perspectives, in differing contexts and frames, in light of other texts that are in some way complementary either through parallelism or contrast or a conjunction of the two. These statements best summarize my style of reading in this volume. In addressing a range of European narratives from the eighteenth to the twentieth centuries, I use a predominantly reader-oriented approach. Reader-oriented is to be distinguished from reader response, which is subjective in its premises, whereas reader orientation denotes an exploration of the cognitive processes on readers' part whereby they construct the text in accordance with the signals it projects.[6] By this means relationships both within and among texts can be evinced so that the complex house of fiction is more clearly illuminated.

Although the readers' lens is ultimately the operative one, other lenses too play their part. That is the volume's underlying theme. One of the lenses is always that of the narrator, presenting its view. Another is that of the protagonists as they envisage their situation within the realm of the fiction. Often readers are placed at such an angle as to see either with the narrator or the protagonists, or at times with both, alternately or even simultaneously. These are the focal points I want to scrutinize in order to discover how the readers' lens is fashioned by the imperatives of the text. This consideration unifies the three parts of the volume.

The first part, "Images Through the Lens," is the most diversified. The opening essay, "Goethe's *Italienische Reise* in its European Context" analyzes Goethe's reading of Italy as compared to that of his near contemporaries, Chateaubriand, Stendhal, Smollett, and Hazlitt, but also our reading of their readings. The central element of the second chapter, "'Paris change!' Perception and Narration," is again a geographic location, albeit a city, not a country. The readers here are internal to the fiction: Rastignac in Balzac's *Le Père Goriot*, Gervaise in Zola's *L'Assommoir*, and the title figure of Rilke's *Die Aufzeichnungen des Malte Laurids Brigge* are all trying to decipher Paris just as we construe their efforts to do so. The third piece, "Reading 'Nasty' Great Books," faces the problem of the images formed through the lens of relatively inexperienced, undergraduate readers, using Flaubert's *Madame Bovary* and Thomas Mann's *Der Tod in Venedig* as examples. As with the travelers and the newcomers to Paris, the purpose is to read the students' readings.

The second part, "Through Green Spectacles," is devoted to Kleist, taking its title from the famous passage in his letter to his fiancée of 22 March 1801. Kleist's hypothesis that we may all be seeing the world through green spectacles offers an apt avenue of access to his narratives. The chiasmus of protagonists' and readers' changing assent and resistance is the topic of the first of these three Kleist essays. It takes up *Der Tod in Venedig* again, but this time places it beside Kleist's *Die Marquise von O—*. Readers' resistance, the focus of "Reading 'Nasty' Great Books," is re-examined here, but now set off against the protagonists' growing assent. *Die Marquise von O—* is then discussed in greater detail in the following chapter to show how the multiplicity of lenses through which the situation is registered internally creates the ironies that confuse and thwart readers. The thwarting of readers and the reasons for it are further discussed in the last piece of this middle section through a comparison of the narrative strategies in Kleist's *Das Bettelweib von Locarno* and Kafka's *Das Urteil*.

The third part, "Mirror Images?" deals with realism. In place of the customary mimetic view, the emphasis is rather on the conventions of re-

alism as a mode of writing and on the ways in which they guide readers
in their construction of the text. The first of the four chapters, "Realism
and its 'code of accreditation,'" lays the theoretical basis. The next two,
"The Game of the Name," and "Not So Long Ago: Historical Allusion in
Realist Fiction," delve more intensively into two key areas already
sketched in "Realism and its 'code of accreditation: '" the role of names
and that of historicity. Finally, "Rereading *Buddenbooks*" is a case study
which illustrates the issues raised in the three previous chapters in relation to one major text. The repetitions in the overlap between the successive chapters are a deliberate part of my approach, a shift of lens as texts
are envisaged from different angles and in differing relationships to each
other.

I want to express my gratitude to Raymond A. Prier and Mihai Spariosu for their encouragement and constructive criticism. I am also grate-
ful for the support given to me by the National Endowment for the Humanities through a fellowship at the National Humanities Center during
1988–89, when much of the first draft was written. All translations are my
own.

I

Images through the Lens

1

Goethe's *Italienische Reise* in its European Context

"A man who has not been to Italy is always conscious of an inferiority, from his not having seen what it is expected a man should see. The grand object of travelling is to see the shores of the Mediterranean."[1] In this dictum Dr. Johnson at once articulated and promoted the vogue for the Italian journey. The visit to Italy became the highlight of the Grand Tour, which began in the later eighteenth century to come more within the economic range of the educated middle class, attracting such men of letters as David Garrick, Adam Smith, John Wilkes, Hume, Gibbon, Fielding, Smollett, Sterne, Johann Caspar Goethe, Winckelmann, Heinse, and Karl Philipp Moritz, to name only a few of the most notable. Travel was stimulated at this time by the perceptible improvement in roads and inns as well as by the relative peacefulness of Europe between the end of the Seven Years War in 1763 and the outbreak of the French Revolution. The Golden Age of travel, as it has been called,[2] witnessed as its by-product an unprecedented efflorescence of travel writing of all kinds. Addison's *Remarks on Several Parts of Italy* (1705) ushered in an era in which nonfiction travel literature not only achieved a commanding popularity, but also attained literary stature as a distinctive genre with recognizable conventions of its own.[3]

Where does Goethe's *Italienische Reise (Italian Journey)* stand in the context of this emergent tradition? This is the question I am here addressing. How did Goethe read Italy, and how does his account relate to those of his predecessors and near contemporaries? In what ways does it conform to, and/or depart from the norms of travel literature of the period? In attempting to site the *Italienische Reise* in this way I am deliberately moving away from the more customary biographical approach, which has focused on its significance for Goethe's life. Its overtly autobiographical nature and its importance in Goethe's development as an artist[4]

9

has led to a certain neglect of its qualities as travel writing which I would like to counteract by reading it in its European literary context.[5]

To do this raises, however, a fundamental methodological problem. It could be described theoretically as a problem of genre. In practical terms it amounts to this: to which part or parts of the mass of later eighteenth and early nineteenth century travel writing should Goethe's *Italienische Reise* be compared? Although travel literature becomes an acknowledged genre in the course of the eighteenth century, it denotes an extremely broad category that encompasses unusually wide variations. At one end of the spectrum are the down-to-earth travel manuals, often by hack journalists; these forerunners of Baedecker sought to provide travelers with concrete information about the best routes, eating places, and accommodations, together with the most noteworthy natural and artistic sights to be seen. This type of writing left its precipitate in all travel literature; there is an instructional streak in almost every account of a journey to Italy. It is not so much the didactic intention as the quality of the writing that makes these pedestrian guidebooks so incommensurable to Goethe as to impair the worth of any comparison that might be made.

One of the first criteria in establishing parallels to the *Italienische Reise* must be that of quality. Goethe's particular characteristics as a travel writer can be understood only by comparing him to other travel writers of high literary standing. To put him alongside James Edward Smith, whose *Sketch of a Tour on the Continent* appeared in 1793, or Marianna Stark, whose *Letters from Italy* date from 1800, would simply be to load the evidence in such a way as to pre-empt the banal conclusion that Goethe was a superior writer. I have therefore sought out contemporaneous accounts of a journey to Italy by major writers. Out of considerations of genre, images of Italy in such fictions as Byron's *Childe Harold's Pilgrimage* (1812 – 18) or Madame de Staël's *Corinne, ou l'Italie* (1807) have also been excluded because their representation of Italy is secondary to a narrational purpose and embedded in a fictional context. From the point of view of genre, the works most congruent to the *Italienische Reise* are Smollett's *Travels Through France and Italy* (1776), Stendhal's *Rome, Naples et Florence* (1817), Hazlitt's *Notes of a Journey Through France and Italy* (1826), and Chateaubriand's *Voyage en Italie* (1827). These works are in consonance with the *Italienische Reise* in three crucial respects: qualitatively, as works by writers of international renown; thematically, as primary accounts of journeys to Italy; and generically, as first person reports poised between the informational and the fictional.

That is the theoretical rationale of my comparison. Its format will be a juxtaposition of certain key features of these five texts. After a brief review of the routes followed, I want to focus on the modes of narrative organization and the choice of material, paying special attention to the perception of the past. In examining these facets, my ulterior agenda is to examine the relationship of the self to the other, or, as the eighteenth century would call it, the balance between reflection and observation. This was becoming a salient issue by Goethe's time. The interest — and, of course, the precariousness — of travel writing stems from the delicate equipoise it has to maintain between the perhaps conflicting demands of the self and the other. The growing cult of the self and of personal sensibility could be seen as a threat, or at least as an erosion, of the conventions of travel writing as they had crystallized in the course of the eighteenth century. For background I want to outline those conventions as the norm that formed the framework for the individual writer.

It was convention, rather than personal wishes or taste, that determined both the writer's actions and his descriptions, dictating the routes to be followed and the sights to be seen as well as the appropriate mode for reporting on them. The itinerary[6] through Italy was more or less prescribed, with a marked preference for the cities over the country. Turin, Milan, Venice, Bologna, Florence, Rome, and Naples were the standard objectives, with Rome as the Mecca for every intellectual traveler. Rome was revered in the later eighteenth century as the very embodiment of Classical antiquity; however, the dearth of a sense for the picturesque in either nature or art resulted in a large measure of indifference to both the Middle Ages and the early Renaissance. Nevertheless, it was curiosity about Italy's past and heritage that inspired most travel writing.

Convention shaped, too, the form of the travel description; which was expected to conform to a certain code that became increasingly well defined with the emergence of travel writing as a genre, even while that code was subject to a continual process of modification. As a sense of species came to be central to eighteenth century literary criticism, readers' understanding depended heavily on their awareness of the author's implied intentions and of the accepted objectives of the form in use. So, for instance, one of the cardinal criteria for the literariness of travel writing was its organization into a narrative, as opposed to a mere dissertation. The two common modes of narrative disposition were the journal format, preferred by Addison and thus of exemplary significance, and the arrangement in letters. But once such a literary organization was instituted, it immediately created a difficulty for travel writing through the tendency to confluence with the novel, particularly with the rise to preeminence of the epistolary novel.[7] So, while the narrative organization in a travel book provided entertainment and continuity, it could also become problematical as soon as it began to blur the distinctions between fiction and non-fiction. As, of course, it was bound to do. The travel writer's unenviable task was to steer the tricky course midway between the reliable but dull dissertation and the vivid but unreliable fictionalization. Likewise, in style the travel account had to aim at a middle range between the solidity of studied discourse and the freedom of colloquial conversation. The underlying tensions inherent in the genre are summarized in the phrase which the eighteenth century itself coined to encapsulate the purpose of travel writing: "pleasurable instruction," which points tellingly to the innate pull between the documentary and the aesthetic, between the obligations of the traveler and those of the writer.

This dichotomy coincides with another that became more and more vexing as the eighteenth century moved into the nineteenth. This second dilemma, which is in effect a restatement of the first in different terms, is named in the title of Hester Lynch Piozzi's book, *Observations and Reflections made in the course of a Journey through France, Italy, and Germany* (1789). Here are those two key words, "observations" and "reflections." It is important to notice that "observations" take priority over "reflections," and that the assumption made is of an easy compatibility between these elements. They were indeed closely linked insofar as "observations" meant specific descriptions of things seen during travels, while "reflections" denoted the philosophical, aesthetic, moral or political thoughts occasioned by those sights. The ratio between the two could vary greatly; what is more, it changed over the years toward a growing receptivity to the writer's "reflections." The interplay between observation and reflection is so central to travel writing because it subsumes another more radical and significant polarity, that between other and self.

This also was undergoing a momentous shift between the mid-eighteenth and the early nineteenth century. The previous convention that a travel writer must not speak about himself or herself was attenuated to such an extent that travelers became as much poets as geographers. In part this was an outcome of the search for novelty in travel writing, which brought new attention to more artistic and ornamental topics. But in large measure it must be recognized as a concomitant and yet another manifestation of the wider drift of sensibility toward the primacy of the individual, the personal, and ultimately the subjective perception. While many reviewers continued to take exception to the autobiographical, to the focus on the traveler's response instead of on description of the actual object, the advent of the so-called 'picturesque' traveler by the closing years of the century confirmed a change of emphasis whose beginnings can be traced back to the enormous impact of Sterne's *Sentimental Journey* (1768). Sterne's fictional technique of emotional self-dramatization impinged on authentic travel accounts to so marked a degree that they came to resemble memoirs, drawing increasingly on the evidence of the writer's own apprehensions rather than on appeals to anterior authorities.

This trend was further fostered by the development of travel itself. As travelers explored areas not charted by their predecessors, such as Italy south of Naples and Sicily, they had to rely first and foremost on their own findings and reactions. Moreover, in order to picture these unfamiliar regions to their readers, they tended to resort to a more elaborate, consciously literary style embellished by imagery associated rather with creative than with reportorial writing. The boundaries between travel writing and fiction had, therefore, become quite porous by the time of Goethe's journey to Italy. Travel literature in fact stood at the crossroads between its traditional allegiance to past models and to external sights presented by a self-effacing observer and its modern privileging of the predilections and responses of an at least partially fictionalized persona.

After this brief survey of the scene at large, let me return to my initial question: where does Goethe's *Italienische Reise* stand within this context? Goethe's own wide familiarity with travel writing has been amply documented by Arthur G. Schultz in an article entitled "Goethe and the Literature of Travel."[8] Over thirteen per cent of Goethe's reading, Schultz argues, citing the evidence of his borrowings from the Weimar library, falls into the category of travel books (457–8). Goethe also had a number of precedents close to home, including his father's *Viaggio per l'Italia*,[9] a collection of forty-two letters covering one thousand and ninety-six quarto pages about his journey in 1739–40, Karl Philip Moritz's *Reise eines Deutschen in Italien in den Jahren 1786–88 (A German's Journey in Italy 1786–88)*, published in 1792–93,[10] Heinse's letters about his Italian journey of 1780–83,[11] and Winckelmann's letters[12] of 1756–57, which Goethe mentions with warm approval while himself in Rome. On the other hand, as an avowed "Todtfeind von Wortschällen"[13] ("arch enemy of verbal outpourings"), he frowns on the effusive sentimentality of Sterne and his imitators. This is very much in keeping with his skeptical reserve toward not only the romantic, but to extremes of any kind. Consequently Goethe maintains a critical detachment from certain popular trends of travel writing of his day, preferring to align himself in a conservative stance more with the older traditions of the genre than with recent innovations.

In his route, too, Goethe conforms largely to the accepted itinerary, though with some notable exceptions. Coming from Germany, he does not enter Italy by either of the gateways customary for British and French travelers: Turin, taken by Chateaubriand and Hazlitt, or the coastal water access via Nice and Genoa adopted by Smollett. Instead, his arrival is through the spectacular scenery of the Brenner Pass. Crossing the Alps straight up and over, so to speak, makes him experience in an immediate, physical way the striking contrast between North and South. The difference is expressed not just in the expected climatic terms — rainy greyness as against blue skies and sunshine — but, significantly, also in terms of fruitfulness as Goethe comments again and again on the prodigious fertility of the North Italian plain, especially the lusciousness of the peaches, the grapes, and above all the figs, for which he has hankered. This connection from the outset between Italy and abundant productivity, metaphorically as well as literally, is a cardinal element in Goethe's image of Italy. After the Brenner and Bolzano, he joins the typical Grand Tour route through Verona, Vincenza, Padua, Venice, Ferrara, Bologna, and Perugia, all of which he visits in barely two months. The glaring omission is Florence, which he decides on the spur of the moment to bypass in order to reach more quickly his primary goal, Rome. His impatience to get to Rome explains his hasty trajectory through the Northern towns. In his fascination with Rome, which finds expression in his extended stay there, he is true to the late eighteenth century pattern, although he gives greater rein to personal preferences than most other travelers. Goethe clearly asserts his individuality in his foray into the deep South beyond Naples, the wonted limit of even enterprising tourists. To venture as far as Sicily was quite a rarity.[14] Goethe's somewhat idiosyncratic progression through Italy may be taken as emblematic of his tendency to follow the dominant paradigm of his day, while at the same time modifying it at will to suit his own inclinations. He allows himself to be guided, but not dictated, by conventions, and he departs from them without hesitation to follow his own desires.

This same blend of conformity and individuality typifies the narrative organization of the *Italienische Reise*. Given the choice between the letter form popular in the eighteenth century and the journal favored by the romantics, most travelers opt fairly unequivocally for the one or the other in outer presentation as well as in inner posture toward the putative audience, though the two do not always wholly coincide. Smollett, for instance, uses the letter form, opening each section with an overt address, "Dear Sir," and closing with "Yours," or "Your affectionate humble servant," or some variant on this formula. Yet despite these allocutory rituals, he shows surprisingly little audience awareness. He writes in the past tense of recently retrospective memory, switching to the continuing present for his descriptions of the sights of Italy. Chateaubriand, too, casts his *Voyage en Italie* into the mold of letters to a named personage, a Monsieur A. M. Joubert, and he intersperses his report, which is entirely in the present tense, with such turns as "mon cher ami"[15] ("my dear friend") to underscore the directness of the writer-reader relationship. Stendhal, on the other hand, chooses the journal format, with dated entries that are at times more like notes than a cohesive account. He writes in the present or the present past in a chatty manner that postulates an intimate rapport with his audience. Hazlitt's writing is the opposite to Stendhal's in its formality and impersonality. His *Notes of a Journey through France and Italy* is arranged in chapters, without dates, and with a prevalence of the historic past tense.

To turn from these works to Goethe's *Italienische Reise* is to realize immediately the complexity of its narrative organization. Outwardly a dated journal, like Stendhal's, it nonetheless bears transparent traces of its origins as letters to his friends in Weimar in its frequent personal invocations, some in the singular, as to an individual, some in the plural, as to a group, and in other vestiges of correspondence in tone and in such formulations as "So viel für diesmal" (187; "That's all for this time"), or "Einen hübschen geschnittenen Stein lege ich bei" (172; "I am enclosing a prettily cut stone").

But Goethe's manifest allegiance to his audience is partnered by a very pronounced and continuing dual consciousness of himself: as an experiencing figure and as a creating persona. This is the feature that most sharply distinguishes his writing from that of any of his contemporaries. The effect of this dualistic consciousness of self is a kind of *déboublement*. This doubling through the extrapolation of a writing self alongside the traveling and experiencing self has momentous implications for the *Italienische Reise*. It leads to an authorial presence quite different from that animating comparable travel accounts. Precisely because Goethe envisages himself primarily as a writer, he does not engage in the sort of dramatization of his personality prevalent — and problematical — in the work of his peers.

The persona of the traveler commonly serves to lend unity to the episodes of the journey, and to forge links between its various parts. However, the traveler's self-dramatization can easily become more than a heuristic device, and begin to intrude on, or indeed overshadow the narrative itself. This is certainly the case with Smollett, who delights in projecting himself as the splenetic traveler, and also, though to a somewhat lesser extent, with Chateaubriand, the itinerant melancholic, and with Stendhal, the savvy and gossipy man-about-Italy. Taken to extremes, as in Sterne's *Sentimental Journey*, the traveler's quirky personality and responses may wholly displace the travel account. That, indeed, was one of the points of Sterne's satire; he was fully aware of the dangers lurking in what would today be called 'the cult of personality,' and in his *Sentimental Journey* he debunks Smollett and his ilk.

On this score Goethe is in concurrence with Sterne. The distance that he interjects in the *Italienische Reise* between the traveler and the writer may well stem in part from the temporal gap between his journey and its final literary format, but more fundamentally it testifies to Goethe's recoil from the contemporary tendency to cultivate an idiosyncratic self that is allowed to dominate the discourse. As a result of his eschewal of an inflated role for the persona of the traveler, the orientation of the *Italienische Reise*, despite its individualistic tone and flavor, remains firmly set toward the object of contemplation and the audience.

The intercalation of the writing self has other important ramifications. It endows the account of travel with a secondary enframing dimension. In this respect the *Italiensiche Reise* is without parallel in the travel writing of the period. Chateaubriand may mention with pride occasions where he is recongized as a poet; Goethe, on the contrary, strives for the utmost anonymity, resorting even to the pseudonym Herr Müller. But while Chateaubriand presents himself as a writer, it is Goethe who truly functions as such. So the *Italiensiche Reise* transcends its origins as a travel record and comes to possess an independent existence as a cohesively organized aesthetic artifact. Nowhere is this more apparent than in its dense web of interlaced motifs and images. I have already mentioned fruitfulness as one such metaphoric complex. Allied to it are the multiple vitalistic images of rebirth, renewal, renaissance, spring, movement, and life that amount to an acquiescence in temporality, but simultaneously also to an affirmation of human beings' capacity to surmount their limits. So while most travel literature depends for its integration solely on the voice and personality of the narrating traveler, in the case of the *Italienische Reise* there is in addition an artistic wholeness that devolves from its shaping by Goethe's creative imagination. Thus it is, as its narrative organization reveals, both a distinctly personal account and an autonomous literary construct obedient to its own internal laws. The traveler Goethe is a manifest presence, but it is the writer Goethe who is in command of the discourse.

I have begun my attempt to contextualize the *Italienische Reise* with an analysis of its narrative organization because this represents in microcosm a paradigm of the work's salient characteristics. The doubleness inherent in the mode of presentation has its complement in the nature of Goethe's vision of Italy, which shows the same extraordinary capacity to embrace apparent opposites and synthesize them into a highly distinctive and harmonious whole. The polarity here is between Italy's past and her present, which Goethe is able to perceive as linked parts of a grandiose continuum rather than as the discrete entities that they seem to his contemporaries. Whereas every other late eighteenth or early nineteenth century travel writer fixes his primary sights on either Italy's past or her present, Goethe alone constantly sees the translucence of the past in the present. His reading of Italy is, therefore, an organic, genetic, and totalizing interpretation, in contrast to the fractionalized images offered by his contemporaries. Before considering Goethe more fully from this angle, we need again to look at his contemporaries to set the context.

Smollett and Hazlitt are similar in their choice of focus and, to some extent, in their attitudes. This may be as much a matter of audience as of nationality, for both are addressing a British readership that they take to be in need of a good deal of concrete information about the present day practicalities of travel on the Continent. They provide far more circumstantial documentation about modes of conveyance, amenities (or otherwise) of inns, quality of food, and prices charged than any of their Continental counterparts. After reading Smollett, you know exactly how to set about hiring a boat and a crew to take you along the coast from Nice to Genoa, where to stay overnight, what provisions to take along, and what hazards to watch out for. On occasion Smollett points to "a necessary piece of information to those who may be inclined to follow the same route,"[16] while Hazlitt states his aim as being "to give the reader some notion of what he might expect to find in travelling the same road."[17] This foregrounding of the business of traveling is not only reminiscent of the manuals of instruction; it is also cumulatively to the detriment of the sightseeing because it seems such a hassle just to get there. Despite their earnestness and their considerable knowledgeability, both Smollett and Hazlitt make the impression of being unwilling travelers, fulfilling a distasteful obligation and finding scant pleasure in it. They give geographic and historical data with expansive accuracy, yet with a marked lack of enthusiasm so that things are not animated by any inner illumination.

Of the two Smollett is the more robust and down-to-earth, often noting specifics of climate, speech, economics, and the appearance of streets and buildings as if to assess what it would be like to live there:

> Pisa is a fine old city that strikes you with the same veneration you might feel at sight of an ancient temple which bears the marks of decay, without being absolutely delapidated. The houses are well built, the streets open, straight, and well paved; the shops well furnished; and the markets well supplied; there are some elegant palaces, designed by great masters. The churches are built with taste, and tolerably ornamented. There is a beautiful wharf of free-stone on each side of the river Arno, which runs through the city, and three bridges thrown over it, of which that in the middle is of marble, a pretty piece of architecture: but the number of inhabitants is inconsiderable; and this very circumstance gives it an air of majestic solitude, which is far from being unpleasant to a man of a contemplative state of mind. For my part, I cannot bear the tumult of a populous commercial city; and the solitude that reigns in Pisa would with me be a strong motive to choose it as a place of residence. (222)

Even this rapid survey shows Smollett's indifference to the antiquities of Italy, which he often regards with an open contempt for their inconvenience. Here is the conclusion of his comment on the Pantheon in Rome:

> the gilding of those colums is said to have cost forty thousand golden crowns: sure money was never worse laid out. Urban VIII likewise added two belfrey towers to the rotunda; and I wonder he did not cover the central hole with glass, as it must be very inconvenient to those who go to the church below, to be exposed to the rain in wet weather, which must also render it very damp and unwholesome. I visited it several times, and each time it looked more gloomy and sepulchral. (270)

No wonder that Smollett came to be the prototype of the splenetic traveler, the model for Sterne's satire of Smellfungus in his *Sentimental Journey*.

Hazlitt is more subtle than Smollett in injecting his negatively tinged reflections into his observations. His perspective is visual insofar as he concentrates on surface appearances and frequently assimilates what he sees to his prior experience of paintings. In Parma, for instance, "We saw, in a flight of steps near one of the barriers, a group of men, women, and children, that for expression, composition, and colouring rivalled any thing in painting" (205). An even more revealing example is his account of the Apennines:

> The Apennines have not the vastness nor the unity of the Alps; but are broken up into a number of abrupt projecting points, that crossing one another, and presenting new combinations as the traveler shifts his position, produce, though a less sublime and imposing, a more varied and picturesque effect. (208)

By placing the traveler vis-à-vis the scene to obtain a "picturesque effect," Hazlitt is enframing and distancing it as it is turned into a picture. So his vision achieves the opposite of the romantic absorption of the phenomena of the outer world into the psyche. Hazlitt, by contrast, dwells on the divide between himself and the other by bringing out its remoteness, its alienism, and particularly its self-contained existence as a tableau to be viewed from afar. The dryness of his descriptions, the dearth of imagery and metaphor, and his recourse to fairly pedestrian adjectives ("beautiful," "delightful," "elegant") all contribute to the overriding sense of stasis, of a deadening flatness that dulls his presentation of Italy. It is as if Hazlitt, like Smollett, were anxious to keep this foreign land at a safe remove: the stance of both signals *Noli me tangere.*

The two French writers have less in common with each other than the two British except for their assumption of a greater prior acquaintance with Italy on their readers' part. They therefore give few details about travel, less so than Goethe, and absolutely no instructive advice. Apart from that they are wholly heterogeneous. In some respects Chateaubriand's Italy is as distanced as Smollett's and Hazlitt's, though for very different reasons. It comes across as a sort of generic Italy because Chateaubriand does not ever really look closely at anything. His tendency is to a generalized survey, heavy with plurals that evoke type, not specifics. This is his introduction to Lombardy:

> Vous voyez d'abord un pays fort riche dans l'ensemble, et vous dites: "C'est bien"; mais quand vous venez à détailler les objets, l'enchantement arrive. Des prairies dont la verdure surpasse la fraîcheur et la finesse des gazons anglois, se mêlent à des champs de maïs, de riz et de froment: ceux-ci sont surmontés de vignes qui passent d'un échalais à l'autre, formant des guirlandes au-dessus des moissons: le tout est semé de mûriers, de noyers, d'orneaux, de saules, de peupliers, et arrosé de rivières et de canaux. (161–62)[18]

This passage contains a crucial clue to the entire work in that phrase: "mais quand vous venez à détailler les objets, l'enchantement arrive" ("but when you come to look at the objects in detail, enchantment overtakes you"). Chateaubriand's "enchantment" with Italy, that is to say, his emotional response, blocks his powers of observation. He makes little or no attempt at the kind of representational account for which Smollett and Hazlitt strive. Indeed, present day Italy is of no interest to him. Arriving in Rome on the eve of the St. Peter's day feast, he sees the crowds thronging the streets, but, unlike Goethe, he looks right beyond them to the remains of the past dimly silhouetted in the moonlight:

> J'ai vu l'illumination et le feu d'artifice qui annoncent pour demain la grande cérémonie consacrée au prince des Apôtres: tandis qu'on prétendoit me faire admirer un feu placé au haut du Vatican, je regardois l'effet de la lune sur le Tibre, sur ces maisons romaines, sur ces ruines qui pendent ici de toute part. (167)[19]

This scene is characteristic of Chateaubriand in its fascination with ruins and also in its absence of human figures, again in contrast to Goethe's lively and populated Rome. What Chateaubriand sees everywhere are "ruines" (178, 179, 181), "débris" (177), "décombres" (193; "rubble"), "une cour délabrée" (173; "a dilapidated courtyard"), "des pierres sépulcrales

chargées d'inscriptions mutilées" (173; "tombstones laden with muti-
lated inscriptions"), things that are "croulant" (176; "crumbling"), "des
fers rouillés ensevelis sous les mêmes décombres" (178; "rusty irons buried under the same rubble"), a "vaste cimetière des siècles avec leurs
monuments funèbres, portant la date de leur déces" (196; "vast cemetery
of the centuries with their funereal monuments bearing the date of their
decease"). The most vivid and effective metaphor for this rampant tran-
sience, for this piercing recognition that "la vie est une mort successive"
(188; "life is a successive death") is contained in the episode of the bird
that precipitates some drops of rain onto a stone, wiping out a newly pen-
cilled name just as Chateaubriand is trying to decipher it. The past, however, has no more autonomous existence in the *Voyage en Italie* than the
present; there is no sense of historical depth, of a layering of the ages, only
a flat surface littered with ruins. This surface acts as the springboard for the
traveler's reflections: "Le lieu est propre à la réflexion et à la rêverie: je re-
monte dans ma vie passée: je sens le poids du présent, et je cherche à
pénétrer mon avenir" (169; "The spot is conducive to reflection and reverie:
I go back over my past life; I feel the weight of the present, and I seek to
pierce into my future").

It is no exaggeration to claim that Italy functions as a prop for Chateaubriand, both a stimulus and a backcloth to his own feelings. The center of the stage — and I use the theatrical term deliberately — is occupied
by the self-dramatizing persona of the poet, who is the coloring filter of
experience. Not the sights of Italy, but his responses and associations
dominate the text, which is an expression of Chateaubriand's "enchantment." So the writing is lyrical and emotive, mellifluous and suggestive, es-
chewing the precision of sharp outlines in favor of the evocative vision.
The looming foreground presence of the traveler's consciousness impels
the *Voyage en Italie* toward a covert fictionalization.

Stendhal is in many ways the dramatic opposite to Chateaubriand,
although he too, as the controlling animator, towers over the entire spec-
tacle he conjures up. But wheras Chateaubriand's fixation is on the past,
Stendhal's is almost exclusively on the present. His commitment is unmistakably to the contemporary scene, to political issues, to social man-
ners (and intrigues), to the performative arts of the day. Even where he
does make an excursus into history, it tends to be hasty and perfunctory,
for his attention rapidly gravitates back to the present. Describing the ca-
thedral in Milan and sketching its history, he suddenly speculates that the
people who meet there as if by chance might be spies.[20] Always the past
is, as it were, personalized, that is to say, envisaged in terms of the individuals involved, not as a conflict of ideas or a struggle for power.

This may well be because Stendhal's engagement with contemporary concerns has an ulterior polemical motive, for the specter of Napo-

leon is never far from his mind. The implicit and at times explicit subtext of his comments on Italy is a critique of France; his admiration for Italian systems of governance is inspired in part at least by his disaffection from his native land. Writing about Italy thus becomes for Stendhal, as for Chateaubriand, a pretext; if for Chateaubriand it provides an outlet for his sensibility, for Stendhal it creates an opportunity for indirect political agitation. Both are in fact appropriating Italy for their own purposes. Stendhal, with his customary passion for masks, conceals his belligerent intentions in the persona he projects as a garrulous, well-informed, but opinionated cicerone, who delights in the anecdotal. His tone is often irreverent and ironic, his manner informal, almost conversational as he darts with mercurial energy from one social gathering to another. That summarizes the order of his priorities: Italy forms the setting, the context for *his* activity; it is the occasion for, rather than the matter of his writing. In short, with Stendhal the other has to take a back seat to the self, just as the past fades before the insistent demands of the present.

This is never the case with Goethe. He alone among all his contemporaries is able to achieve a genuine equipoise not only between self and other (because the self becomes to a certain extent an other as a writer), but also between attention to the past and to the present. The duplicative mode characteristic of the narrative organization becomes even more clearly apparent in Goethe's vision of Italy. The past and the present, as twin and complementary aspects of the same civilization, are totally inseparable for him. This symbiosis of antiquity and modernity is undoubtedly the salient feature of the *Italienische Reise*, and it is also the enabling basis for the more complete and balanced picture of Italy that emerges from this in comparison to other travel reports.

Like Stendhal, Smollett and Hazlitt, Goethe derives his initial impressions of Italy from the scenes momentarily surrounding him. In other words, his primary access is through the present. But in contrast to the critical reserve of many of his contemporaries, Goethe from the outset adopts a posture of enthusiastic openness to the sights and sounds of Italy. At the crossing of the Alps already "ging mir eine neue Welt auf" (13; "a new world opened up to me"), and by the time he reaches Bolzano on the South side of the Brenner Pass he comments: "Mir ist es jetzt nur um die sinnlichen Eindrücke zu tun die kein Buch, kein Bild gibt" (25; "I am concerned only with the sensual impressions that no book, no picture can convey"). It is indeed his animated immersion in immediate sense impressions that is most striking in his response to Italy. He delights in the fruitfulness of the Northern plain, singling out the plump figs, the olives, and the lemons as emblems of the area's natural bounty. He shows an equally spontaneous interest in the everyday life of the common people without any trace of the superciliousness or suspicion of Smollett or Hazlitt, or the snobbishness of Stendhal. It is no coincidence that Goethe's favorite adjective, "lebendig" ("lively"), is so frequently allied to the word "Volk" ("people").

This is a typical passage, the account of the street scenes in Verona:

> Auf den Plätzen ist es an Markttagen sehr voll, Gemüse und Früchte un- übersehlich, Knoblauch und Zwiebeln nach Herzenslust. Übrigens schreien, schäkern und singen sie den ganzen Tag, werfen und balgen sich, jauchzen und lachen unaufhörlich. Die milde Luft, die wohlfeile Nahrung läßt sie leicht leben. Alles, was nur kann, ist unter freiem Him- mel.
>
> Nachts geht nun das Singen und Lärmen recht an. Das Liedchen von Marlborough hört man auf allen Straßen, dann ein Hackbrett, eine Vio- line. Sie üben sich, alle Vögel mit Pfeifen nachzuahmen. Die wunderlich- sten Töne brechen überall hervor. Ein solches Übergefühl des Daseins verleiht ein mildes Klima auch der Armut, und der Schatten des Volkes scheint selbst noch ehrwürdig. (50)[21]

As in this description, so throughout the *Italienische Reise* there is a strong awareness of Italy not as a mere repository of antiquities to be con- templated, or an array of curiosities to be ogled at, but rather as a living present panorama, an actuality that has its concrete incarnation in the people. The famous evocation of the Roman carnival (404–515) as a pop- ular festival is only one of many examples where Goethe observes and records the gusto of the present day population, their appearance, their clothing, their pastimes and games, all the sundry rituals of everyday life. The vividness and dynamism of the *Italienische Reise* stems in no small measure from Goethe's affirmation of the importance of the common- place present reality as the embodiment of Italy's lasting vitality.

If the key word for Goethe's perception of Italy is "Gegenwart" ("present"), as Staiger[22] has maintained, then only because the past is for him subsumed into the present. Again, the duplicative process becomes manifest as Goethe constantly assimilates the past into the present. In viewing the remains of the past, Goethe proceeds in a manner little dif- ferent from his approach to contemporary street scenes. There is none of the self-conscious hushed awe, the estrangement we find in Smollett or Hazlitt, much less the morbid elegiac lyricism of Chateaubriand. Goethe is at once briskly down-to-earth and imaginative. His presentation of the amphiteater at Verona, "das erste bedeutende Monument der alten Zeit, das ich sehe" (40; "the first significant monument of the past that I have seen") is characteristic of his method. He begins by noting its present condition: "so gut erhalten!" ("so well preserved!"). Because of its intact state and its continuing potential as an arena, it should, in Goethe's view, be seen filled with spectators; that is to say, he promptly draws it into practical present use. In his mind's eye Goethe visualizes the amphitheater crowded with "people":

> Denn eigentlich ist so ein Amphitheater recht gemacht, dem Volk mit sich selbst zu imponieren, das Volk mit sich selbst zum besten zu haben.
>
> Wenn irgend etwas Schauwürdiges auf flacher Erden vorgeht und alles zuläuft, suchen die Hintersten auf alle mögliche Weise sich über die Vordersten zu erheben: man tritt auf Bänke, rollt Fäßer herbei, fährt mit Wagen heran, legt Bretter hinüber und herüber, besetzt einen benachbarten Hügel, und es bildet sich in der Geschwindigkeit ein Krater. (40)[21]

Here the term and concept of "the people" becomes the pivot of the description, the ball-bearing, as it were, on which the focus turns from the historic functions of the amphitheater to its latter day possibilities. There is a crucial switch to the present tense as Goethe envisages the timeless, archetypal behavior of the populace in the arena. The transformation of the ancient deserted amphitheater into a modern forum teeming with people is accomplished by a great leap of the imagination. The past is thereby endowed with a visible existence that extends into the present. Far from being relegated to some separate sector for obligatory (and tedious) study by travelers, the past is here experienced as an essential and integral facet of Italy that determines and shapes her present character in a unique way. Goethe's sympathetic understanding of the role of the past in Italy's present allows him to attain a deeper grasp of its particularity. To him it is not just another foreign land, but the site of an ancient civilization whose impact remains a palpable presence.

Goethe's perception of the Verona amphitheater is paradigmatic of his apprehension of the past in the *Italienische Reise*. A whole series of examples could be cited to illustrate the basic uniformity of his procedure. Always the underlying aim is, as he put it himself, "das alte Rom aus dem neuen herauszuklauben" (130; "to pick the old Rome out of the new"), to see the old as immanent in the new, and to bring out their reciprocal dependence. A prominent instance of this temporal fusion occurs when Goethe views Palladio's edifices in the environs of Vicenza. As with the Verona amphitheater, where he first remarks on its fine preservation, so here he is impressed "wie er durch die Gegenwart seiner Werke imponiert" (53; "how he makes an impact through the presence of his works"). The villas are not regarded as relics of a bygone age; on the contrary, what pleases Goethe above all is "den Palladio nach so viel Zeit noch immer als Polarstern und Musterbild von seinen Mitbürgern verehrt zu sehen" (57; "to see Palladio after all this time still honored by his fellow citizens as a guiding star and a model"). He underscores the unbroken continuity of the past into the present, in fact its direct relevance to the present by projecting himself into Palladio's mind in order to retrace the steps wherby he arrived at the solutions he settled on. This imaginative self-reincarnation in an historic persona has the effect once more of forging a powerful link between the past and the present by treating the past not as a closed chapter, but as an open-ended and still challenging subject.

The coalescence of past and present is further reinforced by the homogeneity of Goethe's perceptual and narrative strategies. Whether it be a present day street scene or an ancient monument, the approach is essentially the same. Goethe's dominant sense in the *Italienische Reise* is that of sight; he pointed to the primacy of the visual when he defined his aim in his *Tagebuch (Diary)* of 1786 in that much quoted phrase: "mit einem stillen feinen Auge betrachten"[24] ("to contemplate with a still, subtle gaze"). To fill his eyes with the panorama, he developed the habit of climbing a tower on his arrival in a new place so as to survey it at one sweep and from above. The vantage of the tower afforded the opportunity for a rapid orientation of the entire layout, from which the underlying order and the connections between the various disparate structures could be discerned. This tactic clearly fostered the synthesizing vision so much in evidence in the *Italienische Reise*.

The view from the tower is conducive too, to the kind of distance Goethe sought to establish between himself and the objects of his contemplation. This distancing is very different from that of Smollett and Hazlitt, whose stance denotes reluctance and resistance. Goethe, on the other hand, cultivates detachment in order to put himself into a better position for seeing. "Ich bin den ganzen Tag in einem Gespräch mit den Dingen"[25] ("I spend the whole day in conversation with things"), he notes in his *Tagebuch*. That some of those "things" were products of the contemporary world and some of antiquity does not affect Goethe's *modus operandi*. His predilection for the visual, his habit of distancing himself, and his emphasis on the object itself rather than on its effect are so consistently maintained as to minimize the distinction between the phenomena of the past and those of the present.

This tendency to amalgamation is significantly strengthened by one other factor that must be mentioned briefly, namely Goethe's work as a natural scientist. This was of utmost importance for his perception of Italy, for it led to a quintessentially organic and genetic conceptualization, a disire to comprehend the sights of Italy as the interrelated and interdependent products of natural laws and social forces. Instead of registering a series of disconnected facts, as so many travelers did, Goethe fashions an integrating vision that sees the diverse aspects of Italy as segments of a cultural totality. So history and art, flora, fauna, and geological formations, street scenes and carnivals are all linked as facets of a single entity which can be grasped only holistically through an understanding alive to its reciprocally determining ramifications.

In the *Italienische Reise*, Goethe presents a distinctively personal, yet not introspective image of Italy. The integrity of the other is always maintained in the respect Goethe accords alike to Italy's past and to her present. Reflection partners observation without the one ever occluding the other. Goethe works within the dominant conventions of late eighteenth and early nineteenth century travel writing. However, he transforms those conventions, not by the kind of radical innovation represented by Sterne's *Sentimental Journey*, but rather from within, through the richness of tone, the density of texture, and the depth of his appreciation of Italy, all of which distinguish his reading in the *Italienische Reise* from that of even the most eminent among his contemporaries.

2

"Paris Change!": Perception and Narration

Paris change! mais rien dans sa mélancolie
N'a bougé! palais neufs, échafaudages, blocs
Vieux faubourgs, tout pour moi devient allégorie
Et mes chers souvenirs sont plus lourd que des rocs. [1]

"Paris change!": the opening exclamation to the second part of Baudelaire's poem *Le Cygne (The Swan)* beckons as an encompassing title and cue for another consideration of Paris in nineteenth and early twentieth century literature. The physical appearance of the city was indeed being transformed with the gradual accomplishment of Napoleon's design by Baron Haussmann, and so too was its image in literature. That, however, is not my topic; the links between the city's actual face and its literary portrait have been extensively and scrupulously documented by a host of critics.[2] But some other aspects of changing Paris in literature have been given much less attention. Foremost among them is the correlation between the nature of the literary image and the format of presentation. I want to show how the narrational forms offer a figurative reiteration, virtually an "allégorie," to revert to Baudelaire, of the way the city is perceived by the protagonist. To approach Paris in literature from this angle is in effect to invert the customary procedure of enframing the literary portrayal referentially in an existent (or past) actuality. My argument is that the reader's concept derives not from knowledge of an extratextual reality but from the protagonists' perceptions and from the experience of reading in the particular narrational format. What is more, these two are closely and reciprocally interdependent.

This is the proposition I want to explore in three major fictions in each of which Paris forms a central motivational factor as well as the lo-

27

cation of the action: Balzac's *Le Père Goriot* (1834), Zola's *L'Assommoir* (1877) and Rilke's *Die Aufzeichnungen des Malte Laurids Brigge* (1910). Despite their apparent heterogeneity, these three works have certain similarities, apart from their setting, that support the comparison. All three of them, especially in their opening sections, show the impact of Paris on a young, recently arrived newcomer. Eugène de Rastignac has just come from the Angoulême area to study law; Gervaise Macquart has moved some three months previously from Plassans; and the Dane, Malte, has at the outset been in the city a mere three weeks. All are in their early twenties as they make their initial encounter with Paris, and in their attempts to grasp and order their confusing impressions of the city, they are also trying to construct their lives, assimilating the city into their minds.

Their *prise de conscience* assumes differing forms, determined by the disparity of their background, situation, and personality. Rastignac is the energectic, ambitious, extroverted young man from the provinces,[3] from an impoverished middle-class family, bent on making his career and his fortune through the opportunities for upward mobility afforded by the Paris of 1819–1820. Gervaise, by contrast, is defined, and limited, primarily by her gender; she is a working class woman who has come to Paris not of her own volition, but in the wake of her lover, Lantier, the father of her two illegitimate children. With scant education and a sinister heredity of alcoholism and degeneration, she strives at most to survive in the squalid slums of the mid-century industrializing metropolis. Malte, as the scion of an ancient aristocratic lineage, is wholly devoid of social, worldly ambitions; a highly sensitive, complex, introverted aesthete, he endeavors to come to grips with himself, his past and present beyond the noisy commotion of the turn-of-the-century city.

For each of the three the confrontation with Paris marks a crucial turning-point. Rastignac, with his will to power, decodes the city as an object of desire, challenging, exciting, alluring, and full of promise. To Gervaise, the female possessed both by men and by her environment, Paris is a perplexing script; glimpsed longingly as a possible access to security, it becomes increasingly and predominantly a threatening whirlpool of apprehension. For Malte, as he struggles to gain possession of self and universe, it seems the frightening incarnation of dread. What emerges from each of these encounters with the city is less a substantive image of Paris than a subjective interpretation through the psyche of the protagonist. And it is in the narrative strategies that these widely varying visions of Paris find their objectification.

Of the three, Rastignac's is most clearly the story of an initiation. He is surprised, indeed shocked, by his first experiences in Paris. His bewildered impressions are shaped into a cohesive picture through the help of two self-appointed mentors, Madame de Beauséant and Vautrin. Despite the diametric polarity of their respective positions and language, they in effect reveal to him the same social and moral structure. Their advice, backed by his own observations, opens Rastignac's eyes to Paris as an established, hierarchical system, which rests on the twin pillars of money and class. The Vauquer boarding-house, whose successive floors correspond to the tenants' financial standing, represents in microcosm Parisian society, while the fates of the individual inhabitants, as they move up or down stairs, offer Rastignac exemplary histories of the vicissitudes of life in the city.

Paris, then, is perceived as a place governed by an order that is discernible, though complicated and apparently contradictory in character. On the one hand it is, as Vautrin assures Rastignac, "comme une forêt du nouveau monde" ("like a forest in the new world"), open ground for any fortune-hunter, who will be well received provided he presents himself "avec sa gibecière bien garnie"[4] ("with his bag well filled"). Yet at the same time its social intercourse is regulated by an exacting formal ritualism, by "ces lois draconiennes du code parisien" (1031; "these Draconian laws of the Parisian code"), from which not even love is exempt. It is the duplicity of the city's unwritten code that Rastignac has to learn: that the surface adherence to strict conventions of dress, speech, and deportment only serves the better to mask the underlying law of the jungle. For those like Rastignac, determined to "parvenir" (935; "succeed") at any cost, Paris is not only a challenge and an object of desire, but also a mechanism to be mastered and manipulated. Though the operative system may be cruel and ethically despicable, it can nevertheless be both understood and used by those astute — and ruthless — enough to grasp its workings and opportunities. The mood prompted by Rastignac's perception of Paris is one of cynical optimism.

Because he believes fervently in the possibility of success, Rastignac devotes himself single-mindedly to learning to play the Parisian game as quicky and as adroitly as he can without allowing himself the luxury of reflection, let alone of judgments. He is still sufficiently tenderhearted to be moved by the despoliation of Goriot, who has remained an ignorant outsider to the rules of Parisian society. But even while giving the old man pity and tendance, Rastignac sees in him a cautionary example of failure in Paris. His early recognition that the city is "un bourbier" (886; "a slough") does not undermine his will to conquer it. The sub-text of warfare is underscored by such recurrent terms as "combat" (917, 936), "abordage" (919; "attack"), "champ de bataille" (947, 981; "battlefield"), "un boulet de canon" (936, 947; "a canon ball"), and "lutte" (948; "struggle"). It is perhaps in extension of this masculine vocabulary that Paris is cast into a female role as a sexual quarry.

In Anastasie, who is identified as "si éminemment parisienne" (897; "so eminently Parisian") and in her sister, Delphine, Rastignac sees all the city's entrancing glamor. That they turn out to be Goriot's daughters, who have attained their glitter parasitically, literally at his expense, makes them the most telling incarnation of the exploitative Parisian formula preached by Vautrin. No less symbolical is the final tableau of *Le Père Goriot*, when Rastignac overlooks the city from the heights of the Père Lachaise cemetery where Goriot has just been buried.

The striving for mastery that animates Rastignac within the fiction is practiced by the narrator over his fiction. And just as inside knowledge is the key that opens up to Rastignac the covert order of Paris, so too it is the source of narratorial authority. Through his ubiquitous presence in *Le Père Goriot*, the narrator exercises the kind of control over the fiction that Rastignac longs to acquire over the city. From the outset, in the presentation of the Vauquer boarding-house, the speaking voice at once asserts and displays an intimate familiarity with the scene of the action. He knows Madame Vauquer's past, her maiden name and social standing, he can fix precisely the house's geographic and economic location, he has seen and smelled it from the inside, and he is privy to the lifehistories and family background of its various inhabitants. His encompassing hold on the people and the place fosters his self-image as a reliable guide and as the guarantor that *"All is true"* (848). His frequent direct addresses to readers as he takes them by the hand, as it were, consolidate the narrative contract and affirm his predominance. His later occasional reflections on the story in progresss, for example, his designation of Rastignac's tale as "un des sujets les plus dramatiques de notre civilisation moderne" (948; "one of the most dramatic topics of modern civilization"), far from being inept breaks in the illusion, are further expressions of his power over the narrative. As a skilled reader of the Parisian scene, this audible, directing narrator acts as a correlative model for Rastignac.

A similar consonance exists in *L'Assommoir* between the persona's perception of the city and the narrational mode, however much it differs from *Le Père Goriot* in other respects. Gervaise never has the commanding overview, physically or intellectually, that Rastignac seems to have achieved at the end of *Le Père Goriot*. Significantly, when she surveys the city from the top of the Vendôme Column on her wedding day, her gaze is, almost involuntarily, drawn back to her particular *quartier,* recoiling in trepidation from the larger vista.[5] This episode aptly suggests her marginality to the mainstream of Parisian life; she spends her days and years sequestered in a circumscribed area, moving only as far as her limping legs can carry her, excluded by poverty and ignorance from the splendors of Paris, of whose very existence she appears hardly to be aware. In fact, even though within the shadow of the city walls, Gervaise continues to live as if in a province, with the language and culture of a ghetto subgroup. In contrast to the overriding order that becomes apparent to Rastignac as he grows to know the city and its ways better, it is the jumble of Paris that strikes Gervaise as she wends her slow way through the maze of streets and the labyrinthine corridors of the tenement house. She lacks the capacity ever to marshal this haphazard agglomeration of people and things into any structured sense. Instead, the prevailing moral and physical confusion translates into an intuition of the arbitrariness of fate. Gervaise is destined to be the victim of the city, not its master, like Rastignac.

Her perception of the city changes according to her own situation, and it is the outcome of an instinctive response rather than the cognitive understanding that Rastignac has. From the beginning she has an ominous sense of fear that stems from her view of Paris as an insidious oppressor and imminent danger to its inhabitants. In the opening scene, as she sits at the window waiting until daybreak for Lantier's return, she construes the workmen streaming into the city as a "troupeau" ("herd") of animals going to its death: "la cohue s'engouffrait dans Paris, où elle se noyait continuellement" (377; "the throng was engulfed in Paris, where it drowned endlessly"). The herd moves on, and she sees the men "les joues terreuses, la face tendue vers Paris, qui, un à un, les dévorait, par la rue béante du Faubourg-Poissonière" (378; "their cheeks earth colored, faces turned toward Paris, which was devouring them, one by one, down the gaping street of the Faubourg-Poissonière"). The menacing undertones of "dévorait" and "béante" ("gaping") make Paris into a monster as voracious as the mine in *Germinal*. In *L'Assommoir*, too, there is a machine, the still, which appears to Gervaise like a grim and threatening beast:

> L'alambic, avec ses récipients de forme étrange, ses enroulements sans fin de tuyaux, gardait une mine sombre; pas une fumée ne s'échappait; à peine entendait-on un souffle intérieur, un ronflement souterrain; c'était comme une besogne de nuit faite en plein jour, par un travailleur morne, puissant et muet. (411)[6]

The threat is made palpable by the sustained personification, as if the still were a malicious creature with a will of its own and the intent to do harm, insidiously, but incessantly in its silent, dogged work.

The image of the crouching, greedy brute recurs a third time in Gervaise's first glimpse of the tenement house, which becomes, like the Vauquer boarding-house, a symbolic replica of the city:

> La maison paraissait d'autant plus colossale qu'elle s'élevait entre deux petites constructions basses, chétives, collées contre elle; et, carrée, pareille à un bloc de mortier gâché grossièrement, se pourrissant et s'émiettant sous la pluie, elle profilait sur le ciel clair, au-dessus des toits voisins, son énorme cube brut, ses flancs non crépis, couleur de boue; d'une nudité interminable de murs de prison, où des rangées de pierres d'attente semblaient des mâchoires caduques, bâillant dans le vide. (414)[7]

Through its sheer length and breathless onward rush, this sentence mimics in its effect on readers the brutal impression that the house makes on Gervaise. This lurid metaphorization of the objects she encounters in the city creates a striking vehicle for her perceptions.

Her primary response of apprehension is temporarily suspended after her marriage to Coupeau when it is superseded by hope: hope of success, not on Rastignac's grand scale of a whole fortune, but in the modest form of a small laundry business of her own and a comfortable home. The move to Paris thus assumes for her, as for Rastignac, the guise of an opportunity. Unlike him, Gervaise can hardly be deemed a social climber, yet for a while at least she looks toward the prospect of a better, more secure life for herself and her children through the economic potential afforded by the city. But the hungry monster is still there, and gets to swallow her eventually, as if in contempt of all her efforts to survive. As she slides into the abyss that is Paris for the workers in the slums, she is as devoid of insight into what has happened as of power to stop it. While Rastignac's ascent has its climax in his final commanding panorama of the city, Gervaise's descent hits bottom in her death in a hole under the stairs in the tenement house. The male middleclass path in Paris in the second and third decades of the nineteenth century held the possibility of *parvenir* in the sense of expansion and possession. By contrast, the female working class route around the middle of the century is shown to be inexorably one of restriction, enclosure, and ultimately the self-surrender of *s'abandonner* (*"to give up on oneself"*).

Gervaise's immersion in the city has its narrational counterpart in readers' immersion in her mind. The narrator's voice is less insistently to the forefront in *L'Assommoir* than in *Le Père Goriot*, tending often to merge with the viewpoint of the protagonists. This becomes amply apparent in the episode already mentioned of the wedding party's view from the top of the Vendôme Column, which is registered successively in the third person through the eyes of various participants, then in indirect discourse in their own words ("Non, décidemment, ça vous faisait froid dans les boyaux" [419; "No, for sure, that gave you the creeps"]), back to third person narration, and finally, with the phrase "Paris, autour d'eux, étendait son immensité grise" (450; "Paris, all around them, spread its grey immenseness"), shifts to a poetic description by a narrator far more cultured and sensitive than the wedding group. His patently literary, visionary metaphor of Paris as an ocean is in startling contrast to the wedding guests' myopically detailed fragmentation.

Such shifts in focalization generally take place more directly between the narrator and Gervaise. The opening chapter, for instance, begins with a third person narratorial account of her sitting at the window: "Elle regardait à droite," "Elle regardait à gauche," "elle levait les yeux," "elle apercevait" (376; "She looked to the right," "She looked to the left," "she raised her eyes," "she noticed"). Shortly it glides into a less determinate focalization, which fuses her angle of vision with the narrator's in an intermediary state. The chapter ends, however, within her consciousness in the transposition of the key reiterated sight of the slaughterhouse and the hospital into indirect discourse:

> C'était sur ce pavé, dans cet air de fournaise, qu'on la jetait toute seule avec les petits; et elle enfila d'un regard les boulevards extérieurs, à droite, à gauche, s'arrêtant aux deux bouts, prise d'une épouvante sourde, comme si sa vie, désormais, allait tenir là, entre un abattoir et un hôpital. (403)[8]

The repetition of her act of looking to the right and to the left up and down the boulevards underscores the parallelism of the situation, although by the close of the chapter the perception is an internal one through the lens of Gervaise's mind.

Yet despite the tenses, which clearly indicate the switch to indirect discourse, the appearance of the traditional literary metaphor of Paris as a "fournaise"[9] suggests a certain duality of perception contained within the language. While "fournaise" might conceivably emanate from Gervaise, it seems more likely to attribute it to the narrator. His stealthy intratextual presence can be read as signalling the circumscription of Gervaise's freedom, as if he were insinuating himself into the very core of her being. In her discourse the narrator is performing the same coercion as the forces of the city do in her life. The constant drift from her point of view to his and back, sometimes to the verge of indistinguishability, denotes the tenuousness of self-determination in *L'Assommoir.* Things —

success, Lantier, Coupeau, understanding of Paris—escape Gervaise and slip away, as do her thoughts and her discourse under the sway of an extraneous power. The technique is strongly reminiscent of Flaubert's in *Madame Bovary* with its notoriously subtle slides in and out of Emma's consciousness. Perhaps this insidious narrative mode is indicative of the degree of control exercised over women's minds in the mid-nineteenth century. Certainly, the intrusion of the narrator's voice into Gervaise's stream of consciousness suggests the supplanting of her will. It is the linguistic equivalent of her slump into passivity as well as the embodiment of her impotence. The reader, too, in undergoing the frequent transfers from one mentality to another, is made to share the precariousness that is at the heart of Gervaise's experience of Paris.

Malte Laurids Brigge seems literally worlds away from *L'Assommoir* not only in the personality of its protagonist, but also in its narrative disposition, since the experiencing persona and the narrator are one and the same. There is, however, a line of continuity insofar as Gervaise's dominant response to the city is reiterated in an intensified version in Malte. Her dumb, chronic, instinctive apprehension is transformed in him into an acute, highly verbalized, self-conscious dread. What is more, here again, as in the two French novels, the manner of narration represents an objective correlative to the actual matter.

The intensity of Malte's estrangement is already implicit in the opening sentence: "so, also hierher kommen die Leute, um zu leben, ich würde eher meinen, es stürbe sich hier"[10] ("so this is where people come to live, I would rather think that deathing would take place here"). With this terse inversion of the norm, which has the form and impact of a maxim, Malte sets himself apart from his milieu and from average expectations. His dissenting, querying position as an outsider is conveyed by the antithetical structure of the sentence with its sharp contrast between the constative statement of the common assumption in the indicative tense in the first half and the subjunctive in its closing words, "es stürbe sich hier," unusual both in its impersonal formulation and in its rare conjugation. The association between the city and death, a major motif of *Malte Laurids Brigge*, is thus made at the very outset, simultaneously with that foregrounding of language that is the hallmark of the poetic use of words. The subsequent three sparser declarations corroborate the initial theme and mood: "Ich bin ausgewesen. Ich habe gesehen: Hospitäler. Ich habe einen Menschen gesehen, welcher schwankte und umsank" (7; "I have existed outside. I have seen: hospices. I have seen a person who swayed and sank"). These laconic, fractured observations have the same shock effect on the reader as the city has on Malte. The starkness created by the absence of physical designative detail heightens the emotional momentum, which is further reinforced by the unfamiliar plural, "Hospitäler," that suggests their omnipresence, as though the city were filled with places of dying. The person ("Mensch") who sways and sinks underscores the universal tendency here to falter and to fall (and by extension, to die); not particularized even by gender, this figure has a paradigmatic and puzzling character. The syncretic notation of random street encounters: the pregnant woman pushing herself heavily against a wall, the "Asile de nuit" ("night shelter") in a house personified as "starblind" ("blind from cataract"), the gross, greenish child with eczema on his forehead, the smells of iodine, and of grease from fried potatoes: all these disjointed perceptions express the nauseating revulsion felt by Malte as he takes stock of Paris. In the word "Angst" (8; "anxiety"), which forms the culmination of the opening section, incongruously aligned with "Jodoform, pommes frites" ("iodine, fried potatoes"), the sensation is finally named and avowed. What makes this evocation of Paris so distinctive is its live narrational enactment—as against mere description—of Malte's response to the city. All the disparate elements coalesce to engender nervous tension: the short, staccato sentences, the abrupt starts and stops, the sudden assaults of the unexpected, in short, the discord between the frenetic rush and distressing tumult of the city on the one hand, and on the other the frozen immobility of the individual isolated spectator. This amounts to a narrational mimicry of the agonizing existential fear that threatens to silence Malte.

Paris is for Malte the opposite to what it is for Rastignac: the object of dread, not of desire; the locus of decline and death, not of rising life; the catalyst for disorientation, dissolution, and erosion of selfhood, not the formation of personality. It is only by withdrawing from the immediate sense impressions of the city into the geographic and historic otherness of his past that Malte can stem the loss of his self and his cultural values. Instead of expanding outward into the city, like Rastignac, Malte seeks refuge from it in a return to his memories. Only by taking fuller possession of the recesses of his consciousness can he avert the dangers posed by the city. The radical defamiliarization he experiences in facing "l'épouvante"[11] ("the horror") in and of the modern city can be countered solely by a refamiliarization with his cultural roots and heritage.

This is the context for the central action of *Malte Laurids Brigge*, that of writing. The text represents Malte's *Aufzeichnungen*, his notations of the adventures and journeys of his mind. Repeatedly he emphasizes that things become real ("wirklich") through the act of the imagination ("Einbildung"). It is from within ("von innen"), not from without ("von außen") that true knowledge can be derived. His continued reliance on such inner resources is linked to his status as a reader:

So ist es mir klar geworden, daß ich nie ein richtiger Leser war. In der
Kindheit kam mir das Leben vor wie ein Beruf, den man auf sich nehmen
würde, später einmal, wenn alle die Berufe kamen, einer nach dem an-
dern. Ich hatte, aufrichtig gesagt, keine bestimmte Vorstellung, wann
das sein könnte. Ich verließ mich darauf, daß man es merken würde,
wenn das Leben gewissermaßen umschlug und nur noch von außen
kam, so wie früher von innen. (234–35)[12]

Because this anticipated turn to the outer has never occurred for Malte,
he goes on maintaining his primary allegiance to the realm of fantasy and
memory. The images created by *erinnern* (remembering), visionary *sehen* (seeing) and *erzählen* (telling) are those that have validity for him.

So it is through the inner eye that Malte perceives Paris. His approach is the antithesis to that of Rastignac, who is essentially outer oriented because he believes in the existence of an objective reality anterior
to and independent of his own mental processes. He therefore scrutinizes
the surface appearance of things and people as a means to acquire reliable information. In *Malte Laurids Brigge*, on the contrary, the city is a
product of Malte's mind. The image is internalized, phantasmagoric, disturbed and disturbing, as a projection of Malte's consciousness. The metaphorization of the city, apparent in *L'Assommoir* through the moves
into Gervaise's mental space, is posited in *Malte Laurids Brigge* as the
sole reality. The subjectivity of the first person narrator has annexed and,
in a sense, abolished the actual city to substitute for it a place of his own
making. And that place becomes the repository and embodiment of his
Angst. The decay, disease, dissociation of things, dehumanization of people, and death that he sees in Paris are the disintegrating forces he senses
and dreads in himself. Paris becomes an allegory, just as writing becomes
a bulwark against the threats objectified in the city. Writing denotes association, orientation in time and place, recuperation of the past, acceptance of life and death, and therefore a re-finding of oneself. It involves a
transcendence of the chaotic turbulence of the present to forge a link with
the past in the hope of a future.

The radical subjectivity of this perception and the private nature of
Malte's spiritual quest find appropriate expression in the first person narration. Himself a "wohnlose Seele" (262; "an unhoused soul"), a wan-
derer whose natural intimate bond to place has been disrupted, Malte endeavors through the probing and recording of his inner realm to rescue
the individual from the reification of the masses in the city. His deliberately idiosyncratic voice consciously sets itself apart through its use of
language as potently as through its vision. The searching and tentative aspect of this mode of narration has been aptly described as a "hypothe-

tisches Erzählen" ("hypothetical narration"), characterized by the constant interruption of the narrative by comments "die darauf hinweisen, daß das Erzählte nur eine Hypothese darstellt"[13] ("which point to the fact that what is being narrated represents merely a hypothesis"). Such hypothetical narration conveys the transitoriness, the vulnerability to contingency of Malte's Paris and of his world, yet not without leaving open at least an aperture of hope for the future.

In each of these three texts the central protagonist is engaged in the effort to read his/her life situation in direct relation to the scene in which it is enacted, which in these instances is Paris. The interplay between persona and city amounts to more than mere determinism. The impact of Paris initiates a dynamic chain reaction, which devolves from the characters' interpretation of the sights and experiences of the city, and which then shapes their conduct responsively in specific directions. As external readers, we are drawn by the various narrational strategies I have analyzed to share their vision so that the internal readers act as mediators whose readings are projected into ours.

3

Reading "Nasty" Great Books

The *New York Times* of 1 January 1989 recounts an amusing little story. At the end of a course on Great Books, the students were given a final examination that consisted of just two questions. The first was: "Which work read this semester did you dislike most?" and the second: "To what deficiencies in your intellect and character do you attribute this dislike?"

*   *   *

Whether this anecdote is true or not is immaterial. It serves well to reveal a certain mentality towards that cornerstone of American liberal arts education, the canon of the Great Books. On the one hand, pressures are increasing to expand a canon that is perceived as having hitherto been both limited and tendentious through the inclusion of minority and third world texts. On the other hand, however, there is a persistent and deepseated reluctance to scrutinize the canon in any basic way, such as, for instance, confronting a reaction of "dislike." The orthodox belief has been, as illustrated in those exam questions, that a failure to like the accepted canon could only be attributed to a deficiency in education. The implicit underlying assumption is that once Great Books have been adequately explained and properly grasped, they will *ipso facto* become likable. The better, i.e., more closely and discerningly one is able to read a text, the more one will see its depths and subtleties. To dislike the canon is, therefore, taken automatically as a sign of boorishness, without much inquiry into what is subsumed into the idea of an adequate explanation or a proper grasp, let alone a discerning reading. Nor is there any probing into the possibly legitimate sources of the negative image which the students have formed, unconnected with any shortcoming on their part.

Yet a pronounced rebellion or rejection is a valid starting-point for critical exploration, although it goes against the normative expectations for a work hallowed by the privilege of the canon. "Dislike" as a category comprises an ethical as well as an aesthetic criterion. The canon, indeed, has traditionally rested on the postulate of the supremacy of the aesthetic. To supersede such a supposition is out of the question, for it is precisely the aesthetic qualities of a text that make it worth re-reading, in contrast to yesterday's local newspaper. But the presence of the ethical factor must also be acknowledged, parallel to our recognition of the import of the social, the cultural, and the political. All these diverse elements coalesce into our system of values, which in turn creates the context for our readings/misreadings and for the formation of images. In his recent book, *The Ethics of Reading*, J. Hillis Miller has argued that "there is a necessary ethical moment in the act of reading as such, a moment neither cognitive, nor political, nor social, nor interpersonal, but properly and independently ethical."[1] To heed this ethical moment offers one avenue of renewed inquiry into the images that arise through the lens of the reader.

The nature of the ethical moment is open to speculation. Miller delineates one possible approach in his question: "Does the ethical act of the protagonist inside the book correspond to the ethical acts the reading of the book generates outside the book?"[2] This is perhaps rather a simplistic formula for a complex relationship, as Miller himself seems to concede in the tentativeness of his proposal. His alternative model, while equally hypothetical, leaves greater leeway for differentiated development: "There are analogies among all four of these ethical moments, that of the author, the narrator, the character, and the reader, teacher, critic, though what is the basis of these analogies, what *logos* controls them, remains to be interrogated."[3]

The analysis of these analogies may foster a more precise understanding of apparently deviant reactions to works hallowed by traditional praise. This is what I propose to consider in relation to Flaubert's *Madame Bovary* and Thomas Mann's *Death in Venice*. I choose these as paradigmatic texts because they feature so frequently in Great Books courses, and tend to elicit the objection: "I hate this book! it's so nasty." These are not merely the complaints of mediocre undergraduates who find the reading hard going. Similar comments have come from highly literate and sensitive readers, though evidently in more refined terms. Matthew Arnold, for instance, excoriated *Madame Bovary* as "a work of petrified feeling" over which hangs an atmosphere of bitterness and impotence.[4] Nor are these strictures moral in the narrow sense of the word. In that respect there has been a radical change since 1857 when Flaubert was indicted for "offenses à la morale publique et à la religion" and also since 1911 when homosexuality and pedophilia were unmentionable topics. These moralistic concerns are no longer the crux of the issue nor the root of that instinctive repugnance that grows in some readers' minds and breeds a dislike of these Great Books.

A study of the ethical moment suggests that readers' alienation stems not from their ignorance or idiosyncratic prejudices, but rather from the narrator's posture vis-à-vis his protagonists and, by extension, us as readers. There is a correlation between the narrator's tactics and readers' reactions, although it may comprise opposition alongside and even within identification. At some point readers' growing need to dissociate themselves from the narrating voice causes a disjuncture between narrator and readers. So ultimately readers are stranded in a conflicted position, where they are able to admire the aesthetic brilliance of the artifact's construction, but remain nonetheless deeply troubled by its ethical implications, notably in regard to the narrator's role.

The unresolved tension between aesthetics and ethics is one of the central themes of *Der Tod in Venedig* as of *Madame Bovary*. In admittedly very different ways, the action of both pivots on the emergence of a dissonance between them. This is particularly obvious in *Der Tod in Venedig* because of its overt preoccupation with the interaction of the two spheres. Gustav von Aschenbach has fashioned a personal and professional ethic out of aesthetics, and at the beginning of the *Novelle* he appears to have succeeded in so doing. In his classically lucid prose he has shown a whole generation "die Möglichkeit sittlicher Entschlossenheit jenseits der tiefsten Erkenntnis"[5] ("the possibility of ethical determination beyond the deepest insight"). He conceives life as an assertion of willpower, "als ein Trotzdem" (198; "as a despite"), a heroic thrust beyond ambivalence and irony to "Würde des Geistes" (203; "dignity of spirit"). The phrase "moralische Entschlossenheit" (202; "ethical determination") is repeated in the delineation of his personality, and again linked to a state "jenseits des Wissens, der auflösenden und hemmenden Erkenntnis" (202; "beyond knowledge, beyond dissolving and inhibiting insight"). He is a "Moralist der Leistung" (200; "moralist of achievement") who has attained a highly respected social and artistic position.

The precariousness of his ethic is implicit from the outset. What is most crucial in his system is also what is most dangerous: his cult of beauty of form. It is dangerous because the aesthetic lies outside the bounds of the ethical; as an expression of discipline (as in Aschenbach's polished writing) it may be ethical, but it is decidedly non- and even anti-ethical in its drive to autonomy and in its indifference to normative limitations. The plot of *Der Tod in Venedig* represents the enactment of this dualism. In a well delineated irony of situation, Aschenbach is betrayed by his own creed.

Whether he has knowledge of his self-betrayal is another, more intricate problem. One of the skills that he acquires in the course of his rigorous self-training is that of repressing, denying, and thwarting his innermost wishes. So he goes first to Pola before admitting to himself that it is Venice that is the destination of his longing. Similarly, he makes a pretense, albeit a rather feeble one, of leaving Venice. As he becomes increasingly entranced by Tadzio, he wearies of the struggle to maintain the facade he had painstakingly constructed over the years. To claim that he is a willing accomplice to his own destruction is an overstatement. He simply lets go. The justification that his moralistic ego gives to his rebellious id is an essentially aesthetic one: he is continuing to pursue the cult of beauty, as he always had done, though in a different guise. Ethics are divorced from aesthetics, and the latter is shown to have a dual potential for self-destruction as well as for self-creation.

Emma Bovary is equally enthralled by the lure of the aesthetic, although her drama is played out in the nineteenth century woman's domestic context. Her ethical obligations are, clearly, to her husband, her child, and the welfare of her household. But the role of angel in the house appeals to her only intermittently, when she has a specially bad conscience and makes amends by preparing a favorite dessert for Charles. Otherwise she lets her daughter run around with holes in her stockings, and feels unable to love her because she sees her as "laide"[6] ("ugly"). Her shortcomings as wife and mother are underscored, though not without a strong satirical undercurrent, through the contrast with Mme. Homais, "la meilleure épouse de Normandie" (101; "the best wife in Normandy"), who is totally devoted to her family, and totally devoid of either intelligence or sexuality.

Emma's fascination with the aesthetic becomes apparent in her adolescence in her behavior at the convent, where self-indulgent sentimentality captivates her rather than the altruistic devotion she is supposed to be learning. Her taste is formed—and perverted—by the figures and rhetoric of cheap romance, just as Aschenbach finds his model in Greek culture. The tawdriness of Emma's concept of beauty is a comment on the world in which she lives insofar as it offers her no loftier ideals of aspiration. She tries to satisfy her longings by the daintiness of her appearance, spending immense sums on lemons to whiten her skin, and buying scarves and baubles from Lheureux (whose name means "the happy") to the point of bankruptcy. Her lovers' self-presentation is in marked contrast to her husband's growing sloppiness. With Léon she immediately notices his well-manicured nails, which match her own. The motif of nails recurs when Rodolphe calculates Charles' dirty nails and three-day beard among the factors likely to make Emma an easy prey to his advances.

This fundamental struggle between the claims of the ethical and the aesthetic represents the main analogy between the characters and readers. The narrator's vexatory signals have the effect of trapping readers in their own version of the dilemma between aesthetics and ethics that lies at the core of both these texts. The aesthetics of narration raise the issue of the ethics of the narrator's handling of the characters and, beyond that, the implications of this narrative situation for readers. To document this thesis requires an analysis of the delicate and changing relationship between the narrator and readers.

At the opening of both *Madame Bovary* and *Der Tod in Venedig*, the narrating voice extends to readers an offer of friendship. This intriguing notion of friendship as a means of envisaging the alliance between narrator and readers has recently been put forward by Wayne Booth in his book, *The Company We Keep: An Ethics of Fiction*. Booth maintains that: "Considered under the friendship metaphor, the implied authors of *all* stories, fictional or historical, elevated or vulgar, welcoming or hospitable on the surface, purport to offer friendships."[7] These friendships may vary in a number of ways: in the quantity of the invitations, in the degree of intimacy, in the intensity of the engagement they expect, in the distance or familiarity they project, in the kinds of activities they invite, in the level of responsibility they offer, i.e., reciprocity or domination between author and reader, and, I would add, in the reaction they seek to elicit from readers, i.e., trust, skepticism, playfulness. Booth's concept of friendship is another, more vivid and personal denotation of the narrative contract that binds narrator to readers and enables the fiction. At the same time, through the use of the term "friendship," it introduces into the narrator/ readers relationship notions such as loyalty and mutual respect that are intrinsic to an ethics of reading.

In both *Madame Bovary* and *Der Tod in Venedig*, a supposition of friendly solidarity with the reader is established through the use of the first person plural in the opening paragraph. In *Madame Bovary* it is the enigmatic "nous" ("we") that is the initial word of the text and that recurs through the first chapter, but only once again later near the end of the novel: "Nous étions à l'étude, quand le Proviseur entra, suivi d'un *nouveau*" (3; "We were in class when the headmaster came in, followed by a new boy"). The silent spectators of Charles' arrival in the classroom could be his schoolfellows already seated there. In addition, however, that "we" can also incorporate implied observers/readers being solicited, as it were, to enter the realm of the fiction by looking at Charles with both his schoolfellows and the narrator. That indeterminate "we" is tantamount to a tacit invitation to readers to participate in the narrator's point of view. This shared perspective on Charles forms the basis of the friendly accord between narrator and readers in the opening sections of *Madame Bovary*. Similarly, the first sentence of *Der Tod in Venedig* contains a reference to "unserem Kontinent" (185; "our continent"). That usage is no more casual than Flaubert's "we." Its design is to encourage readers to identify with the narrator's angle of vision as "we" step over the threshold of the fiction, and to stand by his side as we become acquainted with its configuration. The rhetorical questions that Aschenbach addresses to himself in the course of his walk about the sources of his sudden desire to travel serve to stimulate the entente between the narrator and readers. For while Aschenbach gives one set of answers, the potential for quite other ones is suggested by the coyness of the phrasing. Beneath the overt text, articulated by Aschenbach, there is a sub-text shared by the narrating voice and readers alert to the covert signals.

The solidarity fostered by the first person plural also projects a measure of stability. The narrator in both instances seeks to fashion a positive self-image of himself in readers' minds. His voice inspires credibility because it is authoritative, not least on account of the control it is able to exercise. The narrator's power is substantiated through his thorough knowledge of the attendant circumstances as the pre-history of Charles in *Madame Bovary* and of Aschenbach in *Der Tod in Venedig* is unfolded in comfortable detail. The undercurrent of irony towards Charles and the innuendoes in regard to Aschenbach are sufficient to adumbrate the narrator as someone who has aesthetic and ethical standards. However, he does not emerge as a fictional persona with a distinctive personality. Flaubert's own characterization of his role in relation to his fiction in his letter of 18 March 1857 is largely apposite to most of *Der Tod in Venedig* too: that he wanted "être dans son oeuvre comme Dieu dans sa création, invisible et tout-puissant; qu'on le sente partout, mais qu'on ne le voie pas" ("to be in his work like God in his creation, invisible and omnipotent, everywhere felt and nowhere seen").[8] Both narrators mostly keep a rather low profile, in contrast to the self-dramatization characteristic of the self-conscious gamesman who likes to draw attention to his presence and power over the text he is creating and simultaneously undermining. In contrast to such tactics, the opening disposition of *Madame Bovary* and *Der Tod in Venedig* sets out to activate in readers the assumption that they are dealing with a fairly direct narration and a knowing, probably trustworthy narrator.

These assumptions are further encouraged by other features of both narratives that support readers' confidence in their ability to construct the text. Aesthetically *Madame Bovary* and *Der Tod in Venedig* are quite transparent. The plot of *Der Tod in Venedig* is the enactment of an inversion as Aschenbach undergoes the metamorphosis from the public persona he presented to the world at the outset to the other self of the end. A series of doubles—the tempter at the cemetery, the sinister gondolier, the cosmetized old dandy—function as alter egos to map the stages of this reversal. The ready intelligibility of the text is assured by the use of such immediately comprehensible symbols as the decaying city, Venice, sinking into the ocean, or Tadzio's less than perfect teeth, the visible indicator that he, too, is vitally flawed. The intertextual echoes of Platen and Gustav Mahler, as well as the extensive citations from the *Phaidros*, also facilitate reading by locating the narrative in its cultural context. In *Madame Bovary* a similar function is performed by the expansive account (37–42) of Emma's artistic experience during her formative years and of her response to it. The impact of romance as a model for her conduct could hardly be spelled out with greater force and clarity. Likewise, the significance of the reiterated motif of the wedding bouquet needs little explanation. The intricate subtext of food as communication[9] that runs throughout *Madame Bovary* is another example of an accessible code. The translucency of the text boosts readers' faith in both their own reading skills and the narrator's willingness to act as a reliable guide. Through our growing friendly engagement with him, we are imperceptibly drawn into complicity with him.

The narrative situation grows considerably more complicated with the increasing manipulation of indirect discourse as a mode of narration. The immediate access to the characters' own thought processes and speech patterns intensifies readers' capacity to identify with them, and through the temporary empathy creates a greater receptivity to their predicaments. Emma's boredom in Tostes, her disillusionment with marriage, her contempt for Charles, her disdain for the vulgarity of her environment are all perceived through her eyes and expressed in her words. The effect of indirect discourse could be compared to an x-ray of the recesses of her mind as against a picture of its surface given in third person narration. Aschenbach's far more complex mind, too, is portrayed from within as he engages in various strategies of self-justification. His strong and, to him, surprising urge to get away from his disciplined life, his decision to head for the South, and his captivation under the dual spell of Venice and Tadzio are all conveyed to readers through his ratiocinations. So in the indirect discourse the narrator assumes the guise of the characters' intimate confidant through his familiarity with their thoughts and his ability to (re)produce them. After instituting himself as the readers' friend, he goes on to project himself as the characters' friend, and therefore acts as a mediator who enables readers vicariously to enter into the characters' lives. The illusion is thereby created of a triangular understanding between the narrator, the character, and readers.

But the symbiosis of this partnership is disturbed by the constant intervention of irony. It is not only latent in the alternation between direct and indirect discourse; it is also implicit within the indirect discourse as a scuttling of the very words being uttered. In *Madame Bovary* the insistent repetition of the same cliches, linguistic and ideological, points to the shoddiness of Emma's aspirations even as she cherishes them. In *Der Tod in Venedig* evasive understatement has the same effect. Aschenbach's dismissive surmise: "Es war Reiselust, nichts weiter" (189; "It was the urge to travel, nothing more") has a decidedly ironic edge. While he is endeavoring to reassure himself about the innocuousness of his desires, the narrator is, by the insinuation of under/overstatement, inviting readers to do the opposite, precisely to suspect that there is a great deal more here than Aschenbach is willing to concede to himself. The irony simultaneously conceals and reveals Aschenbach's self-deception. Its mainspring lies in the narrator's ulterior knowledge of the characters' mentality. It is at their expense, for it casts doubt on their motivations and exposes their ideals as questionable. To the extent that readers grasp the ironies and assent to the narrator's vision, the bond between them and him is strengthened in a collusive complicity. Through our querying, skeptical withdrawal from the characters we are pulled closer towards the narrator.

Yet at the same time, paradoxically, we begin to harbor reservations about his methods. After posing as the character's friend, he emerges more and more as a sly fox of an ironist who bites with a considerable venom of malice. So the detachment, which is a product of irony, itself ironically initiates readers' distancing not just from the figures but from the narrator himself as well. The superciliousness of a voice that undercuts his characters while expecting to maintain readers' friendship arouses a certain self-protective recoil. It is important to distinguish this narrative situation from that in satiric fictions where the narrator has a good heart beneath his snarling surface, and addresses readers with what amounts to a friendly offer: " 'I would like to give you something for your own good — a nasty medicine that may cure you.' "[10] The therapeutic aspect of that kind of nastiness is operative too in such works as Zola's *L'Assommoir* or Virginia Woolf's *To the Lighthouse*, which students tend to reject as "depressing" because they overlook the authentic compassion held out to the characters. This is not the case in either *Madame Bovary* or *Der Tod in Venedig*, where the hostility embedded in the irony triggers readers' negative reactions. Though we may not particularly like the characters, we come to like the narrator even less for the snide way in which he treats them.

In *Der Tod in Venedig* it is possible to pinpoint exactly where and how the colloquy between narrator, protagonist and readers undergoes a mutation. In the lengthy closing section the narrator switches roles by setting himself wholly apart from Aschenbach through a series of comments that record overt censure of him. He refers to him as "der Verwirrte" (275; "the man gone astray"), "der Betörte" (277; "the spellbound man"), "der Heimgesuchte" (297; "the man destined for a bad fate"), and "der Berückte" (300; "the ensorcered man"). He goes on with pointed cruelty to gloat over Aschenbach's degradation as he portrays the "Meister" (302; "Master") sitting on the beach, his hair colored, his face made up, his eyes avidly following Tadzio's every movement. The note of contempt is unmistakable as Aschenbach's decline is described, detail by detail, each one evoking the contrast with his former high-principled, respected persona. The deterioration of the former Aschenbach into the present self-parody is, aesthetically, a masterpiece of imagination. As readers we marvel at the artfulness of this *Novelle:* it is a superbly crafted, highly organized, and, what is more, economical piece of writing.

Ethically, however, it is dubious. The narrator's duplicity towards the protagonist is disconcerting as he shifts from his earlier position of somewhat ironical but basically friendly understanding into unconcealed aggression. T. J. Reed, in his study *Thomas Mann: The Uses of Tradition,*[11] argues that Mann's concept of the plot underwent a sea change in the course of its development. His original intention was to portray Aschenbach favorably in the light of Plato and Plutarch; he had excerpted all the passages that are positive about love. The matter proved flexible, and eventually the negative came to prevail with the result that the *Novelle* turned in a different direction while retaining its structural outline. "Precisely this negative reworking of what was at first a positive conception," Reed maintains[12] "would account perfectly for the strange mixture *Der Tod in Venedig* actually is, of enthusiasm and criticism, classical beauty and penetration, elevation and sordidness." But Reed simplifies the issue when he envisages the *Novelle* as "a story whose overt intention is to pass a moral judgement" so that the "increasing use of adjectival nouns as judgements — *der Verwirrte, der Betörte* — are (*sic*) also a simple and economical way for the narrator to establish his position as a moralist."[13]

To typecast the narrator as a moralist is to flatten the narrative by opting for a single denotative reading that abolishes its essential ambivalences. The narrator is very much implicated in that slipperiness. His condemnatory castigation of Aschenbach toward the end is in stark contrast to the sympathetic understanding he shows at the opening. It is as if he had carefully set the figure up expressly in order to do him down and in. The friend whom the narrator gave out to be proves to be an enemy. For this reason the negative value judgements on Aschenbach, which prompt readers to scorn and reject him, end by backfiring. Readers' sense of anger is directed not at the reviled character but at the narrator as his treachery is unmasked. Because he betrays his created persona, for whom he has feigned friendship, he forfeits the trust we as readers have invested in him.

In *Madame Bovary* readers face a similar dilemma, though it is less visible because the narrator is so adept at keeping up appearances. Nevertheless, the hostility against Emma becomes increasingly palpable, reaching its climax in the deathbed scene, which has the same destructive pleasure in portraying her at her nadir as the last glimpse of Aschenbach on the beach. Here too the contrast is underscored between her earlier self and her present state. To emphasize the ugliness of her dying, it is set off against the fantasies of ethereal fading she had brought from her reading of romance. The horror of the situation is even greater than in *Der Tod in Venedig* because Emma asks for a mirror and sees her own disfigurement, whereas Aschenbach never consciously confronts what he has become. The big tears that roll down her cheeks as she catches sight of her hideousness are in counterpoint to her raucous, frenetic laughter as she hears the blind man's song outside. As in *Der Tod in Venedig*, the recurrent details are orchestrated with utmost finesse to form a pattern of signification for readers. The aesthetic mastery is undeniable. But the orgiastic delight in excess affords a clue to the underlying violence, even though the Flaubertian narrator is too conscious of his art to admit the overt judgmental statements found in *Der Tod in Venedig*. Through the widespread use of the imperfect tense, the normative tense in French for both indirect discourse and for continuous past narration, the narrator of *Madame Bovary* is able so unobtrusively to slip in and out of the persona's consciousness that it becomes virtually impossible to delineate precisely between the voices. This technique attains its maximum effectiveness in the deathbed scene. John Porter Houston has shown, in his book *Fictional Technique in France 1802 – 1927*,[14] that even the most searchingly meticulous stylistic analysis cannot disentangle the priest's liturgical formulae as he administers the extreme unction from the suggestive, erotically colored phrases of Emma's confused consciousness. It is indeed this aesthetic brilliance of *Madame Bovary* that makes it so difficult to analyze readers' reservations. The narrator's antagonism to the character is more insidious, more insinuating, and more resistant to diagnosis than in *Der Tod in Venedig*, yet just as reductive. It goes far beyond the want of compassion of which Flaubert has often been accused. The narrator's attitude towards the protagonist in both texts must be designated as full of guile.

It is because of this ethical violation of the narrative contract established at the outset that readers retreat from the complicity into which the narrator has endeavored to draw them. His betrayal of the character is, by a metonymic transference, experienced as a betrayal of and by readers too. His record of duplicity in dealing with the characters reveals his essential untrustworthiness. His mode of narration amounts to an act of transgression that activates in readers precisely the kind of revulsion he has sought to elicit against the figures. This ultimate unintentional irony of reader reaction stems from resentment at what is perceived as the narrator's deceitfulness. So readers refuse to assent to his maneuvers or to submit to his manipulation. The bad faith apparent in the narrator's presentation of his characters contains a potential threat to readers also. The analogy that Hillis Miller posits between the narrator, the character and the reader turns out to be one of misgivings. The ill-will generated within the fiction extends beyond it into readers' indistinct sense of aversion.

In Booth's terminology of friendship, readers' reactions could be described as a mixture of grief and anger: grief at the loss of the friendship offered by the narrator, and anger at his behavior toward the characters. In effect, readers feel duped as well as offended by a narrator who has cast them into the position of inferiors and has presumed on the power of his rhetoric not only to carry them along, but also to take them in — or, at least, into complicity. Like the listeners in Michel's account of his life in Gide's *L'Immoraliste*, readers are expected to become "presque complices" ("almost accomplices") because of "ne savoir où la désapprouver"[15] ("not knowing where to disapprove"). Such a posture on the narrator's part is predicated on a certain lack of respect for readers, analogous to his contempt for the fictional world. The hurt to the reader contingent on this kind of narrative situation can be brought more sharply into focus through comparison with narrators such as those of Jane Austen or Henry James, who treat readers as equals and endow them with an independent intelligence. These narratorial voices maintain a pact of generosity with readers, whereas those in *Madame Bovary* and *Der Tod in Venedig* are tainted with meanness.

In construing these texts, readers are playing out a dual drama. On the level of the plot they are engaged in the movements of Emma's and Aschenbach's desires. The indirect discourse, by positioning readers within the protagonists' minds, encourages identification. The intimacy elicits perhaps sympathy, perhaps pity for the pathos of the situation, eventually horror at the self-destructiveness that is the outcome of their self-deception. This participation in the realm of the fiction is, however, partnered by another sort of involvement of readers on the narrational level. This is where readers take an active role to the point of emancipating themselves from the narrator's guidance. In antithesis to the characters, who are totally in his power, readers have the privilege of reflection. They can distance themselves not merely from the characters but from the narrator too, subjecting his tactics and motives to scrutiny through the lens of their own intelligence and sensitivity. The narrator's repressed but palpable anger at the fictional world is in turn played out by readers as a largely unconscious animosity against the narrator, which explodes in the disparagement of "I hate this book! it's so nasty." Despite the naivety of their phraseology, these readers have rightly experienced the treacherous undertow of this mode of narration. Their negative image is by no means either misguided or unjustified.

The result is often an impasse. These readers may become convinced of the extraordinary subtleties of the works in question: the profusion of interlocking detail, the virtuosity in the management of viewpoint, the vivid specificity with which an entire world is evoked. Intellectually they may arrive at an understanding of the aesthetic brilliance of such works, which justifies their continued inclusion in the canon of Great Books. Emotionally they feel differing degrees of engagement with the character, depending on such extraneous factors as their own level of maturity, the breadth of their horizon, their gender, and their life expectations. But ethically they shudder in revulsion against a transgression of the narrative contract of friendship because it connotes a deeper infraction of basic human bonds.

II

Kleist: "Through Green Spectacles"

*Wenn alle Menschen statt der Augen grüne Gläser hät-
ten, so würden sie urteilen müßen, die Gegenstände,
welche sie dadurch erblicken, sind grün—und nie würden sie entscheiden können, ob ihr Aug ihnen die Dinge
zeigt, wie sie sind, oder ob es nicht etwas hinzutut, was
nicht ihnen, sondern dem Auge gehört. So ist es mit
dem Verstande.*

*If everybody had green spectacles instead of eyes, then
they would have to judge the objects they saw through
them to be green—and they would never be able to decide whether their eyes showed them things as they are,
or whether they were not adding something, that did
not belong to them, but to their eyes. So it is with our
understanding.*

Kleist, Letter to his fiancée, 22 March 1801.

4

Assent and Resistance in *Die Marquise Von O*— and *Der Tod in Venedig*

"Vorrei, e non vorrei"

Don Giovanni, Act I, scene iii.

Zerlina's response to Don Giovanni's overtures to her, "I would and would not wish it," is the most succinct expression of archetypal ambivalence toward a proposed seduction. On the one hand, she is flattered and tempted by the attentions of a gentleman, while on the other, she has an instinctive, protective fear of getting into trouble and possibly alienating her betrothed.

This pattern of assent and resistance, enunciated by Zerlina, is repeated in far more complex variants in two canonical works of German literature, both of which have recently become known to a wider audience through the medium of cinema. In Heinrich von Kleist's short story, *Die Marquise von O*— (*The Marquise of O*—, 1810 – 11), the marquise, when questioned about her feelings for Count F, replies: "Er gefällt und mißfällt mir"[1] ("I like and dislike him"). Similarly, at a crucial juncture in Thomas Mann's *Der Tod in Venedig* (*Death in Venice*, 1911), as Aschenbach considers fleeing the city, the phrase "Er will es und will es nicht"[2] ("He wants it and does not want it") again echoes the conflict between desire and withdrawal. The two instances are alike insofar as social prohibition manifests itself as psychic inhibition, although the one is voiced directly in the first person, whereas the other is a third person statement by a narrator with access to the persona's mind. What distinguishes the parallelism between these two texts, taking it beyond a mere comparison of theme, is the possibility of finding analogies to it in the reactions of readers to these narratives. The dualism of assent and resistance, characteristic of the fictive figures, has its echo in the experience of readers, who are as deeply torn as the protagonists between acquiescence in and opposition to the strategies whereby the text seeks to draw them in and along. It may well be this projection of the central tension into the reading process that endows both these works with that compelling magnetism that captivates readers.

The plot of both *Die Marquise von O—* and *Der Tod in Venedig*, reduced to its most basic element, turns on a seduction, or rather a yielding, although in neither narrative is it the straightforward temptation scenario enacted between Don Giovanni and Zerlina. Deviation from accepted social norms as well as sexuality are intrinsic to each. In *Die Marquise von O—* a bizarre situation is rapidly delineated in its bombshell opening sentence:

> In M-, einer bedeutenden Stadt im oberen Italien, ließ die verwitwete Marquise von O-, eine Dame von vortrefflichem Ruf und Mutter von mehreren wohlerzogenen Kindern, durch die Zeitungen bekanntmachen, daß sie ohne ihr Wissen in andre Umstände gekommen sei, daß der Vater zu dem Kinde, das sie gebären würde, sich melden solle und daß sie aus Familienrücksichten entschlossen wäre, ihn zu heiraten. (104)[3]

Residing with her parents in their castle, the marquise had in fact recently been saved from rape by soldiers during a skirmish by the gallant Russian officer, Count F. When he returns within a short time and abruptly but insistently begs for her hand in marriage, the surprised family pleads for a decent interval for reflection. Under her mother's gentle sounding, the marquise, who at first resolutely opposes, on principle, the idea of a second marriage, finally concedes that she is simultaneously attracted to and repelled by the count. With the discovery of her pregnancy and the count's eventual appearance in response to the advertisement, the emphasis of the plot modulates from the initial 'who-done-it?' to the 'why-done-it?' that raises the narrative's underlying epistemological issues.

The other pertinent questions, 'how and when-done it?' are relatively easy to answer, certainly for attentive readers of the original text:

> Man schleppte sie in den hinteren Schloßhof, wo sie eben unter den schändlichsten Mißhandlungen zu Boden sinken wollte, als, von dem Zetergeschrei der Dame herbeigerufen, ein russischer Offizier erschien und die Hunde, die nach solchem Raub lüstern waren, mit wütenden Hieben zerstreute. Der Marquise schien er ein Engel des Himmels zu

sein. Er stieß noch dem letzten viehischen Mordknecht, der ihren
schlanken Leib umfaßt hielt, mit dem Griff des Degens ins Gesicht, daß
er mit aus dem Mund vorquellendem Blut zurücktaumelte, bot dann der
Dame unter einer verbindlichen französischen Anrede den Arm und
führte sie, die von allen solchen Auftritten sprachlos war, in den an-
deren, von der Flamme noch nicht ergriffenen Flügel des Palastes, wo
sie auch völlig bewußtlos niedersank. Hier — traf er, da ihre erschrockenen Frauen erschienen, Anstalten, einen Arzt zu rufen, versicherte, indem er sich den Hut aufsetzte, daß sie sich bald erholen würde, und
kehrte in den Kampf zurück. (105 – 106)[4]

The narration of this scene is curious for its amalgam of detail and ellipsis.
The intercalated mention of the hat, for instance, seems at first an intru-
sive redundancy, while the critical act, his assault on her, is literally concealed under the textual cover of the dash. The count's strange behavior
on his return, his blushing, his embarrassment, the fervor with which he
presses his suit, the speed with which he wants the marriage to be for-
malized, and not least his sexually colored language all arouse readers'
suspicion.

If the perpetrator of the deed can be identified without much trouble,
the marquise's involvement is much more perplexing. First "speechless"
from shock, then "totally unconscious," she seems the prototype of the
female victim. Yet her grudging confession of her partial attraction to
Count F suggests at the very least a lowered level of resistance. The passion that he evidently felt for her at first sight may have been reciprocated.
He did strike her as an "angel," a description which she reiterates retro-
spectively in the closing sentence when she explains to him amidst embraces: "Er würde ihr damals nicht wie ein Teufel erschienen, wenn er ihr
nicht bei seiner ersten Erscheinung wie ein Engel vorgekommen wäre"
(143; "He would not have struck her as a devil if he had not struck her as
an angel at his first appearance"). As Dorrit Cohn has suggested, "This
deliberate denial of his non-angelic, *human* nature must surely apply to
herself even as it applies to him. In this light, her flight into unconscious-
ness appears as an instant reaction to salvage the purity of consciousness
in the moment of emerging eros."[5]

Conjoined to the psychic, there is also a social aspect to her assent/
resistance. The "angel" might well fulfill her unconscious wish for release
from the state of seclusion and tutelage in her parents' home, to which her
widowhood has condemned her in the past three years. There is ample
evidence not only of the tyranny her father exerts over her and of his violent temper, but also of his possessive, positively incestuous stance
toward her. The marquise's refusal to consider a second marriage may be

a conditioned response, implanted in her mind, against which her spontaneous desire rebels. She does, finally, marry the count and bear him a whole string of young Russians. This interpretation gains support from her vehement "Ich *will nichts* wißen" (129; italics are Kleist's — "I do not *want* to know *anything*") when the count comes to make confession. She does not want to know anything because she already has more than a dim awareness of it. Swales[6] and Cohn — interestingly, both female critics — argue that the marquise and her mother, in contrast to the male members of the family, have a shrewd inkling of the culprit's identity before the actual denouement. Cohn ascribes to the marquise "a cognitive duplicity, as though Kleist had endowed her with an unconscious form of knowledge unacknowledged by her conscious self."[7] Her "terrified refusal to know the truth (to know her erotic partner)"[8] stems from her repression from her consciousness of her sexuality. Only under the protection of a swoon can she assent where the social and familial norms predicate resistance.

Aschenbach, too, engages in a programmatic denial; he, too, does not want consciously to consent to what he darkly knows. He rationalizes his fixation on Tadzio as a continuance of his life-long cult of beauty of form:

> Mit Erstaunen bemerkte Aschenbach, daß der Knabe vollkommen schön war. Sein Antlitz, bleich und anmutig verschlossen, von honigfarbenem Haar umringelt, mit der gerade abfallenden Nase, dem lieblichen Munde, dem Ausdruck von holdem und göttlichem Ernst, erinnerte an griechische Bildwerke aus edelster Zeit, und bei reinster Vollendung der Form war es von so einmalig persönlichem Reiz, daß der Schauende weder in Natur noch bildender Kunst etwas ähnlich Geglücktes angetroffen zu haben glaubte. (224)[9]

The reference to Greek statuary immediately provides a cultural context for Aschenbach's passion, a reminder of a milieu where feelings such as his were licit, in antithesis to their interdiction in the society of his time and place. Aschenbach's entrancement by Tadzio is as much an infringement of a taboo as the marquise's acceptance of the count's advances to her. The injunction, though different in kind, is equal in force in the two cases.

Like the marquise, Aschenbach puts up a show of resistance. He makes a half-hearted attempt to leave Venice on the grounds that its climate is injurious to his health. But he lingers so long over breakfast, despite repeated promptings from the hotel staff, that he almost misses the train. When it turns out at the last minute that his luggage has mistakenly been dispatched to the wrong destination, Aschenbach returns to the hotel with apparent stoicism to await its return. "Aschenbach hatte Mühe, die Miene zu bewahren, die unter diesen Umständen einzig begreiflich war. Eine abenteuerliche Freude, eine unglaubliche Heiterkeit erschütterte von innen fast krampfhaft seine Brust" (246; "Aschenbach had difficulty in maintaining the only countenance that was appropriate under these circumstances. A reckless joy, an incredible glee shook his innermost heart almost like a spasm"). As in *Die Marquise von O—*, the language is laden with sexual innuendoes. There is a further similarity in the comic surface details of the psychopathology of everyday life masking the potentially tragic substratum. When the Swiss elevator attendant at the Hotel Excelsior greets Aschenbach with the polite commiseration, "Pas de chance, monsieur" (248; "Hard luck, sir"), the irony of his aborted flight is brilliantly underscored.

This incident of the misdirected luggage serves as a catalyst to Aschenbach's conversion from resistance to assent, as if he felt that fate had played its hand and he should go along with it. In ceasing to resist, Aschenbach is renouncing a life of self-imposed discipline similar to the marquise's, but of far longer duration. Right at the outset, as he is overcome by his sudden lust for travel, he is sufficiently aware of his own situation to ask himself: "Rächte sich nun also die geknechtete Empfindung, indem sie ihn verließ, indem sie seine Kunst fürder zu tragen und zu beflügeln sich weigerte und alle Lust, alles Entzücken an der Form und am Ausdruck mit sich hinwegnahm?" (192–3; "Was the suppressed feeling now taking its revenge by abandoning him, by refusing to sustain and animate his art further, taking away all his pleasure, all his ecstasy in form and expression?"). His yielding to the enchantment of Venice and of Tadzio represents, therefore, a reconfirmation that his vital, instinctual forces have not been dampened beyond revival by the life he has led. His switch from resistance to acquiescence is a performance of the polarity controlling his existence, so graphically contained in the anecdote told of him in the expository section:

> Als er um sein fünfunddreißigstes Jahr in Wien erkrankte, äußerte ein feiner Beobachter über ihn in Gesellschaft: "Sehen Sie, Aschenbach hat von jeher nur so gelebt" — und der Sprecher schloß die Finger seiner Linken fest zur Faust —; "niemals so" — und er ließ die geöffnete Hand bequem von der Lehne des Seßels hängen. (196)[10]

In Tadzio, Aschenbach sees the concrete incarnation of that perfection of form he had always upheld as the goal of his aspirations. What he had thought to be attainable only through dire effort now presents itself as a spontaneous formation. Each day Aschenbach marvels at "die wahrhaft göttliche Schönheit des Menschenkindes" (230; "the truly divine beauty of this human being") until he comes to regard him as the "Standbild und Spiegel der geistigen Schönheit," "Form als Gottesgedanken" (255; "image and mirror of spiritual beauty," "form as divine thought"). Only in his final monologue on the beach does he concede "daß dies ein gefährlich-lieblicher Weg, wahrhaft ein Irr- und Sündenweg, der mit Notwendigkeit in die Irre führt" (303; "that this is a dangerously pleasant path, verily a path of transgression and sin, which necessarily leads astray"). In its tragic conclusion, *Der Tod in Venedig* is the diametric opposite to *Die Marquise von O—* which suddenly comes to a superficially happy, but problematic and unsatisfying end with marriage and family.

The inclination to denial and subterfuge, that is so marked a characteristic of both the marquise and Aschenbach, creates in large measure the ironies of situation in which they become enmeshed. Both protagonists, in the very act of finding what they take to be their salvation, unwittingly precipitate their fall. To the marquise the count appears as a refuge from the soldiers assaulting her, yet her protector himself betrays her trust by promptly raping her. Similarly, Aschenbach has fashioned a personal and professional ethics out of his exaltation of aesthetic form, only to discover that the worship of beauty results in self-deception and eventual catastrophe. In both instances, the shelter that is sought brings instead of the anticipated security a cruel exposure.

The reversals suffered by both characters are contextualized in, and form part of a wider paradigm of dislocation which encompasses their entire universe. The particular is an example of the general, but the former also reinforces the latter in a sinister reciprocity. To aggravate the dichotomy, the normal order seems still to prevail for a while even when it is already so deeply undermined as to be heading for dissolution.

The apparent maintenance of the established order is categorically, though ironically, posited in *Die Marquise von O—* after the departure of the invaders: "Alles kehrte nun in die alte Ordnung zurück" (109; "Everything now reverted to the old order of things"). The as yet concealed irony resides in the fact that the marquise has meanwhile become pregnant so that things can never quite revert to the old order. When her state is diagnosed and she protests her innocence, her mother scoffs at her for trying to invent "ein Märchen von der Umwälzung der Weltordnung" (122; "a fable about the overturning of the order of the world") so as to cover what she deems her daughter's "Fehltritt" (122; "error"). The marquise, persisting in her assertions of bewilderment, then asks the midwife about the likelihood of an immaculate conception, only to be roundly laughed at. This is a benign repetition of the doctor's reaction when he reproves her for her tendency to joke before taking his leave with the formal declaration "daß er ihr die letzten Gründe der Dinge nicht werde zu erklären brauchen" (120; "that he would not need to explain to her the ultimate causes of things").

The doctor's sarcastic rejoinder shifts the problem from the physical onto the metaphysical and ontological plane through its intertextual allusion to Kant.[11] The Kantian resonances of "Dinge" ("things"), as in the earlier "Ordnung der Dinge" (109; "order of things"), stem from Kleist's own reading (and misreading) of Kant. *Die Marquise von O—* is indeed a fable, or an allegory, of the overturning of the normative order of the world when an officer, who approaches a lady with a courteous address in the language of polite society, then immediately proceeds to rape her. It is significant that the term "Ordnung" ("order") of the first half of the story is superseded in the latter part by the more non-committal "Einrichtung" ("set-up"). And "Einrichtung" is qualified first by "groß," "heilig," and "unerklärlich" (126; "great," "sacred," and "inexplicable"), but at the close by the simple and telling adjective, "gebrechlich" (143; "fragile"). It is on account of the fragile set-up of the world that the marquise forgives the count. She for one, perhaps for her children's sake, has come to terms with the brittleness of a social, moral, and metaphysical structure, wherein angels may turn out to be devils, and vice versa.

The same theme permeates *Der Tod in Venedig*, though not with quite the same intensity nor with the metaphysical edge; the perversion of order into chaos takes place here primarily on the physical and moral plane. The exemplary order that has dominated Aschenbach's life has its counterpart in the organization of the Hotel Excelsior, a microcosm of elegant protocol, whose ritualistic formalities assure its pampered guests a harmonious sojourn. To don evening dress, for instance, "eine Uniform der Gesittung" (223; "a uniform of decorum") is the unquestioned custom. Nevertheless, Aschenbach's luggage is misdirected to Como (leaving him, as a byproduct, unable to dress *comme il faut* for several days). Evidently, even in this model system, mistakes occur, however profusely the manager may apologize for what he euphemistically calls the "Zwischenfall" ("incident"), which he considers "äußerst peinlich für ihn und das Institut" (248; "extremely embarrassing to him and the institution"). Things are not as wholly under control either in the hotel or in Aschenbach's life as appearances might initially suggest; "incidents" intervene, with regard to emotions as easily as with luggage.

As in *Die Marquise von O—*, signs of a disturbing dissonance are manifest early on in *Der Tod in Venedig*, though again in a less immediately violent form than the invasion of the castle. During his first walk, in the opening section of the *Novelle*, Aschenbach encounters a mysterious stranger with a skeletal head near the cemetery, a transparent augury of death. Then, on the boat from Pola to Venice, there is a noisy crowd of young people on an outing, one of whom proves at closer quarters to be an elderly man, made up and dressed to masquerade youthfulness. As he gets more drunk, his gestures denote lewd sexual intentions. Aschenbach experiences a sense of numbness "als zeige die Welt eine leichte, doch nicht zu hemmende Neigung, sich ins Sonderbare und Fratzenhafte zu entstellen" (213; "as if the world were showing a slight but inexorable tendency to become distorted into the strange and grotesque"). The expected seemly order is temporarily restored in the ambiance of the Hotel Excelsior, again as in *Die Marquise von O—*, but here also appearances are deceptive. Like the embryo carried by the marquise, the passion nascent in Aschenbach grows implacably under the cloak of impeccable propriety.

When the smell of formaldehyde begins to mingle with the foul odors from the lagoon, Aschenbach makes discreet inquiries, all of which are, naturally, rebuffed. The city, like Aschenbach, is endeavoring to hide its guilty secret. The correspondence between the two is emphasized through the use of the same word, "Heimsuchung" ("doom"), applied to him (258, 297) and to Venice (290). Even after he learns the facts about the cholera epidemic sweeping the city, Aschenbach decides not only to stay himself, but also not to warn the Polish family. The progressive emptying of the hotel, the beach, and the streets is favorable to his passion as it brings him into closer propinquity with Tadzio. He fantasizes himself and the boy as the last survivors in the infected city. The imminent threat of death, together with the corruption of the authorities "brachte eine gewiße Entsittlichung der unteren Schichten hervor, eine Ermutigung lichtscheuer und antisozialer Triebe, die sich in Unmäßigkeit, Schamlosigkeit und wachsender Kriminalität bekundete" (291–2; "induced a certain demoralization of the lower classes, encouraging darker, antisocial drives, which surfaced in intemperance, indecency, and an increase in crime"). The disruption of order that is a concomitant of war in *Die Marquise von O—* is effected in *Der Tod in Venedig* through the incursion of a highly contagious and deadly disease. In both narratives the breakdown of external order is shown to foster a climate conducive to the derangement of values.

That sense of derangement is also, by a metonymic transference, experienced by readers. The impact of both these narratives is profoundly unsettling. Their endings in particular are disturbing: the abrupt romance closure of *Die Marquise von O—* with marriage and a whole string of little Russians is as astonishing as the moralistic conclusion of *Der Tod in Venedig* with the narrator's outspoken condemnation of Aschenbach. In one respect these two narratives are diametrically opposed: the outcome of *Die Marquise von O—* is positive, and its narrating voice carefully eschews judgmental statements and appears, indeed, to be as much in the dark as the protagonists and readers, whereas the denouement of *Der Tod in Venedig* is negative, and its narrator emerges in the last third of the story as a moralist in his evaluations. Yet, curiously, the effect on readers is remarkably similar insofar as both elicit a distinct sense of violation that arouses a discomfited resistance.

This resistance is all the more surprising in light of readers' earlier willingness to assent. While the protagonists modulate from resistance to assent in their acceptance of the essential fragility and deceptiveness of their universe, readers, move in the opposite direction in their increasing recalcitrance to the course of events in the fictive realm and the treatment meted out to them as readers. This results in a chiasmus which heightens the complexity and piquancy of the reading process.

Both narratives initally encourage readers' belief in their ability to construe the text and to make valid inferences. After the shock of its opening sentence, *Die Marquise von O—* settles into a more familiar format with a long retrospective narration of the storming of the castle and its immediate sequels. Count F's behavior in returning to the family in order to press his offer of marriage is so obviously suspect as to make readers identify him as the rapist without much doubt. Yet even after they feel in possession of the answer to the central mystery, the whirlwind speed of the narration carries them along. Indeed, they rather bask in their awareness of their own cleverness, especially in contrast to the family's agonized puzzlement, which comes to appear both comical and ironic. During the first half of *Die Marquise von O—*, therefore, readers tend to develop a security akin to complacency in regard to their capacity to master the fictive situation and the conventions of reading.

The beginning of *Der Tod in Venedig* is even more readily intelligible. An omniscient third person narrator offers readers an uncomplicated narrative contract as he gives ample and precise information about Aschenbach's present state of mind and his personal history. Through the introduction of an apparently casual first person plural in the opening sentence in the phrase "unserem Kontinent" (185; "our continent"), readers are drawn into a closer solidarity with the narrating voice. Its confident and confiding tone projects an image of stability and reliability. Authoritative and competent, this voice remains firmly in control, although such random asides as "Seltsame Zusammenhänge!" (202; "Curious connections!") or "Wie dem auch sei! (203; "Be that as may!") hint at possible ulterior layers not yet divulged to readers. By and large, however, readers have little reason to query the trust they place in this narrator as a knowing and credible teller.

On the contrary, the semiotic transparency of *Der Tod in Venedig* supports readers' assumptions of their competence as well as fostering their complicity with the narrator. This becomes strikingly apparent in the first two sections already. Aschenbach's vision of "eine Art Urwelt-wildnis" (189; "a sort of primitive wilderness world") replete with morasses, exotic vegetation, outlandish birds and a crouching tiger requires as little explanation in this post-Freudian era as his glimpse near the cemetery of the mysteriously appearing and disappearing stranger, whose protruding teeth, empty gaze and prominent forehead are those of a death-head. The resurgent thirst for life in its most crudely vigorous manifestations is not merely a rebellion against the many years of dour self-discipline, but also a fear of incompletion, of never having really lived as the specter of the final closure of death advances toward him. Similarly, the sleaziness that characterizes the boat taking Aschenbach from Pola to Venice — its rusty decrepitude, scruffy crew, surly ticketman, steward in a soiled jacket, and wretched food — merges with the aberrant in the old man masquerading as a youth, whose upper dentures slip while he shouts a ribald greeting to Aschenbach. His misadventure with the gruff, unlicensed gondolier, whose gondola seems to him a softly upholstered coffin of ease, and who vanishes without awaiting payment, is the third in the series of eerie encounters that herald a new phase in his life. Like the image of the clenched hand to denote his previous lifestyle, all these episodes are wholly transparent. Throughout *Der Tod in Venedig* the symbols, not least the references to Greek mythology, are so readily comprehensible as to make the text virtually self-interpreting. Readers willingly assent to this mode of narration, partly on account of the pride it inspires in their skill in decoding the signs. As in *Die Marquise von O—*, readers consent to the role delineated for them because it invests them with an attractive perspicacity. Through their appeal, at some level, to readers' vanity, both texts manipulate their audience into exactly the desired position of compliance.

But this quiescent assent does not prevail throughout. In both instances readers begin to be perturbed through the incidence of indirect discourse, which considerably complicates the narrative disposition. In *Der Tod in Venedig* it opens up an aperture of irony between the narrator and the protagonist, and thus sows in readers' minds seeds of doubt as to his motivation. The most obvious example occurs in the opening section when Aschenbach is made to dismiss his sudden lust for adventure with the innocuous diagnosis: "Es war Reiselust, nichts weiter" (189; "It was the urge to travel, nothing more"). Aschenbach's desire to minimize and contain the extent of his emotional turmoil is evident in his curt phrase; yet by virtue of its overstatement, in the added "nichts weiter" ("nothing more"), it adumbrates the possibility of alternative interpretations with graver implications for his psyche. It is by no means a far-fetched hypothesis, even at this early stage in the narrative, to conjecture that Aschenbach has not only been pushing himself to the verge of breakdown, but has also been practicing a fundamental and systematic self-deception. His dark intuitive apprehensions surface, significantly often as questions, at other points too, notably in the passage already cited in which he wonders whether his long suppressed feelings were now taking their due revenge (192–3). While Aschenbach himself refuses to embark on any radical self-assessment, readers are certainly prompted by these glimpses backstage to engage in a skeptical reconsideration of the surface image of success presented to them. Readers are here still obeying the signals— albeit ambivalent ones—emitted by the narrator, but they are beginning, too, to develop that independence of judgment that will eventually lead to resistance.

In *Die Marquise von O—*, indirect discourse is used more widely and to differing effect, though with the same ultimate outcome of stimulating readers' autonomy. Few writers have practiced indirect discourse as extensively as Kleist, and, perhaps even more important, as dispassionately. Reported speech in Kleist's narratives is precisely that: an account of what characters say or have said without any of the undertones instilled by the narrating voice in *Der Tod in Venedig*. Indirect discourse in *Die Marquise von O—* does not, therefore, serve the purpose of suggestivity. Because of the total absence of evaluative input from the narrator, its impact on readers is to create confusion. The heteroglossia conveys a bewildering multiplicity of views and putative scenarios, all of which carry equal weight since none is privileged through either endorsement or denial. Count F is said to have died of wounds sustained in combat; he reappears as hale and hearty as before. Neither the marquise nor her family knows what to make of his conduct at this point, or indeed later, despite much searching discussion of the contradiction between his prominent good qualities and his estranging idiosyncrasies. Bereft of any of the customary narratorial guidance, readers are left to sort out this multivocality as best they can. Thus, as in *Der Tod in Venedig*, though by a different process, they are driven to cultivate their own capacities for discernment in facing a text that offers a maximum of potentiality and a minimum of definity.

The perplexity is further heightened by a feature that might be expected to simplify matters: the extraordinary precision of Kleist's grammatical constructions and the perfect cohesion of his syntax. Admittedly sentences and paragraphs are frequently long, producing that sense of breathlessness, of pressure, of unrelenting thrust that no reader can escape. But although this style pushes parataxis to its limits, it invariably observes the rules of grammar with an almost exaggerated care. The meticulous interlacing whereby each clause is linked to the preceding and the following one, and sentence to sentence, even as they are piled up in a dizzying array, is without flaw. The rigorous sequentiality of Kleist's prose, with its characteristic markers such as "eben" ("just"), "da" ("as" or "when"), "hierauf" ("thereupon"), and especially "dergestalt daß" ("in such a way that"), is in stark contrast to the fortuity that dominates his fictive world. So readers find themselves able to construe syntactically each individual segment, but utterly unable to join them cognitively into a comprehensible whole. The extreme consequentiality of the linguistic texture, paradoxically, highlights the utter inconsequentiality of human behavior.

Some of these Kleistian strategies are adopted in *Der Tod in Venedig*. The hyperemphatic turn, "dergestalt daß" (188; "with the consequence that"), for instance, is sufficiently unusual in modern discourse to be recognized by German readers as an echo of Kleist. Mann's phraseology does indeed bear the imprint of Kleist in its tendency to parataxis and prolongation as well as in its exactness. Mann also appropriates some of Kleist's favorite ciphers of contingency: "zufällig" (186; "by chance"), "Es fügte sich" (243; "It turned out"), "So geschah es" (230 and 267; "So it happened"). But where the Kleistian narrator, through his insistent neutrality, leaves genuinely open the susceptibility to chance, the narrator in *Der Tod in Venedig* injects an unmistakable undercurrent of irony into these apparently constative statements. He does so by his implicit presence as the teller of Aschenbach's story and by the perception that he has of that story. The coincidences and accidents, that occur through inexplicable hazard in *Die Marquise von O—*, are presented in *Der Tod in Venedig* as engineered, perhaps subconsciously, by Aschenbach so as to allow him to follow his inclinations without pangs of conscience. Thus where readers face a wholly enigmatic scenario in *Die Marquise von O—*, in *Der Tod in Venedig* it is an ironic one, whose calculated reversals become increasingly evident as the plot unfolds.

Because of this discrepancy in the narrator's function in the two narratives, the relationship of narrator to readers is different and, as a corollary, so is the nature of reader resistance. In *Der Tod in Venedig*, that resistance is provoked by the terms in which the last part of the story is told, so that readers' antagonism comes to be directed against the narrator. In *Die Marquise von O—*, on the other hand, there is far less resentment of the narrator, who manages to maintain his stance of detached chronicler. His refusal (or inability) to provide anything other than a romance closure is a source of some irritation, but this is merely one, almost minor, facet of readers' deeper discomposure at being forced to confront on their own the insoluble problem of good and evil raised by the narrative. Readers' resistance is, therefore, more distinct in *Der Tod in Venedig*, but more profoundly motivated in *Die Marquise von O—*.

In *Der Tod in Venedig* the point at which readers' pleasure in the text's subtleties is converted into repugnance at its crassness can be determined with precision. It coincides with the narrator's switch of posture from ironist to moralist. As Aschenbach lets himself increasingly follow the dictates of his instinct rather than his reason, the narrator divorces himself from him in a series of descriptive pronouns that express overt censure of him: "der Heimgesuchte" (288, 297; "the man destined for a bad fate"), "der Berückte" (264,300; "the ensorcered man"), "der Betörte" (272, 277; "the spellbound man"), "der Verwirrte" (275; "the man gone astray"), "der Starrsinnige" (288; "the obdurate man"), and last, "der Hinabgesunkene" (308; "the fallen man"). The final portrait of Aschenbach sitting on the beach, his hair colored, his face made up, his eyes fixed on Tadzio's every gesture, is sharpened in its cruelty by the appellation given to him: "Meister" (302; "master"). He who had indeed been a master of the aesthetic, and who had "aller Ironie entwachsen" (203; "grown beyond all irony"), is now unmasked as having been, ironically, ensnared by the lure of the very thing in which he had sought a defensive bulwark.

This change of the narrator's attitude toward his protagonist is shocking to readers. The very words with which Aschenbach is branded are jarring disclosures of the narrator's aggressiveness which in turn rebounds against him. Even as he is prompting readers to scorn Aschenbach, toppled from his precariously maintained position of eminence, he achieves the very opposite. For his betrayal of Aschenbach reveals an innate treachery, which makes readers wary and distrustful of him. His bad faith in regard to Aschenbach is an act of transgression which infringes and undermines the narrative contract established at the outset. Instead of assenting to the narrator's disparagement of Aschenbach, readers dissociate themselves from it and from the narrator, exercising their freedom of response in their resistance.

The process of inversion is more subtle and more devastating in *Die Marquise von O—*. Here, too, readers are expected to learn a new role as the narrative progresses, and it proves a difficult one. After priding themselves in the first half on their astute powers of detection and deduction, readers gradually come to discover that they are no better able to grasp, let alone to explain "the ultimate causes of things" than the protagonists. In other words, their capacity to read and to interpret is subject to severe limitations because truth is not attainable in the "fragile set-up" that constitutes this world. Extravagant contradictions abound, such as the report of the count's death, followed by his reappearance, not to mention his unfathomable conjunction of chivalry and depravity. So readers are sucked into the epistemological dilemma with which the family is seen to struggle to little avail. The marquise, who has avowed the ambivalence of her feelings for the count, opts ultimately against further attempts to pursue knowledge in her vehement assertion, "Ich *will nichts* wißen" (116; "I do not *want* to know *anything*"), and decides to make her peace with the world as it is. Perhaps she marries the count precisely out of her recognition of the imperfection of all things and beings; or perhaps because she has loved him from the first moment; or perhaps out of consideration for their child.

Whatever her reasons, the happy ending, normatively associated with comedy, sits surprisingly on a story whose coloring has been primarily, though not wholly, dark. The marriage represents, of course, a comfortable resolution of the plot, but it does nothing to solve the radical quandaries embodied in its action. The argument could even be advanced that the final happy outcome exacerbates the underlying problem by suggesting that the sole way to come to terms with an alarming universe is to accept it without excessive ratiocination and to incorporate viciousness into the "order of things" as an integral facet of human life. If this be the case, *Die Marquise von O—* offers an unpalatable view of the world, which readers are likely to resist. What they resist even more strongly, however, is the implication that their own capacity to read and understand is negligible in relation to the enormity of the question. The resultant sense of alienation is as acute in *Die Marquise von O—* as in *Der Tod in Venedig*, although its sources are quite heterogeneous.

In both *Die Marquise von O—* and *Der Tod in Venedig*, readers, through their initial readiness to assent, in effect place themselves within the frame of the narrative. They are not prepared for the consequences of their situation: that they are expected to compromise their beliefs in *Der Tod in Venedig*, and to improvise them in *Die Marquise von O—*. So they become locked into the conflict between the urge to re-read (in order to know?) and the self-protective desire not to know: "vorrei, e non vorrei."

5

Through Multiple Lenses: Ironies in Kleist's *Die Marquise von O—*

*"Und gleichwohl muß es doch notwendig eins oder das
andere gewesen sein." ("And yet it must necessarily
have been the one or the other.")*

My epigraph is a phrase from the mouth of the marquise of *O—*'s
mother which epitomizes an essentially unironic view of existence in its
imperious insistence that everything must necessarily be open to resolution into one or the other alternative. In the course of the narrative, protagonists and readers alike have to face the deconstruction of this simplistic view and the distressing implications of that process.

To students of irony and of reading in general Kleist's *Die Marquise
von O—* has a peculiar fascination. Within the compact form of a quite
short *Novelle* it encompasses an astonishing range of ironies intertwined
into a tight web. Kleist draws largely on the traditional devices and strategies of irony, but he does so with such virtuosity and subtlety as to intensify the possibilities of ironic narration into a haunting metaphor of his
perplexed vision of the universe. The figural means of representation become an allegory of the world represented. There is no surer way to experience the dilemmas of Kleist's world than to wrestle as a reader with
the ironic mobility of his text.

Much of the irony in *Die Marquise von O—* hinges on readers' capacity to work out the situation long before the protagonists are able to
do so. Kleist deliberately manipulates the element of surprise so that *Die
Marquise von O—* can be read at one level as a detective story. In the
opening sentence the reader has the shock of discovering the body, so to
speak. This is followed by an extended retrospective account of the cir-

cumstances leading up to this point: the storming of the citadel, the count's sudden marriage proposal, the diagnosis of the marquise's pregnancy, her conflict with her family, and her retreat with her children to her country estate. It is not until three-fifths of the way through the story that we return to the present time of narration, to "jene sonderbare Forderung" ("that strange summons") in the newspapers of M — "die man am Eingang dieser Erzählung gelesen hat"[1] ("which was read at the beginning of this narration"). This lengthy excursus from the starting-point into the past heightens the tension by delaying the eventual response to the marquise's advertisement for the father of the child she is expecting. However, it also serves another purpose: by giving readers access to the marquise's immediate past it enables them to see through the situation from an early moment on.

The entire disposition of the narrative is, therefore, designed to permit the maximum latitude for the exercise of those kinds of irony which devolve from readers' possession of an understanding superior to that of the duped protagonists. Or rather, as they later discover, from readers' belief that they are in possession of such superior understanding. For that belief in turn is ultimately undercut by an irony of a different dimension from that which dominates the first half of the narrative. Readers find themselves victims of double-dealing: they have been dealt a set of cards with which they engage in a game with whose rules they are conversant; only gradually does it dawn on them that another game is simultaneously being played in which they are as much at a loss as the protagonists. From the role of observers of irony, which they assume through most of the narrative, they are demoted to that of victims of irony. In the jolt of this fall they experience the full impact of Kleist's contingent vision of the universe.

Readers attain their position as observers of irony by virtue of the astuteness of their detective powers. Their awareness of the irony of the situation being enacted depends on their ability to decipher the puzzle of the marquise's pregnancy in advance of her and her family. Readers' suspicions become the organizing center of their interpretation of the narrative in progress as an ironic plot. What is more, their increasing assurance of their own reading creates the pride that comes before the fall.

How soon then are readers able to solve the 'whodunit?' aspect of *Die Marquise von O—*? It has recently been asserted that modern students are "alerted to the true state of affairs after only a few paragraphs."[2] That may well be so, but mainly because Kleist's paragraphs are inordinately long. There are in fact surprisingly few of those stylistic signals of an ironic intent that occur at the beginning of such works as Jane Austen's *Pride and Prejudice* and Byron's *Don Juan*. The opening sentence is startling in its disruption of expectations of behavior for a woman of that class and of that moral standing at that time. It is rife with ironies of situation in the discrepancy between the marquise's impeccably virtuous past and her present position and action, and also in her astonishing decision to publicize her problem and to marry "aus Familienrücksichten" (104; "out of consideration for her family"), when those very considerations might have dictated the diametrically opposite course of discreet secrecy. Yet there is nothing in either that sentence or in the subsequent rapid narration of the attack on the citadel to warrant the assumption that this text is meant to be read in any sense divergent from its overt surface. The narrator's tone is that of the detached chronicler, and the language is devoid of ambiguity.

It is not until after the notorious gap, denoted by a dash that has aptly been likened to "einer spanischen Wand, hinter der der Erzähler erst hervorkommt als 'die erschrockenen Frauen' der Marquise erscheinen"[3] ("a screen from behind which the narrator emerges only when the marquise's 'frightened women servants' appear"), that the timber of the narration modulates as perceptible clues insinuate the presence of irony. The word *Umstände* (circumstances), which crops up no fewer than sixteen times in a relatively brief story, creates an ingenious verbal and ideational link between the marquise and the count. Both have recourse to that conveniently capacious term to characterize the duress prompting their actions. The imperatives of the marquise's "andere Umstände"[4] (104; "other circumstances") is echoed by the count's constraint "daß er sich der Frau Marquise unter diesen Umständen gehorsamst empfehlen müsse" (108; "that under these circumstances he must submissively take leave of the marquise"). Similarly, the pressures exerted by her recognition "daß sie in gesegneten Leibesumständen wäre" (109; "that she was in blessed bodily circumstances") are countered by his concession that he is "durch die Umstände gezwungen" (110; "forced by circumstances"). Such stealthy lexical indicators reinforce the suppositions aroused in readers' minds by the count's bizarre conduct and by the urgency not just of his proposal but of his wish for an instantaneous marriage.

The conjecture of an ironic subtext is corroborated by a striking and curious phrase in the conversation between the marquise's father and the count when the latter is pressing his precipitate suit. To the count's assurances about his integrity, veracity, etc.: "Der Kommandant erwiderte, indem er ein wenig, obschon ohne Ironie, lächelte, daß er alle diese Äußerungen unterschreibe" (112; "The commander replied, smiling a little, though without irony, that he subscribed to all these assertions"). The parenthetically inserted "obschon ohne Ironie" ("though without irony") is conspicuous as one of the very few interpretative comments regarding a character's inner attitude in a story where it is the notation of external, often physical responses, such as gestures, blushing, fainting, or silence that predominates. Given the economy of the narration in *Die Marquise von O—*, this deliberate reference to irony can hardly be accidental. It seems as if Kleist specifically names the trope in order to confirm the idea in readers' minds. Its posited absence suggests *per contrariam* its possible presence. The context of the phrase bears out this hypothesis for it comes at the moment when the count is making the most grossly ironic assertions of his rectitude. To which the marquise's father replies with that non-ironic smile and the confident statement: "Noch hätte er keines jungen Mannes Bekanntschaft gemacht, der in so kurzer Zeit so viele vortreffliche Eigenschaften des Charakters entwickelt hätte" (112; "He had never met a young man, who had in so short a time shown such an excellent character"). That this peerless young man had in an equally short time demonstrated the opposite by violating his daughter is patently the last thought that would cross his mind. Hence his lack of any sense of the ironic implications of his own bearing or the count's, or indeed of any alternative interpretation of the situation. To readers, however, to whom that alternative has already occurred, the evocation of "Ironie" at this point acts as an endorsement of their increasingly probable surmise. Kleist has here introduced a phrase into his narration that is of no more than marginal significance for the progression of the narrative, but of crucial importance for its reading.

Readers' growing confidence in the validity of their inferences brings a pronounced dramatic irony into play. The audience commands knowledge denied to the protagonists. This is underscored by the repeated insistence on the family's utter bewilderment: "Die Familie wußte nicht, was sie zu dieser Äußerung sagen sollte" (113; "The family did not know what to respond to this statement"); "Als er das Zimmer verlassen, wußte die Familie nicht, was sie aus dieser Erscheinung machen solle" (113–14; "When he had left the room, the family did not know what to make of his appearance"); "Inzwischen war die Familie in der lebhaftesten Unruhe... Der Kommandant sagte, daß er von der Sache nichts verstehe": (115; "Meanwhile the family was in extreme agitation... The commander said that he understood nothing of this matter"). The unknowing actors are contrasted with the knowing readers, who are able to assess things from the vantage point of their superior insight. The irony is, therefore, at the expense of the characters as they grope toward an understanding already attained by the audience. The disparity between the internal and the external interpreters of the situation is most flagrant in the scene following the count's surprising return after his reported death and his abrupt proposal of marriage (109 – 119). To initiated readers the discussion among the members of the family is at once farcical and tragic.

As readers become ever more convinced of the appropriateness of their construction, the dramatic irony intensifies to a pitch where it begins to create a problem of credibility. It is hard for modern readers to accept the characters' protracted blindness, even within the framework of early nineteen century trust in the conduct proper to a gentleman. There is evidence to support the argument[5] that the marquise, and indeed her mother, have begun to have a shrewd inkling of the culprit's identity considerably before the actual denouement. In the last resort, however, such a pseudo-realistic question as 'when does she begin to know?' is beside the point in the most literal sense of the word. For the point of *Die Marquise von O—* is not so much 'when?' or even 'what?' do the protagonists know, as how can they deal with the knowledge they acquire, how can they accommodate it to their cherished world view. So the marquise's lasting ignorance can be seen as a form of denial. Even more important, with this displacement of interest from 'what?' and 'when?' to 'how?', the dramatic irony loses its momentum. The distance between readers and protagonists is suddenly and drastically foreshortened. The superior insight on which readers have relied proves to be of limited worth, maybe even mistaken. In an irony of reversal, the tables have been turned on them; they have been ousted from their privileged observation tower and thrown into the maelstrom of uncertainty.

This ironic manipulation of the dramatic irony is paradigmatic of the shifting nature of the irony in *Die Marquise von O—*. Through Kleist's use of many devices traditional to irony, readers are first encouraged to develop certain consistent patterns of reading derived from the established strategies for recognizing and constructing ironies. However, this primary level of seemingly stable irony is itself subject to ironic subversion through other narrative tactics which undermine the authority of the constructed meaning. So the characteristic dualities of irony are sharpened in *Die Marquise von O—* into duplicities that thwart the reading process and leave readers in a quandary parallel to that of the characters.

A good example of this complicated double-dealing is the handling of verbal irony. The extraordinarily dense linguistic texture of *Die Marquise von O—* is a major source of its ironies. It is through his distinctive use of words that Kleist opens up an aperture of irony, and he does so by the rhetorical means generally associated with ironic discourse. His favorite procedure is the simplest and most common device of irony, *double entendre*, which he exploits with the utmost inventiveness. Innocuous words and phrases such "Folgen" ("consequences"), "verbindlich"

("binding"), "empfangen" ("to receive"), "ergeben" ("submissive"), "nä-
here Bekanntschaft" ("closer acquaintance") are given an ambiguous aspect through the context of dramatic irony in which they are embedded.
It is an outcome of this practice "daß keine Bemerkung unverfänglich
bleibt, daß jede neben dem gemeinten noch einen zweiten Sinn erhält, der
zwar dem Sprechenden verborgen bleibt — dafür aber Autor und Leser
um so größeres Vergnügen bereitet"[6] ("that no phrase remains innocuous, that each one contains beside the obvious meaning a second one,
which remains hidden from the speaker — but therefore gives the author
and reader added pleasure").

Often Kleist has recourse to variants on the ironic *double entendre*.
What is said, far from being the opposite to what is meant, is exactly what
is meant, at least in the mind of the speaker, but is not understood as such.
The count's statements are frequently the object of failure to understand
on the hearer's part. When he tells the family of his need "über eine not-
wendige Forderung seine Seele ins Reine zu sein" (111; "to come clean in
a compelling demand of his soul"), when he claims to have "entschei-
dende" (115; "decisive") reasons for his actions, and finally, when he de-
clares, "es würde ein Tag kommen, wo sie ihn verstehen würde!" (119; "a
day would come when she would understand him!"): in all these instances he is in fact speaking without any ironic intent. The irony arises,
contrary to his purpose, through the listener's refusal to take his words
at their face value. There is then a further layer of irony in the disparity
between the responses of the fictional hearers within the text and those
of the readers outside the text who can see the literalness of the meaning.
The marquise's misperception of her name "Julietta!" on the count's lips
as referring to some unfortunate "Namensschwester" (108; "sister in
name") is one more example of such misinterpretation. Another kind of
double entendre occurs when a protagonist speaks with ironic intent, yet
— ironically — hits the nail on the head without realizing it. The most
prominent instance of such unconscious irony is the father's dictum: "Sie
hat es im Schlaf getan" (131; "She did it in her sleep"), which is put forward as a scathing sarcasm, but is nearer to the truth than the speaker
believes. The marquise's mother, too, makes comments that come unwittingly close to the heart of the matter: "Sein heftiger, auf einen Punkt hin-
treibender Wille, meinte sie, scheine ihr einer solchen Tat fähig" (114;
"His violent will, fixated on a single issue, she said, seemed to her to make
him capable of such a deed"); "ob er nicht kommen, seine leichtsinnige
Tat bereuen und wieder gutmachen werde" (115; "whether he would not
come, regretting his frivolous deed and making amends for it"); "ein uner-
hörtes Spiel des Schicksals" (132; "an unheard of trick of fate"); "en jun-
ger, sonst wohlerzogener Mensch, dem wir eine solche Nichtswürdigkeit

niemals zugetraut hätten" (134; "a young, well brought up person, to whom we would never have imputed such a vile deed"). In these numerous cases of *double entendre* irony appears in its characteristic guise as "a form of utterance that postulates a double audience, consisting of one party that hearing shall hear and not understand, and another party that when more is meant than meets the ear, is aware both of that more and of the outsiders' incomprehension."[7]

Another rather more subtle type of *double entendre* also plays an important part in *Die Marquise von O——*. Words are introduced which, either in themselves or in the combination in which they are placed, have certain associative overtones. In itself this is so familiar a feature of any poetic discourse as to warrant no special mention. What distinguishes it in *Die Marquise von O—* is the consistent referent and position of such connotative language. The connotation is invariably sexual, and its locus is the count. He addresses the marquise "mit einer aufflammenden Freude" (110; "with a blazing joy"); he had thought of her constantly after he had been wounded, and he tells her:

> daß er die Lust und den Schmerz nicht beschreiben könnte, die sich in dieser Vorstellung umarmt hätten, daß er endlich nach seiner Wiederherstellung wieder zur Armee gegangen wäre; daß er daselbst die lebhafteste Unruhe empfunden hätte. (110–111)[8]

His boyhood memories of the swan whom he had tried in vain "an sich zu locken" ("to entice toward himself") after besmirching her with mud come to him "in der Hitze des Wundfiebers" (116; "in the heat of the fever from the wound"), when he confuses the marquise with the swan. The subliminal resonance of the phrase "in der Hitze des Gefechts" ("in the heat of combat") adumbrates the parallel between the count's behavior toward the swan and toward the marquise. The unmistakable sexual coloring of the count's speech is a pointer to the powerful, barely repressed erotic undertow of his personality, which breaks through in his crucial deed. His penchant for such diction represents an ironic inversion of the highly stylized discourse of his class and time;[9] his ritualistic "untertänigst" (114; "most obediently") and "gefälligst" (115; "most compliantly") are contravened by his instinctive and instinctual vocabulary.

The evidence of the rhetoric therefore suggests that *Die Marquise von O—* is governed by a web of literary ironies which are relatively transparent to readers once they have grasped the fundamental situation. The ambiguities of the language seem to be the appropriate expression for the discrepancy between the masking appearance and the ulterior reality. Seen in this light, *Die Marquise von O—* conforms to the classical paradigm of irony. But in a characteristically Kleistian double-dealing a further dimension becomes palpable, where this legible irony is itself severely undercut. The cutting instrument in the case of the rhetoric is indirect discourse, which produces a distinctively dualistic effect. On the one hand, it serves to lend credibility to the characters' utterances. In page after page of reported speech the narrator presents their words and thoughts through the lens of their perception. The tone is cool and detached; the narrating voice refrains from explicit comment or ostensible interpretation. What Wolfgang Kayser has noted of a passage in *Das Erdbeben in Chili (The Earthquake in Chile)* holds true for *Die Marquise von O—* too: "Der Erzähler hat sich mit der Wendung ganz auf die Gestalt, von der er spricht, eingestellt, er wertet aus ihrer Perspektive"[10] ("The narrator has with this turn positioned himself wholly with the figure of whom he speaks; he evaluates from the figure's perspective"). Kayser later elaborates on this argument: "Er wertet hier — soll man sagen: wie einer oder als einer, der das Vorhergehende nicht kennt und nun vor den Mandaten steht"[11] ("He evaluates here — should one say: like or as one who has no knowledge of the foregoing and faces only the briefs"). This very aptly captures the posture of the Kleistian narrator. Maintaining his aesthetic distance through an austere non-involvement, he assumes the role of the neutral, factual chronicler whose function is solely to report. He retreats behind the events narrated, speaking indeed almost as if his back were turned to the audience.[12] Yet the air of authenticity that is created thereby is in itself more questionable than may at first appear. Kleist, long before Flaubert, exploited the ironic potential of indirect discourse as a mode of narration. What is reported is, notwithstanding its semblance of veracity, after all nothing other than subjective perceptions through the eyes of various characters. The wide range of their views of the predicament already hints at the elusiveness of any authoritative position. The essential precariousness of all that is being so meticulously registered is implied in the high incidence of the form "es schien" ("it seemed") as well as by such interpolations as "wie sie meinte" (108; "as she thought"), "meinte sie" (114; "she thought"), "wie er meinte" (133; "as he thought"). It is a realm of conjecture that is being represented in indirect discourse. These characters judge and are judged both by the image they present to the world and by the image ("Vorstellung" is another recurrent key word) of each other that they hold. Because the narrator records their voices and their perceptions, and because, moreover, he abstains from evaluative elucidation, readers are left to face the text on their own. The more closely they examine that terse, compact text, the more urgently do they become aware of its innate slipperiness. What confronts them is a narrative that not only uses irony, but that is also intrinsically ironic in its structure.

Readers' difficulty in achieving a reliable interpretation of the text reiterates the protagonists' problems in disengaging appearance and reality. Double-dealing subverts both these endeavors to arrive at any definitive clarity. 'Reality' in *Die Marquise von O—* can at best be posited as a provisional, tentative state, subject always to additional modification, and therefore always beyond the reach of certainty. As a result, such fundamental concepts as *Sein* (being) and *Schein* (appearance) cannot be retrieved from the instability in which they float. The outcome of these equivocations is a mobility that extends from the literary into the metaphysical sphere.

In centering its axis on the dichotomy between appearance and reality, *Die Marquise von O—* is following the archetypal plot of irony. A disagreeable surface masks an admirable personality, and vice versa. The comic social ramifications of this scenario are enacted in Jane Austen's *Pride and Prejudice.* Darcy is eventually recognized, despite his flaws, as a generous man of honor, while Wickham is exposed as the unscrupulous cad that he is. The initial misjudgments are corrected, and painful though that process is to those involved, all's well that ends well. *Die Marquise von O—* also ends well in an apparently conventional way with the marriage of the marquise and the count and "eine ganze Reihe von jungen Russen" (143; "a whole succession of young Russians"). However, this outward reconciliation is not accompanied by a genuine resolution of the problem. Unlike Darcy, the count is never fully rehabilitated; he seems *and* is angel *and* devil. Appearance and reality, instead of being finally disjoined, as is customary in irony, are in *Die Marquise von O—* inextricably conjoined. Their contours, far from possessing distinct, circumscribed limits, are so blurred as to be fused. So readers are forced to confront a *coincidentia oppositorum* that can neither be harmonized nor dissolved.

Because the lines of demarcation are so fluid, the notion of the role is of primary importance in *Die Marquise von O—*. As an intermediary performative stage, the role erodes distinctions by hovering at times closer to appearance, at others closer to reality. Since the characters must assess each other (and we them) from the evidence of manifest conduct, the foregrounding of the role compounds the confusion surrounding both the pursuit of specific certainties and the larger issues of *Sein* and *Schein.* For instance, the count is first seen in circumstances encumbered with doubt: "Der russische Offizier, der, nach *der Rolle zu urteilen, die er spielte,* einer der Anführer des Sturms zu sein *schien*" (106; "the Russian officer, who, *judging by the role he played, seemed* to be one of the leaders of the assault" [italics are mine]). His entreaties for the marquise's hand in marriage are regarded, successively and separately, by the marquise and her father as an "Aufführung" (110 and 111; "performance").

Leopardo has a role foisted onto him—or perhaps it is an appearance that betrays a reality in the same way as the count's apparent "performance" belies a reality. For the scenario proposed by the marquise's mother is sufficiently feasible to be seriously considered as a viable possibility by the marquise herself. On the other hand, the marquise's mother opposes the presence of her father and brother when the respondent to the advertisement is expected because of the "Unschicklichkeit der Rollen, die der Vater und der Bruder dabei zu spielen haben würden" (138; "the unseemliness of the roles which the father and the brother would have to play in such a scene"). The impossibility of accurately distinguishing between appearance and reality is also evinced in the erroneous report of the count's death, which is never explained, or even referred to again. The implication is that the evidence of the senses and of the mind may be wholly misleading. The criteria by which men and women judge each other, like the categories in which they think, prove to be brittle constructs that do not stand the test of experience. Nor are readers granted the privilege of exercising a discrimination superior to that of the protagonists. As readers we, too, are playing a role: the role of readers of irony. And we are as liable as the protagonists to become the victims of our own readings/misreadings because our lens is no more reliable than theirs.

So the attempt to grapple with the ironies in *Die Marquise von O—* leads back to its central problem of knowledge. Not just the protagonists' scant and fallacious knowledge, but also ours as readers. For we come to realize that, like the characters, we are in a dilemma not readily amenable to resolution. Once we are in possession of the knowledge that the count, who seems an angel, is a devil, we believe ourselves capable of grasping the irony implicit in *Die Marquise von O—*. But gradually we learn that this is not so, that there is far more than meets even the clever eye. So we are made aware of the fragility of our initial sense of reasonable assurance vis-a-vis the text we are interpreting. Our confident superiority to the protagonists evaporates as we find ourselves confronting perplexities *with* them. Their predicaments are projected onto us as we begin to discover that we have been dealt not a manageable set of dualisms, but double-dealt, as it were, a refractory knot of enigmas. The irony of *Die Marquise von O—* is, therefore, an irony of duplicity, itself double and duplicitous. Its neat, almost schematic surface of dualities acts as a mask for the epistemological and ontological crises which it delineates. Kleist has adopted the guise and devices traditional to irony, but for his own ulterior purposes, for the covert exposition of problems far beyond the overt matter of his story. The ironic game being played with readers is a complex and hazardous one.

The narrative refutes the confident assertion of the marquise's mother: "Und gleichwohl muß es doch notwendig eins oder das andere gewesen sein" (121; "And yet it must necessarily have been one or the other"). Things in *Die Marquise von O—* defy such "necessary" division into antithetical classes. The riposte to that assertion, which stands as my epigraph, comes in the marquise's evasive: "Er gefällt and mißfällt mir" (117; "I like and dislike him"), which denotes an acquiescence in the contradictoriness of feelings and relationships. For the ironic dualities in this text do not cancel each other out; they go on co-existing. Not a single one of the major issues in this *Novelle* is ever resolved into a univalent statement. The prevailing format is not a straightforward dialectical system, in which "eins oder das andere" ("one or the other") prevails, but rather an oxymoronic one *and* the other. Ultimately the only consistency in *Die Marquise von O—* lies in its obsessively reiterated grid of ambivalences. Whichever facet of the text we analyze, we come up repeatedly with a set of discordant options, which echo each other to form an unsettling hidden agenda, and which effectively block our desire to read as one or the other. In its place we are driven to accept the predominance of simultaneity and discordance.

That the count seems *and* is angel *and* devil is the central cipher for ambiguity. The duality is resistant to even so ingenious an interpretation as Thomas Fries' Lacanian account in his comparison of *Les Liaisons dangereuses* and *Die Marquise von O—*. Fries sees the count as a divine "symbolic father"[13] who replaces in the marquise's mind the actual father whom she rejects as representative of the traditional social order. The identification of the count as the real father of her child confounds his symbolic standing; his acknowledgement of paternity also makes him an accessory to the social order, and hence an innately contradictory person, at once a rebellious innovator and a conformist conservator. A parallel polarity is inherent in the marquise herself: she is the "Vortreffliche" ("excellent one") *and* the "Nichtswürdige" (135; "worthless one"). She not only protests her innocence; she is actually aligned with the Madonna as a "wunderliches Weib" (121; "a wondrous woman"). The terminology here points unmistakably to the religious realm: "du reinere als Engel" (135; "you purer than angels"), "du Herrliche, Überirdische" (135; "you glorious, supernatural one"). She regards her child as "göttlicher" ("more divine") because he is "geheimnißvoller" (126; "more mysterious"), and she asks the midwife about "die Möglichkeit einer unwißentlichen Empfängnis" (124; "the possibilty of an unknowing conception").[14] The complementary other to this image is as crassly abusive as this one is idealized: "die Schändliche! ... die verschmitzte Heuchlerin!" (132; "the infamous one ... the wily hypocrite!"), "die abgefeimteste Verräterin!" (133; "the craftiest traitor!") with the "Schamlosigkeit einer Hündin" (132; "shamelessness of a she-dog"), a fallen woman, a whore, who has been a willing participant in the rape, but who hypocritically persists in denying her responsibility. Even if such extremes are eschewed, there is a more concrete discrepancy in her attitude to a second marriage: at the outset she is said to have decided against it, yet she does nevertheless enter into it, and she may well subconsciously have wished for it. It could be her father who originates the opposition to the idea of a second marriage out of his urge to repossess his widowed daughter.[15] This would tie up with the Lacanian perception of him as the incarnation of an old order ripe for rejection.

The figure of the father is the most controversial one in *Die Marquise von O—*. On the surface at least his actions are less open to doubt than most: he does grab a pistol, even though the shot goes off accidentally, and he is seen to press "lange, heiße und lechzende Küße" (138; "long, hot, and longing kisses") onto his daughter's lips. There is no mistaking the erotic message of those words. So is he the stern father, the disciplinarian, the "Kommandant" ("commander") of his generic name, or/and is he the jealous lover? The incest scene between father and daughter, which has perplexed generations of critics, can perhaps best be read as an exemplar of readers' inability ever to know anything for sure. It is greatly complicated by its context: it is witnessed by the mother. In a situation that verges on the obscene, she is a voyeuse through a key-hole. Her spontaneous and unequivocal delight in what she sees is a further source of bewilderment for readers. The mother here functions as an oblique filter of the father/daughter relationship, an interpreting lens between the happening and readers, in counterpart to the effect of the sustained indirect discourse as a linguistic mediation.

Nor is the mother herself exempt from the dominant dualistic schemata. At the beginning she and the other women are portrayed as vacillating: the processes "auf der Waage der weiblichen Überlegung" (104; "in the balance of female reflection") are so sluggish that they are overtaken by the assault on the citadel. Against the background of martial combat the women are, perforce, subjugated to male orders, specifically to the "commander." So they are manipulated, and in the rape victimized, rape being the archetypal act of exploitation and domination, the expression of the male will to power over the female. As the narrative progresses, however, this proportion is reversed until the women assume the position of entrepreneurial manipulators. The marquise initiates her emancipation by leaving the parental home after her confrontation with her father. She asserts her own will by taking her children with her, and in the country she designs an independent existence with such success that "das Gefühl ihrer Selbstständigkeit" (127; "her sense of independence") prompts her to take the step of advertising for her child's father. Her mother's transformation is even more striking: it is she who takes the initiative in testing her daughter, she who is the shrewd decision-maker at crucial moments, she who shows presence of mind and the capacity for control in the arrangement of the marriage. She knows, too, just how to manage her irascible husband:

> Sie kochte ihm für den Abend alles, was sie nur Stärkendes und Beruhigendes aufzutreiben wußte, in der Küche zusammen, bereitete und wärmte ihm das Bett, um ihn sogleich hineinzulegen, sobald er nur an der Hand ihrer Tochter erscheinen würde. (138)[16]

The verbs are in the active; she is the doer, director, indeed manipulator, for by cossetting and *de facto* infantilizing him, she demotes him from his authority as "commander." Her image and position are finally as equivocal as the count's, as her daughter's and her husband's.

The famous oxymoron then,[17] "Ein reines Bewußtsein und eine Hebamme!" (122; "a clear conscience and a midwife!") designates a dilemma which irony can deconstruct but not transcend. No one in *Die Marquise von O—*, including the narrator, commands the firm perspective that would support a confident reading of the situation. All is perspectivism, conjecture, possibility, that finds its linguistic equivalent in indirect discourse and conjunctions of doubt. This impasse in the search for knowledge within the fiction extends also to the interpretation of the fiction. Readers are caught in the same epistemological straits as the protagonists and the narrator: that of coping with the disturbing information they have acquired. Unwilling though they are to adopt the marquise's stance of "Ich *will nichts* wißen!" (129; "I don't *want* to know *anything!*"), they have nonetheless to come to terms with the limits of their knowledge and of their powers of interpretation. The irony continuously deflects and scuttles our accustomed reading stratagems. The *écriture* does not, however, as Carol Jacobs maintains,[18] incise and erase at the same time. Erasure is too strong a term, and an inappropriate one because it leaves a *tabula rasa* and hence the opportunity for a fresh start. What makes Kleist's writing so deeply disconcerting is precisely that its irony does not erase, but erode. It incises and erodes so that no possibility is ever definitively eliminated. As a result, all the alternatives remain in a tantalizing state of potentiality.

The conflicted images projected by all the main protagonists point to a deeper schism intrinsic to the problematics of reading *Die Marquise von O—*. On the cosmic level readers face as difficult a choice as in the interpretation of the characters. Is this a tale of human error or of metaphysical dislocation? The key terms are, on the one hand, "Irrtum" (110; "mistake") and "Fehltritt" (117; "error"), and on the other, "Umwälzung der Weltordnung" (122; "overturning of the order of the world"). It in this latter possibility that is for the marquise, as for readers, "das Entsetzliche, mich Vernichtende" (107; "the terrible that destroys me"). At stake here is certainly not the physical feasibility of what happened; such a literal reading would, absurdly turn *Die Marquise von O—* into an inquiry into quick sexual fixes! Taken figuratively, however, the count's act becomes an allegory of the moral and ethical syntaxis of the world. The doctor's sarcastic comment about not needing to explain the ultimate causes of things refers to the physical and social plane, but it is equally pertinent to the metaphysical and ontological. This other potential is contained in the word "Dinge" (120; "things"), which here, as in the earlier "Ordnung der Dinge" (109; "order of things"), has a decided Kantian echo as a thinly veiled allusion to Kleist's own quest for a valid order. In this context Kleist's Kant crisis may be seen as a problem of reading insofar as it hinges on the issue of decidability/undecidability. Because the "Einrichtung" (126; "set-up") of this world is so "gebrechlich" (143; "fragile"), the ultimate causes of things, while in little need of physical explanation, are on the psychological and metaphysical plane beyond explanation. Even if the count is correctly identified as the father of the marquise's child, a larger ulterior mystery looms as to the motivation of his action, which raises troubling questions about the nature of both good and evil.

None of these oppositions is ever resolved in *Die Marquise von O—*; everything remains in a state of suspension because of the predominance of paradox. That the count is angel *and* devil, capable within a few moments of French courtesies to a lady in distress and of raping the woman he is purporting to protect: this inconceivable combination shatters not only the ethical framework within which this society has operated, but also the ontological beliefs on which it has rested. Once the security of the entire system has thus been put into jeopardy by the incursion of paradox, it cannot be reconstituted by a facile claim such as: "die Wirklichkeit manifestiert sich als das Zugleich des Widersprüchlichen"[19] ("reality manifests itself as the simultaneity of contraries"). A proposition of this kind, though not strictly speaking untrue, derives from flawed logic: the reign of paradox precludes, by its very nature, the establishment of a stable "reality." It also precludes a purposeful irony of exposure, which can stem only from a reasonably assured position. What paradox fosters is a duplicitous irony of double-dealing that distrusts and subverts every possibility. Instead of being "notwendig eins oder das andere" ("necessarily the one or the other"), things dangle in indeterminacy and contradiction. The dualities of irony are here potentiated into the dissonances of paradox.

In *Die Marquise von O—* "Ironie ist die Form des Paradoxen"[20] ("Irony is the form that paradox takes"), though not in the implicitly positive sense in which Friedrich Schlegel conceived it. For Schlegel immediately qualified his aphorism with the rider: "Paradox ist alles, was zugleich gut und groß ist" ("Paradoxical is everything that is at once good and great"). This assessment of the role of paradox and irony adumbrates a Hegelian movement from thesis through antithesis to synthesis. Paradox and irony are alike for Schlegel vital instruments of romantic idealism. It is a measure not merely of Kleist's distance from his romantic contemporaries in Germany but also of his amazing modernity that his irony, far from being the agency of transcendence envisaged by Schlegel, is rather the means for a *mise en abîme*, or, at least, a radical throwing into question of the conventionally accepted order of things.

Yet despite this inversion of Schlegel's postulated meaning, his phrase forfeits none of its cogency for *Die Marquise von O—*. Irony *is* the narrational form that paradox assumes in this text. Its importance resides therefore not so much in its function as a dramatic tool of deflation and disparagement as in its position as the fulcrum of the epistemological and ontological question marks that are at the heart of this *Novelle*. Because the irony queries and queers its own ploys, it has the cumulative effect of diminishing the confidence that readers may invest in the narrator and in the narrative process as well as in the world itself. The comfortable entente between narrator and readers, that animates the ready recognition of the ironic insinuations of a discourse, yields to the anxiety that this ironist is himself the butt of the cruellest irony. For though he is able to perceive and to represent the paradoxicality of the human and the cosmic system, he is as unable as the protagonists (or, for that matter, readers) to decipher, let alone to fathom it. An irony that might be deemed "progressive"[21] is the most appropriate mode in which to record the obdurate paradoxicality of the precarious arrangement of this universe. Irony thus asserts its supremacy in *Die Marquise von O—* as the locus of the paramount rift in the narrative — the rift that is both a hazard and a thrill for readers to negotiate.

6

Reading Kleist and Kafka

In a review of *Die Verwandlung* (*The Metamorphosis*) and *Der Heizer* (*The Stoker*), published in the *Berliner Beiträge* of 6 July 1916, Oskar Walzel suggested that "die kleine Erzählung (*Der Heizer*) hat etwas Kleistisches"[1] ("the little narrative (*The Stoker*) has something Kleistian"). The context of Walzel's observation is significant: "Feinfühlige, denen ich Franz Kafkas 'Heizer' vorlas, bestätigten mir, was mir beim Vorlesen noch stärker auffiel als beim stillen Lesen: die kleine Erzählung hat etwas Kleistisches" ("Sensitive people, to whom I read Kafka's 'Stoker' aloud, confirmed even more strongly what had occurred to me in reading it silently: the little narrative has something Kleistian"). The resemblance between Kleist and Kafka is here not the outcome of critical analysis, but the impression of listeners. The association suggests itself, spontaneously, as it were, to minds well-stocked with the classics of German literature.

This reaction to Kafka's early stories is reiterated in Beda Allemann's more recent experiences with students:

> Zu den wiederkehrenden Erfahrungen in Kafka wie in Kleist-Seminaren gehört es aber auch, daß früher oder später ein besonders begabter Student sich zu Wort meldet und fragt: Ließe sich Ähnliches nicht auch bei Kleist (respektiv bei Kafka) feststellen?[2]

A considerable number of critical studies have already sought to fathom the correlation between Kleist and Kafka. Moreover, critics concerned primarily with either Kleist or Kafka also tend to make comparisons with the other.[3]

What is one to make of the insistent awareness of an analogy between Kleist and Kafka on the part of readers over several decades? Is it merely a vague, perhaps erroneous impression, or can it be substantiated through an analysis of the process of reading the texts? What is it in the way both tell a story that makes readers sense the likeness? Does a consideration of their rhetoric and its impact on readers offer a sounder basis for understanding a resemblance so often perceived intuitively, yet so resistant to conclusive demonstration? Before assaying a rhetorical and narratological reading, I want to survey the differing routes by which critics have so far endeavored, with varying success, to arrive at a recognition of the nature of the affinity between Kleist and Kafka.

Nearly always such attempts are buttressed by references to Kafka's avowed fascination with Kleist. His attraction to his literary ancestor, particularly in the formative years 1911–13, toward the beginnings of his own creative activity, is cited to validate rapprochements between these two writers despite the great historical and social differences separating them. Kafka certainly had an intimate familiarity with Kleist's work. He edited the Rowohlt edition of Kleist's *Anekdoten* in 1912, and of the three recitations he gave during his lifetime, the one on 11 December 1913 was devoted to *Michael Kohlhaas*, evidently his favorite among Kleist's narratives. In early February 1914 he apologizes to Felice Bauer for not having written the previous evening "weil es über Michael Kohlhaas zu spät geworden ist"[4] ("because it grew too late on account of Michael Kohlhaas"), adding that although he was reading it "wohl schon zum zehnten Mal" ("probably for the tenth time"), it still gripped him "mit wirklicher Todesfurcht" ("with a genuine terror").

Kafka also has a perceptive lens for Kleist's letters. In a diary entry of 11 February 1911,[5] when he has been reading the letters Kleist wrote at the age of twenty-two, after he had decided to give up the traditional family career in the army, Kafka slips into indirect speech before giving a direct first person quotation from Kleist, as if he were re-enacting the scene between Kleist and his family. Here there is a strong hint of that psychological identification with Kleist which he voiced in a memorable image in a letter to Max Brod less than a month earlier on 27 January 1911: "Kleist bläst in mich wie in eine alte Schweinsblase"[6] ("Kleist blows into me as into an old pig's bladder"). The frequent allusions to Kleist in Kafka's diaries and letters attest to his preoccupation with his predecessor and amply support Kafka's contention that Kleist was one of his "eigentlichen Blutsverwandten"[7] ("true blood relations"). Yet it is important to note that Kafka uses the phrase in an autobiographical context as he tells Felice Bauer that of his four blood relations — Grillparzer, Dostoyevsky, Kleist, and Flaubert — only Dostoevsky had ever married. He concludes that perhaps Kleist alone, when he shot himself, had found "den richtigen Weg" ("the right way"). Kafka's personal feeling of inward brotherhood with Kleist can thus be convincingly documented; much more contentious, however, is the matter of the literary similitude between their writings.

Kafka's own testimony may well have prompted the earliest and most persistent comparison between himself and Kleist on biographical grounds. A short but influential article by Max Brod, Kafka's friend and literary executor, entitled "Infantilismus: Kleist und Kafka" appeared in *Die literarische Welt* 28 of 15 July 1927. Applying a Freudian matrix, Brod dwells on "die seelische Nähe der Grundhaltung" (4; "the psychic similarity of their basic stance"). Their abnormally powerful ties to the parental family, he argues, proved prejudicial to their development toward independence, leading in both cases to a lack of self-confidence, manifest in their recoil from marriage and in their constant need for self-confirmation. Such personal parallels, hinging on their troubled relationships to their families and their rejection of the career path expected of them have become the stock-in-trade of Kleist/Kafka comparisons. Reference is repeatedly made either to "die Verwandtschaft der persönlichen Lebensproblematik beider Dichter"[8] ("the relatedness of the two writers' personal problems"), or to that permanent "Identitätskrise"[9] ("identity crisis") said to beset them throughout their lives. Recent critics have been more circumspect in focusing on specific aspects of the biographical analogy. Jörg Dittkrist, for instance, using a socio-biographical approach, seeks to determine the role in their writing of certain common traits of their existence such as their isolation, their dream of the 'simple' life, their ethical rigor, and their self-stylization.[10] Mark Harman, drawing to some extent on the methods of psychobiography, presents an interesting juxtaposition of their autobiographical self-images.[11]

Aside from the biographical, the most popular means to link Kleist and Kafka has been through the exploration of thematic parallels. As in the field of biography, so here too the earliest studies produced large and vague generalizations. Notably in the immediate postwar period, when Kafka was discovered by the existentialists, he was aligned with Kleist on the basis of their alienation, their anxiety, their acceptance of contingency, and their sense of paradox. Although such connections are fully warranted, their usefulness as a basis for comparison is undercut by their wide validity for a great many writers not just of the postwar but of the post-Kantian era. Alienation and a sense of paradox are by no means specific to Kleist and Kafka alone. The presence of these qualities testifies to an overall family resemblance without, however, pinpointing a particular fraternal kinship. Subsequently, again as in the biographical sphere, the focus has sharpened with a shift from grandiose claims to the juxtapositions of specific works, as in J. M. Lindsay's article "Kohlhaas and K: Two Men in Search of Justice," which shows the "remarkable parallels of situation and content."[12]

The essentially literary aspects of the resemblance between Kleist and Kafka have not been extensively analyzed, although some provocative ideas have been put forward. They have, for instance, been singled out as "Meister in der Kunst des Anfangs"[13] ("masters in the art of the opening"). Another interesting correlation has been discerned in their common use of physical gestures as an expression of inner states.[14] Fainting, silence, pallor, blushing, and palpitations in Kleist, like taking a hand, rummaging in pockets, holding one's head in hands in Kafka, amount to a secondary sign language, whose function is to fill the gap left by the narrator's abdication of omniscient insight. The recourse to gestures is, therefore, a corollary to the narrator's detachment from the protagonists, whom he observes from the outside. The same detachment underlies the predominantly dramatic presentation and the marked preference for dramatic effects, which Harman[15] has examined.

The thorniest issue in the entire field centers on the question of their rhetoric. In sketching the web of affinities Max Brod insists on the similarity of their prose styles. Because of Kafka's predilection for Kleist, it has been tempting to assume a direct influence on his writing. Several attempts have been made to define the nature of the stylistic likeness. Wolfgang Jahn[16] has shown how both writers exploit the potential of syntax to create tension. Harman maps the syntactic parallels within the context of their dramatic prose style, and makes acute observations on the way in which the revelation of the verb is habitually delayed by the hypotactic grammatical patterns favored by both Kleist and Kafka.

But the stylistic resemblance has also been sharply disputed, and with it by implication the hypothesis of a *literary* affinity between Kleist and Kafka, as distinct from a merely biographical or thematic one. The dissenting voices are sufficiently vigorous to demand attention. Kafka's "Abstand zu Kleist"[17] ("distance from Kleist") is underscored by Hermann Pongs, who sets off Kafka's "analytical" style against Kleist's "symbolical" style. Likewise, Hartmut Binder[18] contrasts the uniformity of the Kleistian chronicler's report with the variety of narrative levels in Kafka's work, and concludes that there is little evidence of any stylistic parallel between them. Allemann emphasizes the divergence in their relative sentence structure and contests the viability of any literary parallel when he maintains "daß zwischen der intuitiv erfaßten und von Kafka bestätigten 'Blutsverwandtschaft' und ihrem konkreten Nachweis durch Textvergleichung eine Diskrepanz besteht"[19] ("that there is a discrepancy between the intuitively perceived 'blood relationship,' confirmed by Kafka, and its concrete proof through the comparison of tests").

I would argue against this: the intuitively perceived affinity between Kleist and Kafka **can** indeed by corroborated by a rhetorically oriented comparison, i.e., by a consideration of the similarities in their manner of narration and its effect on readers. I choose to work with *Das Bettelweib von Locarno (The Beggarwoman of Locarno)* and *Das Urteil (The Judgment)* partly because these works have never been subjected to comparison, but mainly because of the very difficulty of establishing a convincing correspondence between them along more traditional lines. In contrast to *Das Urteil*, *Das Bettelweib von Locarno* does not lend itself to any psychobiographical interpretation. To connect them thematically is feasible: both can be deemed to center on guilt and atonement, ending in violence and suicide. Yet such a reductive summation only serves to illustrate the inherent weakness of a purely thematic link since dozens of other narratives could be assembled under the same heading. What is more, the two stories diverge widely in their narratorial stance. *Das Bettelweib von Locarno* is told in a reportorial tone by an impersonal chronicler, who sees the protagonists and the action almost wholly from the viewpoint of an external observer, and who recounts happenings at a certain remove and by means of indirect discourse. *Das Urteil*, on the other hand, apart from the short introductory paragraph and the one sentence conclusion, is told from Georg's angle of vision and with an extensive use of dialogue that reinforces the immediacy of its dramatic impact. The disparities between these two texts in certain respects only intensify the challenge of uncovering the deeper, hidden affinities.

They reside principally in the mode of narration itself. What has been said of Kleist is equally apposite to Kafka: "Vom Erzählen, von diesem besonderen Erzählen her bekommen sie auch erst ihren Sinn"[20] ("From the narration, only from this special narration do they attain their meaning"). The particular character of this narration arises from the tension between what is told and what is *not*. In this there is a pronounced consonance between Kleist and Kafka. The simultaneous overabundance and dearth of information given to readers is the cardinal trait common to Kleist and Kafka. In *Das Urteil* as in *Das Bettelweib von Locarno* "ist alles oder gar nichts der Erklärung bedürftig"[21] ("everything or nothing is in need of explanation"). Readers find themselves knowing everything— and nothing. The meticulous specificity of all the peripheral minor circumstances is in the crassest contrast to the elliptic gaps on the central question of motivation. The legalistic precision of the telling, with its tight syntax, is a cover for the essentially enigmatic nature of what is being told. Concealment is practiced in language that purports to reveal. On the one hand, much more information is included than readers need; the wealth of material is such as to complicate and obstruct the task of reading. Yet, on the other hand, less information is available than would be necessary for the confident construction of an interpretation. The ample documentation of physical detail fosters an illusion of knowledge which hides the central blanks at the heart of the text. This curious amalgam of informational glut and want is characteristic of the narrative discourse of both Kleist and Kafka, and represents a major confluence between them.

The most conspicuous manifestation of this parallelism is in the luxuriance of the circumstantial detail. Both *Das Bettelweib von Locarno* and *Das Urteil* are rich in specific information from their beginning onward. In *Das Bettelweib von Locarno* the geographic location ("Am Fuße der Alpen bei Locarno"[22] ["At the foot of the Alps near Locarno"]) is established with a scrupulousness evident too in the handling of time, in the pivotal switch from the castle's past state ("befand sich" — "used to lie") to its present ruination ("liegen sieht" — "be seen to stand"). *Das Urteil* starts likewise with time: "an einem Sonntagsvormittag im schönsten Frühjahr"[23] ("on a Sunday morning in a beautiful spring") and place in the punctilious description of the position of the apartment, and the appearance, build, and situation of the house: "im ersten Stock eines der niedrigen, leichtgebauten Häuser, die entlang des Flußes in einer langen Reihe, fast nur in der Höhe und Färbung unterschieden, sich hinzogen" ("on the first floor of one of those low, flimsily built houses that stretched in a long row along the river, and were distinguishable from each other only in height and color"). Of this careful designation, only one fact proves relevant to the action: that the house is by the river, where Georg will drown himself.

This procedure is characteristic of *Das Urteil*, where readers often have difficulty in discerning which details fulfill a purpose in the narration, and which may be redundant. To take just three examples: that the house where Georg and his father live is low, flimsily built, and undistinguished may be denotative of their social level, but this seems peripheral to the plot. The fact that Georg sits for a while after finishing his letter to his friend "den Ellbogen auf den Schreibtisch gestützt" (53; "his elbows resting on the desk") could suggest the unusual consequentiality of the letter just completed by implying deep deliberation about it. Similarly, it is hard to decide whether the initial phrase in the sentence: "Auf seinen Armen trug er den Vater ins Bett" (61; "On his arms he carried his father to bed") has any particular force; it could be a manifestation of Georg's momentary superiority over his father, or it could be simply another physical descriptive detail. If the adverbial prelude were stripped or even moved from its inceptive position, the sentence would lose its vividness, but not its meaning. So readers find themselves in possession of information they do not know where or how to accommodate. The malaise induced by confronting narrational elements that may be superfluous has its own vital role to play by exposing readers to a direct experience of uncertainty analogous to that of Kafka's protagonists.

In Kleist the informational overload is even more readily apparent because the redundancies are often linguistically distinct, in subordinate clauses or in encapsulated phrases. In the latter half of the opening sentence of *Das Bettelweib von Locarno*, for instance, the beggarwoman is bedded on "Stroh, das man ihr unterschütte" (196; "straw that was spread under her"); in their second vigil in the haunted room the marquis and his wife are accompanied by "einem treuen Bedienten, den sie mitgenommen hatten" (197; "a loyal servant, whom they had taken with them"); on the third occasion it is "der Haushund, den man von der Kette losgelaßen hatte" (196–7; "the house dog, who had been let loose from his chain") and "Pistolen, die er aus dem Schrank genommen hatte" ("pistols, which he had taken out of the cupboard"). In each case the inserted qualifying phrase heightens the precision, yet retards the narration. As in *Das Urteil*, readers are acquainted with all sorts of data that do not contribute to the solution of the intrinsic enigma. This mass of circumstantial detail in both Kleist and Kafka acts as a decoy, prompting readers to believe that they command a great deal of information, as indeed they do, but not of a kind amenable to a consistent reading.

The effect of precision created by the abundance of detail is reinforced by the immaculate cohesiveness of the syntax. Kafka's German was clearly shaped by his training as a lawyer in its compulsion to exactitude. As for Kleist, his is "eine Prosa, die bis ins Letzte gegliedert, deren Teile mit schärfster Logik gefügt und auf einander bezogen sind"[24] ("prose that is structured in every filament, whose parts are integrated with utmost logic and connected to each other"). No sentence in either Kleist or Kafka is allowed to stand on its own: each is riveted into its position through links to what has preceded it and to what follows it. Kleist makes frequent and striking use of such conjunctions as *während* (while), *indem* (just then), *kaum* (hardly), and *indeßen* (meantime). His signature favorite is the construction *dergestalt daß* (in such a way that), which has pronounced legalistic undertones. Some of the same devices recur in Kafka's prose: "Währenddeßen" (61; "In the meantime"), "Kaum war er aber" (61; "But hardly had he") and "In diesem Augenblick" (66; "At that moment") in *Das Urteil* could come straight out of a Kleistian text. Kafka resorts to other means too to attain the same close-knit coalescence between the units of his narrative. The smoothness of the transitions in *Das Urteil*, thematically as well as grammatically, is remarkable. Paragraphs begin with such phrases as "Aus diesen Gründen" (54; "For these reasons"); "Mit diesem Brief in der Hand" (57; "Holding this letter in his hand"); "So bechränkte sich Georg darauf" (55; "George therefore limited himself to"). The syntactic disposition is designed to foster the impression of sequentiality.

In the hyperstructured prose of both Kleist and Kafka, the protracted hypotactic sentences with their plethora of surbordinate and parenthetical clauses, conjoined into long breathless paragraphs, move forward with an unrelenting, compelling logic. The tight interlacement of the syntax projects a high degree of control. Like the wealth of circumstantial detail, the devious syntax gives the appearance of reproducing a universe governed by stringent order. That appearance, however, is deceptive. The discipline of the syntax serves as a bulwark against disorder, an attempt to hold it back, yet simultaneously also an indicator of the impossibility of so doing.

The very sentences where the syntax is at its most complex are those that obliquely disclose what is being suppressed. A fine example comes in this convoluted sentence toward the middle of *Das Bettelweib von Locarno:*

> Dieser Vorfall, der außerordentliches Aufsehen machte, schreckte auf eine dem Marchese höchst unangenehme Weise mehrere Käufer ab; dergestalt, daß, da sich unter seinem eigenen Hausgesinde, befremdend und unbegreiflich, das Gerücht erhob, daß es in dem Zimmer zur Mitternachtstunde umgehe, er, um es mit einem entscheidenden Verfahren niederzuschlagen, beschloß, die Sache in der nächsten Nacht selbst zu untersuchen. (197)[25]

The cause and effect succession of the syntax echoes the marquis' endeavor to stem the advance of the irrational. But at the same time the grotesque extremism of the sentence structure signals the desperateness of his attempt to quell the dark forces engulfing him. Rationality reaches such an absurd pitch of intensity as to refute itself.

Kafka's extended sentences have the same capacity for paradoxical self-contradiction. As Georg, with his letter to his friend in his pocket, walks into his father's room for the first time in months, he muses:

> Es bestand auch sonst keine Nötigung dazu, denn er verkehrte mit seinem Vater ständig im Geschäft, das Mittagessen nahmen sie gleichzeitig in einem Speisehaus ein, abends versorgte sich zwar jeder nach Belieben, doch saßen sie dann meistens, wenn nicht Georg, wie es am häufigsten geschah, mit Freunden beisammen war oder jetzt seine Braut besuchte, noch ein Weilchen, jeder mit seiner Zeitung, im gemeinsamen Wohnzimmer. (57)[26]

The final upshot of this sentence is the opposite to what it overtly says; it bears out the neglect of the father that Georg is trying to conceal from himself in the same way that the marquis in *Das Bettelweib von Locarno* is denying the encroachment of the ghost. The syncopated surface with its profusion of qualifying clauses acts as a diversion that breaks the thread of the supposedly rational argument and covers its speciousness. The logic of the syntactical construction in Kleist and Kafka is, as much as the accuracy of the documentary detail, an aspect of the rhetoric of deception that (mis)leads readers into the belief that they are dealing with a taut, rigorous narration, while actually leaving them to face a tantalizingly cryptic discourse disrupted by omissions and lacunae.

The lacuna at the heart of *Das Bettelweib von Locarno* becomes manifest in the very first sentence in the ambivalence of the link between its first and second parts:

> Am Fuße der Alpen bei Locarno im oberen Italien befand sich ein altes, einem Marchese gehöriges Schloß, das man jetzt, wenn man von St. Gotthard kommt, in Schutt und Trümmern liegen sieht: ein Schloß mit hohen und weitläufigen Zimmern, in deren einem einst auf Stroh, das man ihr unterschüttete, eine alte kranke Frau, die sich bettelnd vor der Tür eingefunden hatte, von der Hausfrau aus Mitleid gebettet worden war. (196)[27]

The contrast between the castle's proud past and its derelict present immediately arouses readers' curiosity, prompting the crucial question as to how it fell into its forlorn state. It is a question that will be answered on the practical but not on the moral level. After a colon that induces readers to expect amplification of the statement made in the first half, the second half of that lengthy sentence begins by picking up the motif of the castle by elaborating on its former splendor. But then it takes a great disjunctive leap from its main theme, the ruin of the castle, to the apparently trivial incident of the old beggarwoman who is given shelter by the mistress of the house. Syntactically there is no fracture; the move from the rooms of the castle to the old woman is accomplished via a subsidiary clause ("in deren einem"; "in one of which"). The syntactic infibulation is visible, not only here but throughout the narrative; however, it does not correspond to a conceptual connection. The syntactic continuity serves precisely to cover the cognitive discontinuity. Here, in the very first sentence, readers encounter the intrinsic mystery that will frustrate construction of the narrative: what is the nature of the conjunction between the two halves of the sentence, between the two happenings, the advent of the beggarwoman and the destruction of the castle? Is there a causal connection between them, or are they fortuitous *faits divers?* The grammatical structure, despite its tightness, does not offer any clues. The gap is overlaid by a plethora of circumstantial information, such as the castle's geographic location, the size of the rooms, the straw that was spread under her, that has no direct bearing on the central problem. Only the phrase "aus Mitleiden" ("out of pity"), which gives fleeting insight into a protagonist's mind, hints at the inherent moral issue.

The second shorter sentence is intercalated between the two ponderous ones with which the paragraph begins and ends:

> Der Marchese, der bei der Rückkehr von der Jagd zufällig in das Zimmer trat, wo er seine Büchse abzusetzen pflegte, befahl der Frau unwillig, aus dem Winkel in welchem sie lag, aufzustehn und sich hinter den Ofen zu verfügen.[28]

If the first sentence contains the crucial gap, the second presents the critical act, and it, too, is highly perplexing. The marquis, on his return from hunting, "by chance" enters the room where he is used to keeping his gun. There is a contradiction here: the word "pflegte" ("used to") expresses the habitual aspect, the repetitiveness of his action. The predictability of his entering the room subverts the "zufällig" ("by chance"). And *why* does he order the beggarwoman to move? The floating adverb "unwillig" ("unwillingly") is puzzling. It refers to the marquis, but does it describe the tone of his command or the state of his mind? Luke and Reeves translate it as "angrily";[29] Greenberg opts for "irritably."[30] If these interpretations are correct, then the marquis' stance could be contrasted with his wife's benign, pitying attitude. Yet "unwillig" could also denote "reluctantly," which would complicate the question as to why he orders her to move. This question, like so much else in *Das Bettelweib von Locarno*, remains unanswered.

The third and final sentence of the opening paragraph of *Das Bettelweib von Locarno* recounts the beggarwoman's accident:

> Die Frau, da sie sich erhob, glitschte mit der Krücke auf dem glatten Boden aus und beschädigte sich auf eine gefährliche Weise das Kreuz: dergestalt, daß sie zwar noch mit unsäglicher Mühe aufstand und quer, wie es ihr vorgeschrieben war, über das Zimmer ging, hinter dem Ofen aber unter Stöhnen und Ächzen niedersank und verschied.[31]

Again the disposition of the narrative is extraordinarily open. The crux of the dilemma in this instance resides in the conjunction "da," generally rendered in English by "as." In German, however, "da" has a dual potential, the capacity to denote either a consecutive temporal or a consequential, causal link. In this case, the interpretation of "da" is decisive: did she slip *as* she arose, or *because* she arose? "As" is chosen by the translators;

nevertheless, the alternative in German is important for it allows a direct causal relationship to be made between the woman's rising in accordance with the marquis' command and her fatal fall. Such an ambivalent "da" ("as") crops up no fewer than six further times in a narrative whose total length is three pages. The discourse is poised in such a way as to admit multiple readings, although its patina of rigorous grammatical cohesiveness screens its ambivalences from readers. The interlocking syntactical units with their abundance of precise information act as cement to hold together a story full of holes.

The narration of the beggarwoman's fall is a good example of rhetorical duplicity. Although the ulterior sense of "da" ("because") may tempt readers to ascribe the woman's accident to the marquis' command, the incident is in fact written in the active voice: "glitschte mit der Krücke... und schädigte sich... das Kreuz" ("slipped with her crutch... and injured her back"). It is she who injures herself. The fall is not directly attributed to the polished floor, which may be just another of those concrete details, although it could be taken as pointing to some responsibility on the part of the hosts. The second half of the sentence begins with a suggestion of consequentiality in the "dergestalt, daß" ("with the result that"). Yet the situation is inscrutable as this packed sentence rushes onward with utmost urgency to its astonishing concluding phrase: "und verschied" ("and passed away"). This, its climax, is rhetorically an anti-climax in the sparseness of its formulation, especially in contrast to the previous clauses, complicated by a concessive "zwar noch" (translated as: "she did manage"), a lengthy encapsulated phrase, "wie es ihr vorgeschrieben war" ("as had been prescribed to her"), a precise indication of her trajectory across the room, and a duplicative auditory description of her arrival by the stove "unter Stöhnen und Ächzen" ("amidst moans and groans"). Here we have the typical Kleistian alliance of, on the one hand, abundant explanatory documentation of the 'how' of the happening with, on the other hand, an utter dearth of information about the 'why.' Did the beggarwoman die of her injuries, or was she dying anyway? Probably a combination of both, but there is no way of knowing. At the heart of Kleist's vision of the universe, as critics have frequently pointed out, lies "das Unerkennbare, das Rätsel, das man nur erfahren, nicht denken kann"[32] ("the imperceivable, the puzzle, that can only be experienced but not thought out"). Issues of motivation, responsibility, and causation are mooted, but never resolved. The precision of Kleist's discourse tends to beguile readers through its pressing grammatical logic into the assumption of a corresponding sequentiality of thought.

The syntactical, lexical, and narrational strategies of the opening paragraph recur throughout *Das Bettelweib von Locarno*. The hyperstructured sentences represent a strenuous quest for logic in the face of an incursion of the irrational. Words carry echoes and foreshadowings that may yield some clues as to the possible connection between the beggarwoman's mishap and the marquis' misfortune. For instance, the crackling of the straw that announces the ghost's visitation could allude forward to the crackling of the fire that consumes the castle ("knistern" is applied in German to the sounds of straw and fire alike). A deeper ambiguity is implicit in the marquis' comment to his wife "daß es mit dem Spuk seine Richtigkeit habe" (197; "that it was right about the ghost"). Does this mean that the prospective buyer was right in complaining about the presence of the ghost, or indeed that the ghost is right in haunting the castle?

To the very end, the discourse teases readers with its contradictory juxtaposition of gaps and redundancies. When the marquis, "vom Entsetzen überreizt" (198; "frenzied with horror"), sets fire to the castle, is his death caused by the ghost, or is that episode only a contributory precipitating factor, just as his command to the beggarwoman had been in her demise? Is he "müde des Lebens" (198; "weary of life") because of the ghost, or because of his financial worries, or do these, too, devolve indirectly from the beggarwoman? As if in compensation for this axial hiatus, the peripheral detail is lavish: that the marquis lit the fire with a candle, that the room was paneled in wood, that he set it alight in all four corners. Could this be taken as a reference to the location of the beggarwoman in a corner? Finally, what are readers to make of the closing words:

> und noch jetzt liegen, von den Landleuten zusammengetragen, seine weißen Gebeine in dem Winkel des Zimmers, von welchem er das Bettelweib von Locarno hatte aufstehen heißen. (198)[33]

This highly dramatic ending again associates the fate of the marquis with that of the beggarwoman, yet wholly evades the issue of cause and effect. Readers are lured toward the conjecture that the beggarwoman is claiming vengeance on the marquis, although the elliptical texture permits no substantiation of such an hypothesis.

The same motivational lacunae become apparent in *Das Urteil*, though more gradually than in *Das Bettelweib von Locarno*. Its beginning reverses Kafka's customary practice, which in, for instance, *Die Verwandlung (The Metamorphosis)* and *Der Prozess (The Trial)*, is very reminiscent of Kleist's opening thunderbolts. In *Das Urteil* the first paragraph is hardly arresting; the pedestrian situation might herald a quite ordinary tale. Even Georg's ruminations about his friend in Russia seem not too unusual initially; it is the friend more than Georg who appears eccentric.

Only with the third paragraph, "Was sollte man einem solchen Mann schreiben … " (53 – 4; "what should one write to such a man … ") does Georg himself become suspect. His overt attitude toward his friend is one of consideration, empathy, and pity. Yet his rhetoric betrays a degree of vacillation that portends a more conflicted stance than he openly admits. The unanswered and unanswerable questions and unwieldly subjunctives of doubt combine with the reiterated "vielleicht" ("perhaps") to create a sense of indeterminacy. Georg's irresoluteness about his friend fosters a double image of him as both caringly concerned and anxiously uneasy.

Despite the syntactical clarity of the discourse, readers, like Georg, confront "nicht die sogenannte Wirklichkeit … , sondern ein System von Einräumungen, Bedingungen, Möglichkeiten und Weiterungen"[34] ("not so called reality, but a system of qualifications, conditions, possibilities and expansions"). The outcome of readers' assessment in the face of these multiple possibilities is, again like Georg, the impossibility of any tenable conclusion. Just as Georg feels that his lack of knowledge about his friend's inclinations, health, and circumstances puts him into a paralyzing position, so readers, partly because they perforce see through Georg's lens, do not command the sorts of information (e.g. about his character and motivations) that would enable them to form any judgment. In an essentially self-defeating rhetoric, statements are progressively qualified and undermined so as to cancel each other out:

> Aus diesen Gründen konnte man ihm, wenn man noch überhaupt die briefliche Verbindung aufrechterhalten wollte, keine eigentlichen Mitteilungen machen, wie man sie auch ohne Scheu dem entferntesten Bekannten machen würde. (54)[35]

The weighty interpolated concessive clause may infer that Georg does not really want to maintain the correspondence. However, the quasi-logical "Aus diesen Gründen" discourages such a reading by providing a reasoned justification for his position. The internal contradictions of Kafka's prose render every reading no more than conjectural.

This is well illustrated in the summary of Georg's shrinking communication with his friend over the previous three years. Although Georg has informed his friend of his mother's death, he has told him nothing of his own increasing success in business. In another string of "vielleicht" ("perhaps") constructions he gives a variety of reasons for this omission. As a result, his friend misreads Georg's situation to such an extent that he has made the wholly inappropriate suggestion that Georg too should emigrate to Russia. Far from having to seek his fortune abroad, Georg is about to crown his growing prosperity with his forthcoming marriage. He has not disclosed this to his friend, whereas he has written to him of the engagement of two marginal persons no fewer than three times already. Georg's correspondence thus mirrors the imbalance between an excess of incidental information and a paucity of vital facts that readers experience in relation to the text itself. Since this disproportion is seen to beget a radical misapprehension on the part of Georg's friend, readers, dealing with a similar pattern of reticence and effusiveness in their text, must envisage the possibility (likelihhood?) of their own misreading.

Readers' uncertainty is heightened by the conversation between Georg and his bride about the friend in Russia (56). Georg is, as usual, full of hesitations and vacillations; his speech abounds in such turns as "vielleicht" ("perhaps"), "wahrscheinlich" ("probably"), "wenigstens" ("at least"), "allerdings" ("at any rate") as well as a spate of conjunctives of doubt. His bride, Frieda's response is, by contrast, refreshingly blunt but deeply disconcerting: "Wenn du solche Freunde hast, Georg, hättest du dich überhaupt nicht verloben sollen" ("If you have such friends, Georg, you should not have got engaged at all"). The cryptic baldness of this pronouncement foreshadows that other judgment that will bring the story to its climax and conclusion. Frieda's remark, tendered as it is without any explanation, leaves readers entirely to their own speculations: Is it an expression of jealousy on her part? Or of her fear that Georg is a confirmed bachelor who will not adjust to marriage? Or is there some other ulterior sense? Georg's reply: "Ja, das ist unser beider Schuld; aber ich wollte es auch jetzt nicht anders haben" ("Yes, that is the fault of us both; but I wouldn't now want it otherwise") compounds the perplexity by introducing the notions of guilt and willfulness. As if to block further pursuit of such ideas, the following sentence gives a glimpse of Frieda "rasch atmend unter seinen Küßen" ("breathing heavily under his kisses").

The scene between Georg and his father is an intensified repetition of his relationship to his friend. Georg's attitude toward his father is made up of the same mixture of caring concern and unease amounting to guilt as toward his friend. His encounter with his father rises in a crescendo from a calm, intelligible beginning to an outrageous, baffling conclusion. Again it is the details that are documented, while the essentials remain a blank. As Georg enters his father's room, he is amazed how dark it is: "Einen solchen Schatten warf also die hohe Mauer, die sich jenseits des schmalen Hofes erhob" (58; "This then was the shadow cast by the high wall on the other side of the narrow courtyard"). The explanation is immediate, specific, and physical; the insertion of "also" ("then") makes it seem a natural, logical inference. The material reason for the room's darkness diverts from consideration of the larger implicit issue of the father's seclusion in this dim rear cell, when Georg himself enjoys a sunny room with a pleasing view.

The concentration on the surface visible aspects to the displacement of the latent psychological dimension continues throughout the dramatic dialogue between Georg and his father, in which readers are cast in the role of spectators. Georg himself exemplifies the tendency to privilege the practical over the intangible; in dealing with his father he thinks only of the mechanics of where and how to get him to lie down. The expansive continuity of the descriptive notation of the changing scene sets into relief the absence of interpretative comment. Readers learn, for instance, what sort of underwear the father has (61); that he has a scar from a war wound on his upper thigh (63); that he holds only one hand lightly on the ceiling as he stands on the bed (62); that Georg notices him playing with his watch chain as he is being carried to bed (61); that he bites his tongue while keeping his eyes closed (63).

Such data are by no means insignificant; they indicate Georg's fluctuating perception of his father, and even something of his emotional state. Yet this sheer abundance of external information provokes and simultaneously averts the fundamental questions: Why does Georg make a point of telling his father about the letter to his friend? Is he seeking approval in childlike dependence? Or do father and son have so little to talk about that they seize on whatever comes to hand? Why does the father suddenly blurt out: "Hast du wirklich diesen Freund in Petersburg?" (59; "Do you really have this friend in Petersburg?"). Is this a symptom of senility, or perhaps some kind of malice? Why does he then go on to claim: "Ich war sein Vertreter hier am Ort" (63; "I was his local representative here"). Finally, why does the father announce his verdict: "Und darum wiße: Ich verurteile dich jetzt zum Tode des Ertrinkens" (65; "And therefore know: I now sentence you to death by drowning"). Is this a further sign of dementia? What is the terrible guilt for which Georg has to atone? Here, as in *Das Bettelweib von Locarno*, the syntactical continuity camouflages the cognitive discontinuity; the two linking terms "und" ("and") and "darum" ("therefore") suggest that this sentence (in both senses of the word) follows consequentially from what has gone before: "Ein unschuldiges Kind warst du ja eigentlich, aber noch eigentlicher warst du ein teuflischer Mensch" ("You were truly an innocent child, but even more truly you were a diabolical being"). Ideationally, however, there is none of the inevitability implied by the grammatical structuration.

In the closing section the syntactical construction and the distribution of information is such as to preclude insight into Georg's mental processes. The verbal forms are impersonal: Georg "fühlte sich aus dem Zimmer gejagt" (65; "felt himself chased out of the room"), "zum Waßer trieb es ihn" (65; "driven to the water") and "ließ sich hinabfallen" (66; "let himself drop"). It is impossible to tell either the degree of Georg's conscious volition or his mental state; he behaves like an automaton, or as if in a trance. The seeing lens is that of an external observer, as at the opening of the narrative, registering Georg's moves, but excluded from his thoughts. Yet even as readers grapple with this stunning gap, they are told that Georg, as he rushes downstairs, runs into the cleaning woman, who is just coming up to tidy the apartment after the night (65). So we learn exactly why she is coming, but are left to guess why he is going. To the very end, as in *Das Bettelweib von Locarno*, the central lacuna is surrounded by a welter of circumstantial peripheral detail: Georg swings himself over the railing with the gymnastic skill of which his parents had been proud in his youth. His last words: "Liebe Eltern, ich habe euch doch immer geliebt" (66; "Dear parents, I did always love you") are a riposte to his father's accusations; the interpolation of the emphatic and concessive "doch"[36] adumbrates perhaps the difficulty he has had in so doing, or could be a rejoinder to his father's indictment of him. The unadorned statement of an apparently indifferent fact in the final sentence: "In diesem Augenblick ging über die Brücke ein geradezu unendlicher Verkehr" (66; "At that moment an unending stream of traffic was going over the bridge") upholds the supremacy of physical notation in *Das Urteil*. A minute record of the outer course of the action takes the place of the suppressed internal motivation.

This pattern of informational feast and famine in Kleist's and Kafka's narratives poses an acute challenge to readers, who must infer, by scrutiny through their own lens, what connections, if any, exist between the discrete happenings that make up the action. Being in command of a considerable amount of diverse information, readers incline to suppose that they should eventually be able to attain a reasonably credible interpretation. However, the information at their disposal, though voluminous, turns out to be highly inadequate. Its very quantity aggravates readers' difficulties by forcing them to decide what is of central importance. Like Georg's friend in Russia, readers may misfocus on some marginal strand while failing to pay sufficient attention to developments that may be of greater moment. Such deflection represents in effect a tactic of decentering, and it is systematically fostered by the syntactic disposition. Kleist likes to banish a foremost fact into the depths of a subsidiary clause of a complex construction. So in the opening sentence of *Die Marquise von O*— the news of the marquise's pregnancy is submerged in the flood of surrounding data. In Kafka's prose the compulsive inclusion of circumstantial detail often disrupts the movement of the sentence, and confounds readers, not least through the delay of the final verb.

The impact of this mode of narration is to hold readers in a state of suspense, engaging them in an endless quest. As readers become as unsure of their own readings as the marquise and Georg are of theirs, the protagonists' dilemma of deciphering an undecipherable situation is transferred onto them. No guidance is offered from a narratorial viewpoint. Though present as a reporting voice, the narrator in both Kleist and Kafka abdicates superior insight and interpretative responsibility, standing, as it were, with his back to readers.[37] Unlike more traditional narrators, who choose to impart to readers a selected corpus of significant information, which can be fitted together like the pieces of a mosaic, both Kleist and Kafka offer a vastly larger quantity in what seems like a random manner, thereby compelling readers to distinguish between what may and what may not be pertinent to any reading. Thus a far greater onus falls on to individual readers. But at the same time, their confidence in their ability to read is eroded first by having to wrestle with the rhetoric of paradox and equivocation, and then by the realization of the ulterior obligation of having to attempt to organize this puzzling fabric of excess and dearth.

Readers are, therefore, driven to constant rereading. Camus' comment on Kafka applies just as much to Kleist: "Tout l'art de Kafka est d'obliger le lecteur à relire"[38] ("Kafka's art consists essentially in obliging the reader to reread"). Not that rereading advances us very far. Our interpretative processes are repeatedly thwarted by the conflicting signals of the ambiguous internal exegetic models. The coexistence of contradictory evaluations is the hallmark of both Kleist's and Kafka's mode of narration, and indeed of their universe. Unable to find consistent models within the text, readers have no reliable prototypes to guide their metaexegetic strategies. The system in which they are initiated is one of indeterminacy. The text becomes not an end in itself but rather the means of inducing and provoking the work of interpretation and understanding. It sets in motion and throws into relief the consciousness of reading, the laborious business of construing, surmising, articulating, and hypothesizing an elusive and possibly unattainable meaning. Its significance resides precisely in its evocation of the mental state of hesitation and bewilderment.

In other words, to read Kleist's and Kafka's narratives is, as it were, to be forced to don the notorious "green glasses" of which Kleist wrote in his letter of 22 March 1801. But, unlike the recipient of Kleist's letter, readers are never explicitly forewarned of the metaphoric green glasses. Trying to read the text through their own lens, they find themselves thrust without notice into the strange land of the green glasses. It is a land characterized by a singular interplay of presence and absence, of physical precision and cognitive multivalence. The "force with which it exacts interpretation" clashes with "the abyss of meaning it conceals."[39] Readers end up knowing at once far too much and far too little.

III

Mirror Images

Words may be said, after all, to be the finest things in the world. Things themselves are but a lower species of words, exhibiting the grossness and details of matter.

William Hazlitt

7

Realism and its "Code of Accreditation"

The term "code of accreditation" ("code d'accréditement") was coined by Roland Barthes at the Colloque de Cérisy of 1977, where his own writings formed the "pretext." In his reply to a comment on his analysis of Edgar Allan Poe's story, *The Case of M. Valdemar*, Barthes outlines a binary typology of narrative:

> Tout récit est donc soumis à cette alternative: construire son orientation rhétorique en soulignant que "ce n'est qu'une histoire" (celle-ci n'ayant alors de réalité qu'à faire médiation entre sa source et ses déstinataires ...); ou au contraire en se donnant les moyens (par vraisemblance, réalisme (procédures d'accréditement) de s'effacer en tant que récit.[1]

In the ensuing discussion Barthes develops this notion of accreditation procedures, although he ascribes the code of accreditation solely to the first kind of narrative, the text aware of its own status as a literary construct, and constantly signalling to readers that "this is only a story." Such privileging of overtly self-conscious narration is in keeping with the preferences of most post-structuralist critics. What is surprising is Barthes' rider:

> En fonction du problème d'accréditement, il faudrait réinterpreter le réalisme, car paradoxalement ce qu'on appelle couramment le réalisme est un genre littéraire qui rejette le code d'accréditement. Dans Balzac et dans Flaubert il n'y a pas d'accréditement et c'est pour cela en un sens que c'est réaliste.[2]

Barthes' assertions about realism need to be examined, and on two scores: first his contention that realism does not engage in accreditation, that indeed it rejects any such code, and secondly, that this is precisely what distinguishes it from other forms of narration. Curiously, Barthes does not appear in any way to envisage the possibility of a discrepancy between realism's proclaimed tenets and its actual practices. Yet realism's earlier reputation as a sort of kindergarten genre, essentially simple, transparent, and naive, has largely been refuted by the reassessment that has been taking place over the past twenty years or so.[3] Nonetheless, it is still often made to take a back seat to more obviously intricate narrative structures more immediately attractive to avant-garde critics. Barthes' exclusion of realism from the code of accreditation is an instance of discriminatory misreading. To endow realist fiction with such a code is to accede to a willingness to problematize it by recognizing that its manipulation of readers is just as adroit, though much less obtrusive, than in those texts that insistently declare themselves to be "only a story."

The complexity of realist fiction was for long underestimated partly because of its own self-image of ingenuousness which it pointedly cultivated. In contrast to the self-conscious artifact, which accentuates its artificiality by flaunting its artifices, realist fiction deliberately presents itself as free from literariness. Its theoretical statements underscore its artlessness as a straightforward, accurate account of a preexistent, stable, external, knowable entity recognizable as 'reality.' The narrator's assurances to readers near the beginning of Balzac's *Le Père Goriot* that *"All is true"*[4] is the most concise and emphatic summary of the realist position. On the printed page the phrase is foregrounded through its resort to a foreign language and its typographical set in italics. By insisting, moreover, that "ce drame n'est ni une fiction ni un roman" (848; "this drama is neither a fiction nor a novel"), Balzac establishes an explicit dichotomy between the 'true' and the 'fictive,' and endeavors to place his novel squarely under the former heading.

Similar conceptualizations of the novel as a direct, authentic transcription of real life resonate through the nineteenth century. Often it is the image of the mirror that serves as an emblem of the mimetic function of realist narrative. Stendhal's definition of the novel in the epigraph to chapter XIII of *Le Rouge et le noir (The Red and the Black)* is a striking example: "un miroir qu'on promène le long d'un chemin" ("a mirror that is walked along a road"); though ascribed to Saint-Réal (i.e., the saint of the real), it is actually Stendhal's own invention. The "great looking-glass" in the second chapter of Dickens' *Our Mutual Friend*[5] is another instance of the same idea. It crops up again in the famous passage in chapter XVII of *Adam Bede*, where George Eliot formulates her aim as being "to give a faithful account of man and things as they have mirrored themselves in my mind."[6] A parallel view is inherent in Zola's reiterated declaration: "Un oeuvre d'art est un coin de la nature vu à travers un tempérament"[7] ("a work of art is a corner of nature seen through a temperament"). Realism thus claims to be reality as seen through the lens of the writers. Their pronouncements are designed to program readers to perceive the text not as a literary construct, but as a record of the vicissitudes of human existence under the given circumstances of a particular place at a particular time.[8] In other words, they encourage a referential reading, that in effect discounts (i.e., fails to count) the literary aspects of the representation.

To discuss the problems and fallacies embedded in the tenets of realism is beyond my scope here. Suffice it to point out that Zola's idea of "tempérament," like George Eliot's of "mind," introduces the subjective element of a personal, perhaps idiosyncratic filter, while the mirror, as Eliot herself concedes, "is doubtless defective,"[9] an evaluating, potentially distorting prism rather than a dispassionately registering instrument. Even more important is the essentially deceptive nature of realism's self-image. As a result of its own asseverations, realism becomes the victim of its precept of unpretentiousness. By opting for an unassuming posture, it leads — misleads — readers into the belief that it is an innocent mode. As Ian Watt realized, "the poverty of the novel's formal conventions would seem to be the price it must pay for its realism."[10] So it is a paradoxical outcome of realism's success in projecting its chosen image that it comes to appear devoid of the more sophisticated narrational stratagems, including the code of accreditation.

To grant realism a code of accreditation entails a basic change in our standpoint toward it as well as in our suppositions. The reading of realist fiction must be envisaged not as an exercise in referentiality, an excuse for a kind of amateur detective spree in relating the fictional construct to a specific socio-historico-geographic model. Instead, it has to be perceived primarily as a **literary** quest, not for meaning, but for an understanding of a verbal structure governed by its own internal laws and codes. This reorientation directs attention away from the epistemological issues of truthfulness and imitation in favor of a focus on the aesthetic aspects of the realist enterprise.

In practical terms, such a change is initiated by a shift of perspective from that of the writer to that of readers. This does not mean an acceptance of the hypothesis that there is no *énonciateur,* only an act of *énonciation* resulting in an *énoncé.* [11] There was a historic personage called Honoré de Balzac, who was born in Tours in 1799 and died in Paris in 1850, and who wrote a novel entitled *Le Père Goriot,* published in 1834 and set in contemporary Paris. It is evident that Balzac drew on his intimate knowledge of the city, for instance the social standing of certain streets and quarters that are named, not only for the setting of his novel but also for its plot dynamics. The same order of facts can be established about Dickens and London, Zola and the French scene under the Second Empire, or Thomas Mann and Lübeck. This does not, however, necessitate either an investigation of the author's source materials or the reconstruction of a remote locale as a prerequisite for a reading of the text. To support this argument, one need only consider the large number of readers of European fiction who have never seen the sites of the novels' action, and who may have notions of European geography as vague as those held by Europeans about the United States.

Fictive places exist not through their dependence on actual locations; they come alive, i.e., become 'real' to readers by virtue of the convincing illusion that has been created through the medium of language. The primary focus of inquiry should, therefore, be on the way in which the words are disposed in order to produce that illusion and to nurture readers' credence in it. The questions to be addressed to realism must center not on its origins in a past actuality, but on its present force as a literary text. By what combination of means does it attain the illusion, the so-called "effet de réel"?[12] What sort of language is used? Is it predominantly connotative or denotative? metonymic or metaphoric? What information is offered? Almost equally telling, what is omitted, or taken for granted? How much detail is included? Whose is the speaking voice and the focalization? That of the narrator or of a protagonist? A single protagonist, whose consciousness forms the organizing center, or a multiplicity of figures ranging over a spectrum? These questions expose realism to the scrutiny of a literary, rather than the hitherto more customary mimetic lens.

Such an amendment of standpoint involves a fundamental modification in the approach to realist narrative. However 'realistic' a fiction may strive to appear, it is ultimately, and forever remains, a "fiction mimant la vérité"[13] ("fiction miming the truth"). At stake here is its ontological status, the acknowledgment of the element of pretense intrinsic to all storytelling. The realist narrative **pretends** to give a true and faithful account of an existent reality. We as readers acquiesce and enter into that pretense, sometimes to the point of repressing the recognition that it is indeed a pretense. This stance is less a matter of suspending disbelief than of pretending belief. This hypothesis has been put forward by Kendall L. Walton, who has explored the problem with great subtlety in a series of articles on the aesthetics of illusion. "To play the game," Walton maintains, "is to pretend that it is not a game, and it is crucial to realize that it is one."[14] Obviously it is easier to remember in reading that a fiction is a fiction if it keeps reminding us of its status at intervals. On the other hand, with a realist fiction that makes every effort to uphold the integrity of the illusion with consistency, we are far more likely to slip into "our strangely persistent inclination to think of fictions as sharing reality with us."[15] Our strong tendency to regard fictions as parts, maybe extensions of our reality, despite our knowledge at some level that they are not, results in a blurring of the concept of truth. Truth within the world of the fiction cannot be equated in a cavalier manner with truth in reality. To forestall "our habit of playing along with fictions, of fictionally asserting, pretending to assert, what we know to be only fictionally the case,"[16] Walton argues for the introduction of a separate category of fictional truth:

> Propositions which are 'true in a novel,' 'true in (the world of) a picture,' etc. are *fictionally true.* A novel or picture determines what is fictionally true; it *generates* fictional truths ... Roughly, a fictional world consists of the fictional truths generated by a single work.[17]

This concept of fictional truth as a discrete ontological level is useful, but it also has certain limitations, especially in regard to realist narrative. While it is apparent that the Julius Caesar of Shakespeare's play has a fictional life besides, and probably different from the literal existence he had in ancient Rome,[18] the position is much less clear-cut when it comes to Balzac's or Zola's Paris, or the London of Dickens. Like Julius Caesar, these cities have had a literal existence, and they continue to have it in a changing form, besides their fictional existence. What is more, that fictional existence may seem to correspond quite closely to the historical model so that we speak of the accuracy of the representation.

There is no neat way to resolve this dilemma. To resort to Meinong's distinction[19] between *Sein* properties, i.e., existence and non-existence, and *Sosein* properties, i.e., being golden, being a mountain, is helpful to some degree. The distinction works well with a statement such as: "Mrs. Gamp is fat,"[20] where Mrs. Gamp is recognized without reservation as a fictional persona created by Dickens, who has chosen to ascribe to her the quality of fatness, although the only property she herself can have is a literary one, such as being introduced in chapter three. The situation is, however, much more complicated in the case of London or Paris in the nineteenth century since they existed actually as well as now existing fictionally. It may well be, as Hayden White has insisted in *Metahistory*,[21] that all historical images partake of the fictional. This compounds the problem by impugning the relative stability of the historical model, which in turn must intensify the dubiousness of the fictional image, certainly insofar as it purports to reflect a historical reality. Walton, too, concedes that "the barrier between worlds is not airtight."[22] This could be applied to the barrier between the historical and the fictional as well as between the real and the fictional. Walton suggests an ingenious solution by conjecturing the possibility of what he describes as "*crossworld* saving."[23] This accounts effectively for the genuine emotions felt, for instance, by a person seeing a horror movie which he knows to be fictional. With the literary text, such crossing of the worlds is accomplished through the mediation of the narrator, who has the singular capacity of being able to belong to both worlds. It is he who acts as the source and guarantor of the *Sosein* of the fictional object, but not necessarily of its *Sein*. In Meinong's terms, the *Sosein* of an object is not affected by its *Nichtsein* (non-existence). The only finally valid *Sein* in a narrative, however realistic, are the words printed on the page; through them we attain access to the fictional world, through them fictional truths are generated, and the illusion of authenticity conveyed. Through their rhetorical power of persuasion the words draw readers into the fictional realm and convince them of its 'reality.' It is only in this open ontological context that the question of realism and its code of accreditation can fruitfully be addressed.

Realist fiction seeks to accredit itself first and foremost as a fulfillment and confirmation of its stated tenets, that is to say, as a truthful record of actuality. Its code of accreditation amounts to an elaborate and deliberate pretense that it is indeed what it claims to be: a mimesis of life. The underlying thrust of the various strategies that make up the code of accreditation is to authenticate and sustain the central kernel of illusion on which realism is predicated. In large measure the tactics prove successful: we as readers come to believe in the reality of the representation. We can almost smell the odors of Zola's Paris, we grasp the socio-ethical imperatives of the society Mann presents in *Buddenbrooks*, the workings of power and human foibles in *Middlemarch*, and the moral and social tensions between North and South, and between Boston and New York in James' *The Bostonians*, to cite a few major examples. Yet even while directed primarily at the vitality of the illusion, the devices of accreditation, by virtue of their coalescence into a code, testify, ironically, to the innate literariness of realism. The paradox is not, as Barthes asserted, that realism rejects the code of accreditation, and thereby becomes, in his words, "en un sens ... réaliste,"[24] but rather that it embraces that code, and in so doing betrays what it is trying to conceal: its nature as make-believe.

Before that paradox can be explored, the major constituents of realism's code of accreditation must be identified. Its main axis lies at the intersection of time and place. In antithesis to the formulaic 'Long ago and far away' or 'Once upon a time,' that usher entry through the gates of ivory into a sphere of fantasy and romance at a remove from actuality, passage through the gates of horn takes readers to a well demarcated location. The temporal is generally an ancillary dimension because realism has a marked preference for the close-to-hand, the familiar and the common-place, found in the contemporaneous or nearly contemporaneous to the time of writing. But although realist fiction does not turn as programmat-ically on the period of the action as does the historical novel, nonetheless it takes care to fix at the very least its decade, more often its year, and occasionally its month and day, generally at or near the opening. An alter-native, more oblique method of temporal contextualization is practiced by those texts that incorporate identifiable historical events into the fic-tive plot. Instances of this kind include Elizabeth Gaskell's *Mary Barton*, in which John Barton participates as a delegate in the march on London during the Chartist movement of the early 1840s, Dickens' *Hard Times*, which draws on the Preston weavers' strike of 1853, and the 1884 miners' strike near Lille that forms the model for Zola's *Germinal*. In all these novels the protagonists engage in a lively debate of the political contro-versies of their day. The same procedures are used in *Middlemarch*, which is most precisely rooted in the recent past some forty years ante-rior to the date of composition, and which abounds in extensive allusions to the political, social, economic, religious, medical, and legislative con-ditions of its time.

As these examples suggest, there are considerable variations in the amount of attention and the degree of prominence invested in the tem-poral placement. In some cases, as in *Middlemarch, Mary Barton, Ger-minal,* and *Buddenbrooks*, the period of the action is pivotal to the de-velopment of the plot. In other instances, as in James' *The Europeans* or *The Portrait of a Lady*, or Trollope's *Barchester Towers*, it plays a less leading role. Nevertheless, the explicit presence of the temporal factor serves one and the same purpose in all these narratives: its cardinal func-tion is to accredit the fiction, i.e., to authenticate the veracity of the illu-sion by anchoring it in verifiable events. The point in time operates as a bridge between the actual and the fictive worlds. The process can be des-ignated, to borrow cinematic terms, as one of montage, when an invented realm is grafted onto a known situation. This technique is at its most ob-vious in Balzac, who habitually starts his novels with thirty-page descrip-tions that are in effect the hawsers holding the fictive action to a platform of actuality. Through its connection to specific public facts open to cor-roboration in the temporal dimension, the simulated world of the fiction is, by means of a kind of osmosis, endowed with a more substantive cred-ibility. Jane Austen surely understood this when she made precise calcu-lations of time in her novels in relation to calendar dates with the help of an almanac.[25]

Austen knew also the need for equal meticulousness in the handling of place. In a letter of 29 January 1813 she begs her sister Cassandra: "If you could discover whether Northamptonshire is a country of Hedge-rows, I should be glad again."[26] Particularity of place forms the second essential strand in realism's code of accreditation. Though long accepted as one of the hallmarks of realism, it has been curiously neglected as a topic for critical consideration. Compared to the amount of attention given to time in literature, that devoted to place is scant. One reason for this disparity may lie in the inherent "asymmetry of time and space in the narrative."[27] Space has been the object of phenomenological readings in the wake of Gaston Bachelard's *Poétique de l'espace* (Paris: Presses universitaires de France, 1974). More recently semiotic interpretations of space have appeared in abundance. As a subcategory of the larger dimension of space, place has been accorded only limited and often specialized analysis, such as historical reconstruction, or the ecologically motivated essays of Leo Lutwack.[28] The rhetoric of place and its literary presentation has not been much discussed except in relation to particular classes such as the city, or town and country. Yet the importance of place as a means of accreditation can hardly be overstated. While its function is in many respects parallel to that of the temporal mooring, its modes of manifestation run a wider gamut. In its most rudimentary form, it consists of name-dropping: the names of cities and towns, great and small, of districts in those cities, of provinces and regions, of landmarks of all sorts, of streets, comprising both the well- and the little known. The use of names is indeed so crucial an issue that it will be discussed separately in a subsequent chapter.

Nomination is a common and cardinal device of realist fiction for a number of reasons. It reiterates in regard to space the technique of montage in relation to time. The fiction is, literally, grounded in an externally identifiable reality: when the place cited can be found on a map, it has a scientifically proven reality. So the fictive action derives from its geographic siting a decisive legitimation. In addition, the names as sound patterns have an effect akin to magic. The act of naming is like the performance of a ritual, invoking the participants' powers of imagination. The appeal to readers' imagination is a key element in the creation of the fictional world. On the one hand, the names become a cipher for an extraneously valid system, and hence carry a warranty of truthfulness. At the same time, as a code of accreditation they exert another kind of persuasion insofar as they stimulate readers to active input in the construction of the fictive scenario.

But not all realist narratives are sited in a geographically well-known location; many are set in places which appear invented or at least open to doubt, as for instance Middlemarch, Yonville in *Madame Bovary*, and Kessin in Fontane's *Effi Briest*. How does this affect the process of accreditation? The question is important theoretically because it confronts head-on the problem of referentiality. Analysis of specific cases reveals, however, that it is less of a discrete issue than a question of intensification as the fictitious names operate through a mimicry of the actual. Since all fiction demands of the reader a pretense of belief, the difference between reference to actual names and use of invented names is a matter of degree rather than of principle. *Madame Bovary* and *Effi Briest* ask readers to take the further step of pretending that the names are authentic. As the component of outer referentiality wanes, that of pretense increases. While recognizable places function in part as a shorthand code of legitimation, invented ones, specially those that sound as though they could be real, like Yonville and Kessin, derive their credibility from the creation of a fictional space whose accreditation is internal to the boundaries of the fiction.

Pretense is most potently called into play once a name is recognized as literary, i.e., more connotative than denotative, as is, for example, Middlemarch. Whether or not its model is Coventry is irrelevant. Though subtitled "A Study of Provincial Life," and though liberal in its allusions to such actual places as London, Rome, Lyons, Avignon, Manchester, and Leeds, the text consistently eschews the identifiable for the local scene of the action. Besides Middlemarch, there is Tipton, with Freshitt and Lowick, all in "the north-east corner of Loamshire."[29] Loamshire, not an existent English county, offers a legible clue to the figurative import of these invented names. The transparently symbolic nomenclature, Middlemarch, in the county of Loam-shire, clearly evokes the ordinary, down-to-earth, in short, the prototypical, unremarkable English country town of thirty to forty years back. Its very commonness bears on one of the novel's main themes: the contrast between the microcosm of the restricted fictional forum and the macrocosm of the expansive world on the horizon. Tipton strikes Dorothea as a "little pool" compared to the "lake"[30] beyond; the adjectives appropriate to it are "narrow," "petty," and "small," and the images those of confinement ("hemmed in," "a labyrinth," "a walled-in maze") as against "the grandest path" and "the greatest things"[31] ascribed to what transcends the boundaries of the provinces. These dichotomies prove to be misconceptions on Dorothea's part, as she comes to learn through painful experience. But they are not merely the foolish mirages of an innocent young woman for they are echoed and repeated, *mutatis mutandis,* in the career of Lydgate, whose lofty ideals are thwarted in the encounter with the mentality of Middlemarch. For both Dorothea and Lydgate Middlemarch turns out to be not just the arena where their lives are enacted, but itself a determining agent.

Through its commanding role in the plot, the fictive place comes to validate itself internally as Middlemarch is transformed from a static frame of the action into a dynamic force. The novel starts, like so many

realist narratives, with the montage of the fictive Middlemarch in Loamshire temporally into the concerns of 1829 and spatially in relation to London and Paris although no precise distances are ever mentioned. The
known external factors form an accrediting entrance into the fiction. But
when Middlemarch becomes an increasingly insistent presence as a critical consensus in the protagonists' reckoning, a change of orientation
from an outer to an inner accreditation is accomplished. As Dorothea and
Lydgate, Fred Vincy, Mary Garth, and Bulstrode each in turn has to acknowledge and submit to the pressures exerted on the individual by his/
her environment, Middlemarch assumes an active part independent of its
moorings in any sphere extraneous to the fiction. Place in fiction becomes plausible and alive for readers not through its referential connection to an outer existent location, but through the reality it attains intrinsically within the parameters of the fiction as a motivating influence in the
minds of the characters.

This type of accreditation has a different basis from that which seeks
to authenticate the illusion by looking outward to an order of reality anterior to the fiction. The two are, however, neither antithetical nor mutually exclusive. Virtually every realist narrative draws on both external
and internal accreditation. *Middlemarch* is a good illustration not only
because it is often deemed the leading English realist novel, but even
more because it raises issues fundamental to the whole question of accreditation. Its delicate equipoise between the actual and the fictive allows it to keep a footing in the known world, yet without inhibiting its capacity to create a distinctive place of its own for the purposes of the
fiction. It does so by virtue of the power granted to Middlemarch in the
lives and minds of the protagonists. Through the ethical and social charge
it carries as a complex system of values, Middlemarch is invested with a
reality more vital than any merely geographic name could ever possess.
As the incarnation of a certain limited mentality, it dominates the action,
shaping both character and the course of lives. It takes on a metaphoric
stature as a place of the mind, continuous and coexistent with contemporary circumstances, yet unconstrained by the imperatives of mimesis.

The dual accreditation found in *Middlemarch*, deriving in part from
an acknowledgment of an extraneous actuality, and in part from allegiance to its own created field of reference,[32] is characteristic of realist
fiction. A dual accreditation parallel to that in *Middlemarch* is at work in
Zola's *L'Assommoir*, as has been outlined in chapter 2. Another example,
that of Thomas Mann's *Buddenbrooks*, will be analyzed in more detail in
the final chapter precisely because it is such an outstanding incarnation
of the fusion of external and internal fields of reference and their welding
into a fictionalized entity, vividly 'real' to readers.

If the main axis of realism's code of accreditation lies at the intersection of time and place, its primary agent is the narrator. Even where the narrator remains invisible as an individuated figure, as in *L'Assommoir* and *Buddenbrooks*, it is nonetheless his voice that is the source of the accrediting information given to readers. In this area as well, there is urgent need to re-examine some of the traditional tenets about realism, such as the alleged absence of the narrator. Granted that his presence has nothing of the capriciously insistent cult of his own personality characteristic of the self-conscious, self-dramatizing gamesman, who parades in the foreground of the fiction, intruding on the progress of the narration and mischievously disrupting the reading process. By comparison, the narrating persona of nineteenth century realism is a model of reserve and sobriety. His voice remains low-key, anonymous, disembodied, as it were. But nothing could be more erroneous than to conclude from his unobtrusiveness that his function in realist narrative is negligible. It is through the narrator that the procedures of accreditation are activated.

Readers' acceptance of time and place as vehicles of accreditation depends on their assured relationship to the narrator. His proven trustworthiness is the paramount criterion of our readiness to believe what he tells us; our faith in his honesty underpins our credence in the illusion. So the narrative can become 'real,' i.e., persuasively convincing, only if a stable contract is established and sustained between narrator and readers. As the narrator imparts his knowledge to readers with plausible consistency, the latter reciprocate by a growing confidence in the friendly guiding voice of the storyteller. It is the narrator's reliability that is crucial to realist narrative, not his invisibility.

The narrator presents himself from the outset, where the focalization is almost without exception through his lens, as literally an eyewitness in possession of firsthand knowledge of the places, things, and people of which he writes. Often that is in fact the case, but even where the author did not have intelligence of the kind he claims, as in Balzac's *La Recherche de l'absolu* (Balzac had never been to Douai), the narrator continues assiduously to foster the self-image of expertise. So the persona of the narrator already partakes to a lesser or a greater degree of the process of fictionalization, and therefore functions as a bridge between the two worlds on a level beyond the overt one.[33] What matters is the semblance of encompassing knowledge so that he be perceived by readers as well versed as he stands astride the two worlds, that of experienced reality and the parallel one of the fiction. From his vantage point in and of both, the narrator indicates that he is able through his privileged insight to provide accreditation. Once his credibility as the virtually omniscient repository of information has been firmly instituted, he can present himself as not merely the enunciator but also the guarantor of truth. For this reason his role is fundamental to realism's entire tactics of accreditation.

But the narrator's function goes beyond a discrete presence as pedagogue, expositor, and moderator. By inspiring and nurturing the trust we as readers invest in him, he gradually draws us into the realm of the fiction. In this respect the narrator is instrumental in the process of montage that is one of realism's main devices of accreditation. With the cumulative formation of a consensus, a merger of the two adjacent worlds, the actual and the fictive, is consummated. One common way to achieve this passage is by a shift of focalization through the lens of the protagonist, as in the opening chapter of *L'Assommoir.* As soon as readers are persuaded to subscribe to Gervaise's perception of Paris, they have, without consciously realizing it, been transported into the fiction.

The same effect is produced by narrator's allocution of readers. This is a frequent occurrence in *Middlemarch:* "She was blind, you see, to many things obvious to others" (408); "Mr. Casaubon, we know, had a sense of rectitude" (458); "You may well ask why ... " (462); "most of whom, like our acquaintance, Mr. Bambridge" (721). Through these addresses readers become immediate participants in the action, asked to exercise their judgment alongside the narrator. Even more overt invitations to enter the world of the fiction are issued in some other realist novels: in *Mary Barton*, for example: "if you can picture all this with a washy, but clean stencilled pattern on the walls, you can form some idea of John Barton's home";[34] in *Le Père Goriot:* "si vous le compariez à la salle à manger, qui lui est contiguë, vous trouveriez ce salon élégant et parfumé comme doit l'être un boudoir"[35] ("if you were to compare it to the dining-room, which is next door, you would find this living-room as elegant and scented as a boudoir should be"); in *Eugénie Grandet:* "Vous verrez un marchand ... vous n'obtiendriez pas un sou de marchandise chez ces braves industriels"[36] ("You will see a merchant... you would not get a cent of merchandise from these good manufacturers"). In each instance the well-informed witnessing narrator is asking readers to identify vicariously through an effort of the imagination with his own physical experience of the scene. It is as if the narrator's conviction of the reality of the fiction were being projected onto readers. A similar transference occurs when the narrator repeatedly refers to Isabel Archer in *The Portrait of a Lady* as "our heroine" or to Basil Ransom in *The Bostonians* as "our young man." In every case the bond forged between the narrator and readers serves to cement the code of accreditation through the shared perspective. The narrator's appeals to readers amount to an act of seduction on behalf of the fiction.

So the narrator in realist fiction proves a mainstay in the creation of the illusion. It is he who choreographs readers' entry into the fiction. His claim to mastery over the actual and the fictive worlds enables him to act as the spokesman of both and as the agent of readers' initiation into the fiction as well as the instrument of closure. At the opening of *Eugénie Grandet*, for example, the narrator announces:

> Il se trouve dans certaines villes de province des maisons dont la vue inspire une mélancolie égale à celle que provoquent les cloîtres les plus sombres, les landes les plus ternes ou les ruines les plus tristes.[37]

The narrator goes on to describe the place and time of the action, offering his own intimacy as validation, yet actually creating his impact on readers less by his testimony than through the coalescence of images and reiterated personifications. The melancholy atmosphere of the sinister house is potently evoked by the emphasis on silence, stasis, and gloom as well as by the reference to cloisters, heaths, and ruins. These pointers to dessication and death hint immediately at the Gothic undercurrents in this domestic drama of provincial life. With the naming of Saumur in Touraine, the sketch of the historical background and the specifics of its economy, the narrative is accredited in relation to an extraneous reality. Yet at the same time it has, through the intertextual resonances in the description of the house, also been sited in a literary and mythological context. Perhaps no other novel, except possibly *Le Père Goriot*, which follows a similar pattern, illustrates as clearly the way the narrator ushers readers into the realm of the fiction while simultaneously welding it to a reality. Almost twenty pages elapse in *Eugénie Grandet* before the formal start of the action: "En 1819, vers le commencement de la soirée, au milieu du mois de novembre, la grande Nanon alluma le feu pour la première fois"[38] ("In 1819, early in the evening, in the middle of November, big Nanon lit the fire for the first time"). Again, the precise date is a procedure of accreditation, but here it is attached to a fictive act, the lighting of the season's first fire by Nanon. The mounting of the fiction into a context of geographic, economic, and historical data has been accomplished.

The celebration that evening of Eugénie's twenty-third birthday marks the beginning of the plot in the speculations on her likely marriage. It ends nine years later in the same house with Eugénie as yellow and faded as her mother had been, still enclosed in the same house, which is now openly presented as the objective correlative of her life: "La maison de Saumur, maison sans soleil, sans chaleur, sans cesse ombragée, mélancolique, est l'image de sa vie"[39] ("The house in Saumur, a house devoid of sun or warmth, always shaded and melancholy, is the image of her life"). The external accreditation ("Saumur") is still there, albeit in the background; the effective force of the correlation springs rather from the internal accreditation, from the associative momentum the house has gathered as the scene of the fictive drama. With the return at the finale not only to the house but also to the present tense, the arch encircling the action, spanning from the opening to the close, has been completed. The phrase in the concluding paragraph: "Telle est l'histoire de cette femme"[40] ("Such is the story of this woman") is an echo of "événements de cette histoire"[41] ("happenings of this story") at the outset. A frame has been placed round the narrative, and it is put there by the narrating voice.

Eugénie Grandet, as one of the earliest and foremost examples of realism, is of paradigmatic importance in revealing the enframing of the narrative transacted by the narrator. In *Middlemarch*, the invocation of Saint Teresa in the Prelude sets Dorothea's life into a religious, historical, and mythical frame of aspiration. Less readily apparent but equally significant is the frame created by the narrating voice. This is manifest in *Middlemarch* obliquely in the epigraphs to each chapter, which form a meta-level of commentary, and directly in the recounting but occasionally also reflective "I" of "the diligent narrator" (375). This "I," in addressing a "you" and in assuming an "us," posits an audience that denotes another kind of frame. This facet is even more pronounced in Henry James, where an articulate, sometimes opinionated, authoritative (though not invariably omniscient) narratorial "I" is both in control of the fiction and in immediate rapport with readers. James' narration is continuously punctuated by such interpolated turns as "I say," or "I must add," or "as I have intimated." These locutions show the narrator acting as an observer, strategically placed at the margins of the action, sufficiently close to it to have intimate insight, yet in his relationship to readers patently detached from it. In this characteristic posture he, too, represents an enframing device to the fiction.

A frame both connects a picture to its surroundings and separates it from them, thereby confirming its status as an aesthetic artifact. So the narrator in realist fiction, in the very act of accrediting its 'reality,' also discloses its essence as make-believe. He does so not merely by his own position, simultaneously within but without the narrative, but perhaps even more by drawing readers into the same ambivalent situation. Like the narrator, the audience too is subject to a process of fictionalization.[42] As readers we become a presence in the text because it invites, and at times indeed compels our participation. The "you," whose experience, judgment, and reading capacity are invoked by the narrator, overlaps with "us"; in other words, actual readers merge with fictive readers. We sit[43]

within the confines of the world created in the narrative, even while continuing to maintain our sense of separateness. Our double location repli-
cates that of the narrator. This sets further stepping stones between the
actual and the fictional worlds. On the one hand, it encourages interpel-
lation of readers' own experience as a means of authentication, although
this tactic is usable only in direct proportion to the individual reader's
range, and, therefore, ultimately inconsequential for the code of accreditation. On the other hand, paradoxically, it increases the viability of the
fictional world by moving readers away from their reality into its reality.
The " 'engaging' "[44] narrator, in closing the gaps between the narratee, the
addressee, and the receiver, is at the same time de facto closing the gaps
between their respective worlds. The recognition and identification
evoked in the "you," which coincides with "us," results in a deeper assent
to the fiction. Readers' involvement forms the final segment of the frame
that holds the fiction.

   The silhouette of the frame indicates that what we are dealing with
is a story in which our part is that of readers. This should not, however,
prompt the immediate assumption that the fiction is necessarily an-
nouncing itself as "only a story." A narrative that presents itself as "only
a story" may well lend itself to playful self-deconstruction and reconstruction. But within the frame of reference that marks its ontological status as a fiction, a story may take itself seriously as a story, in an attempt
perhaps to raise its own standing, particularly in an age such as the mid-
nineteenth century, that did not place a high value on art for art's sake. Yet
the fact that a story chooses for purposes of credibility to pass itself off
as a literal imitation of actuality, as realism did, does not authorize us to
read it as such. Its posture does not alter its essential condition as a fiction, although it does lead to the sustained endeavor to accredit the authenticity of the illusion by relating it by metonymic extension to a known
system of reference beyond the boundaries of the fiction.

   To acknowledge that realist fiction has a code of accreditation is by
implication to query the traditional dichotomy between the two dominant
distinctive modes of narration: that which operates on the agenda "this
is only a story," and the other which takes for its devise *"All is true."* Such
a dualism is at the least an overstatement, and more likely a fallacy. For
realism's code of accreditation is arguably parallel in function to that of
self-conscious narration insofar as the purpose in each case is to buttress
the self-image projected by the fiction. Although the thrust of the two images is antithetical, they are alike in serving to foster the underlying pretense as well as to signal to readers the context of supposition in which
the text is to be read. What differentiates realism is not the absence of a
code of accreditation, but its covertness. As a narrational strategy and as

an *écriture*, realism is directed toward concealment, indeed denial of its literariness. That it has often inveigled readers into accepting it at its own face value, into believing in its so-called simplicity and transparency, is an ironic measure of its success at the game it is playing. It is, however, a game, no less than that of self-conscious fiction, even if its name is 'truth' and its code of accreditation is designed to cover its tracks and to screen out its scaffolding devices.

8

The Game of the Name[1]

"Fiction depends for its life on place. Location is the crossroads of circumstances."

Eudora Welty

In a highly suggestive essay on "Place in Fiction," Eudora Welty interjects a provocative question: "Might not the magic lie partly in the *name* of the place -?"[2] She immediately answers in the affirmative by pointing to the far greater evocative force of "The Hanging Gardens of Babylon" than just "The Hanging Gardens." In this instance, clearly, the name, with its allusions to mythical and Biblical narratives adds intertextual and associative dimensions to the phrase. What Welty illustrates does indeed amount to a kind of magic in readers' reaction to place names. Since naming is one of the recurrent devices of realist fiction, it needs to be further sounded. What are the sources of this "magic?" How does it work? Specifically, in what ways and to what effects are place names introduced into realist narrative?

The hitherto dominant view has taken its cue from a comment by Henry James in the preface to *Roderick Hudson:* "To name a place in fiction, is to pretend in some degree to represent it."[3] The emphasis has, under the sway of mimetic readings of realism, traditionally been on the representational aspects of names. But in the wake of the post-structuralist perception of realist fictions as verbal compositions rather than as imitations of reality, the time has come to look from a different angle at the deployment and function of names. Once their automatic referential conjunction with a reality is queried, they forfeit something of their status as emblematic icons. The change of focus can best be summarized by going back to James in order now to put the spotlight onto the idea "pretend" instead of onto "represent." To discern how that pretense operates is to go a long way toward understanding the innate mechanisms of realist fiction. Names are an excellent starting point because they play so crucial a role in the game of pretense that lies at the heart of realism.

It is no coincidence that so many nineteenth century novels include a place name or an element of localization in their titles: *Mansfield Park, Northanger Abbey, Wuthering Heights, La Chartreuse de Parme, Middlemarch, Barchester Towers, The Bostonians, The Europeans, The Spoils of Poynton, Le Curé de Tours, The Mayor of Casterbridge, The Master of Ballantrae, Tartarin de Tarascon, Die Leute von Seldwyla, Immensee, Cranford, North and South, Lourdes, Rome,* and *Paris,* are a few random examples. In part this tendency reflects the reduction of interest in the journey, the picaresque adventures common in the fiction of the previous century. The greater proportion of female protagonists also fosters stasis since women, with the exception of a few unconventional adventuresses, had far less freedom and mobility than men. The typical woman's life was often indeed a tale of confinement amounting almost to imprisonment. So the nineteenth century novel is more stationary, more rooted in a single central location as well as enmeshed in domestic trammels. With the growth of belief in determinism, moreover, place comes to be an increasingly important element in the action as it is transformed from mere decor to formative milieu.

Name-dropping is a ubiquitous practice within the novels, too, as is evident in the abundance of geographic appellations: Paris, London, Berlin, Venice, Rome, Florence, Manchester, Liverpool, Southampton, San Remo, Le Havre, Chinon, Azay, New York, Boston, Cape Cod, Topeka, Hamburg, Rostock, Travemünde, Munich, Smithfield, Cheapside, the Louvre, Notre-Dame, Versailles, Vesuvius, Charles Street, the Fischergrube, etc. These place names are handled in widely varying ways. At one end of the gamut Balzac insists on telling readers more about Saumur (in *Eugénie Grandet*) than most of them care to hear. At the other end of the spectrum Henry James will introduce names without a word of explanation. These differences stem from divergent hidden assumptions about readers: the Balzacian narrator opts for a didactic stance because he perceives his readers as needing instruction, whereas the Jamesian narrator projects readers as cosmopolitan as he himself is.

In the last resort, however, irrespective of the amount of information tendered, a place name is marked by one unmistakable and unambiguous clue to its presence: the capital letter at its beginning at once lifts it out of its textual environment. As a visible typographical symbol the capital letter is an objective signal in the text wholly divorced from epistemological questions about the ontological standing of what it denotes. London, Paris, Middlemarch, Yonville-l'Abbaye in *Madame Bovary*, the M — in Kleist's *Die Marquise von O—* share the capital letter as their lowest common denominator without regard to the degree of their correspondence to a putative reality. The ability to grasp the import of the capital letter, i.e., that it denotes a proper name, is the sole absolute prerequisite that can properly be made of the lens of readers in their construction of the text.

The reason for the profusion of names is closely related to the realist novel's underlying purpose. As Welty points out: "Being shown how to locate, to place any account is what does most toward *making* us believe it."[4] The intimate connection between localization and plausibility is one of the cornerstones of realism. Particularity of place has been singled out ever since Ian Watt's *The Rise of the Novel* as one of the quintessential hallmarks of the emergent realist novel.[5] The posture of realism is predicated on its insistent endeavor to stabilize the illusion it seeks to foster. The strong and reiterated emphasis on the truth quotient of the fiction by such writers as Balzac, George Eliot, and Zola, is a cogent expression of the image that realism wishes to sponsor. One immediate way for the novel to enhance the plausibility of its created universe is by investing it with specificity of both time and place. Their cardinal importance devolves from their efficacy in validating the probability of the fiction by anchoring it in an order existent extraneous to the realm of the fiction. "Place," Welty concludes, "is the named, identified, concrete, exact and exacting, and therefore credible gathering-spot of all that has been felt, is about to be experienced, in the novel's progress."[6] The intersection of time and place forms the "chronotope"[7] at which the fictive action develops. The plausibility of the entire fiction is buttressed by, and to a considerable extent dependent upon, the probability of time and place. If the attendant circumstances are convincingly posited, readers will be likely to extend their belief in them onto the fictive world which they encompass. In this larger context the persuasive power invested in names becomes a vital instrument for the successful establishment of a trustworthy illusion.

Naming place and describing or evoking it is thus a central tactic for the creation of what Barthes has deemed the "effet de réel"[8] ("reality effect"). A name as such does not produce a fictive reality; rather it adumbrates a landscape of possibility in readers' minds. The impact of naming is similar to that ascribed by Philippe Hamon to description: "dans le texte lisible-réaliste ... la description est aussi chargée de neutraliser le faux, de provoquer un 'effet de vérité' "[9] ("in the readable realist text ... description also has the task of neutralizing the false, of provoking an 'effect of truth' "). The ambivalence implied by Hamon is present too, though rarely noted, in Henry James' phrase: "the air of truth."[10] This suggests, rightly, that fiction cannot be true, only appear so. In the confirmation of that semblance, names are a potent tool. The invocation of names is an important facet of that delineation of the here and now that is the *conditio sine qua non* of realist fiction. Naming a place is, in the last re-sort, an act akin to conjuration.

Through their capacity to conjure up "the air of truth" names exert a quasi magic power. Indeed, they perform in ways beyond what Welty claimed. For not only is location "the crossroads of circumstances,"[11] where the dynamics of the plot can begin to unfold. It also marks, quite literally, a crossroads for readers' construction of the text, one of the main points where readers imperceptibly cross the boundaries between the world of reality, where they sit reading, and the realm of the fiction, inhab-ited by the protagonists. Because of its potential dual existence in both actuality and the fiction, the name can act as a bridge of continuity, along which readers may move from one sphere to the other without becoming conscious of the transition.

In this respect the realist text differs from, and is far more elusive than its romantic antecedents. The romantic text characteristically ex-hibits "junctures of pronounced discontinuity where the act of validation or establishment is most explicit."[12] In Coleridge's *Kubla Khan*, for in-stance, that discontinuity is at once exposed through the incongruence between the subtitle, "A Vision in a Dream," and the paratextual introduc-tion. The words "vision" and "dream" remove the fictive location from readers' common domain into a decidedly private, subjective dimension. The scene of the vision is designated in the autobiographical preface in prose as "a lonely farm-house between Porlock and Linton, on the Ex-moor confines of Somerset and Devonshire." While Porlock and Linton could equally well be invented or actual names, Somerset and Devonshire are existent British counties, with which Coleridge could expect his read-ers to be familiar. So he is contextualizing the "vision in a dream" of his poem in a knowable location, and at the same time disengaging it from this homely environment.

"Xanadu," the second word of the poem, compels immediate atten-tion by its acoustic strangeness. The contrast between the plainness of the "farm-house between Porlock and Linton, on the Exmoor confines of Somerset and Devonshire" and the exoticism of Xanadu with its "sacred river" Alph, its "caverns measureless to man" and its "sunless sea" is a measure of the distance between them. The physical description of Xan-adu remains so general and schematic as to discourage any material con-cretization in readers' minds:

> And here were forests ancient as hills
> Enfolding sunny spots of greenery.

On the other hand, the atmospheric animation is forceful, not least be-cause of the recourse to constative statements:

> A savage place! as holy and enchanted
> As e'er beneath a waning moon was haunted
> By woman wailing for her demon-lover!

or:

> It was a miracle of rare device,
> A sunny pleasure-dome with caves of ice!

The reiterated emphasis on the outlandishness of Xanadu underscores its remoteness from everyday reality. What is exacted of readers is a leap of faith: they have to believe in Xanadu as a place of the imagination experienced by the poet in a vision in a dream, and mediated through recollection. Through its very differentness from those in the preface, its name signals entry into a realm of vision. In *Kubla Khan* the distinction between the two spheres also becomes visually and aurally manifest in the switch from prose to verse.

The disjunction between real and fictive place is rarely as plain as in Coleridge's poem. More often, romantic fiction juxtaposes the two, sometimes letting them overlap, yet maintaining their separate identities. E.T.A. Hoffmann's *Der goldene Topf (The Golden Vase)*, for example, is specifically located in Dresden, which is mentioned in the first sentence. Various geographic landmarks are cited as the action progresses with the student Anselmus moving about the city: the bridge over the Elbe, the bathing resort on the left bank about a mile above the bridge, the Kosel Garden with its open-air restaurants and concerts, the Prince Anton Gardens in the southeast suburb of Pirna, Konradi's pastry-shop in the Schloßgasse which connects the old marketplace to the main square, the Neumarkt, the Moritzstrasse, and taverns such as the Golden Angel, the Helmet, and the City of Naumburg. Mention of the black gate in the northwest of the newer area of the city ("Neustadt") even allows limitation of the temporal frame since it was erected in 1802 and demolished in 1812.

The absence of physical description does not diminish readers' belief that *Der goldene Topf* is grounded in a particular place at a particular time, but it leaves the scene the more open to the transformations that are the crux of the plot. For the tale is presented as "ein Märchen aus der neuen Zeit" ("a latter day romance"), and this subtitle fulfills a function parallel to that of the preface in *Kubla Khan* as a reading cue. Like the mysterious transformation of the face on the doorknocker under Anselmus' gaze, and like Veronika's metamorphosis into the snake, Serpentina, so the concrete Dresden of the physical world is transfigured into the mysterious Atlantis of imagination and myth. As Anselmus shuttles from the one to the other and back again, the names of locations map both his whereabouts and the stages of his quest. Each of the two spheres, as in *Kubla Khan*, has its own aura and validity; but though conjoined, they are held in discrete suspension as the opposing poles in a tension, or the twin sides of a coin. Yet despite its incessant shifts, the disposition of the romantic text is relatively transparent compared to the more devious design of the realist text.

For realist fiction, in an attempt to enact its own claims to truthfulness, practices the art of disguise by taking pretense to its uttermost limits. In pretending to be a faithful representation of reality, its proceeds on the unvoiced hypothesis of a natural continuity between actuality and fiction. What is more, it actively encourages readers to make the same assumption. Place names can serve as an ideal link between the two spheres since they have meanings in both the adjacent worlds extraneous and intrinsic to the fiction. The continuum, and the concomitant blurring of the boundaries, only enhances the importance of names in the game of pretense being played in realist fiction. The "magic" of names resides precisely in their aptitude for luring readers to join in that game by inducing them to believe in the reality of the fictional construct.

The naming of places inaugurates a system of slippages through which the fluid interchange between reality and fiction is enabled to develop. This porosity is fostered by the relative independence of names as elements of discourse free of the embedment that defines, and limits, the scope of most other verbal units. Thus they hold out the possibility of an open space in which readers' imagination may engage simultaneously with prior experience and with the text. Hence names represent the forum where the process of fictionalization itself can be observed.

Great though the fundamental elasticity of names is, some broad distinctions must be drawn for heuristic purposes. The first category of names cited in nineteenth century fiction comprises places of world renown such as London, Paris, New York, or Berlin. It is safe to presume that all readers, then and now, would recognize these names as denotative of real locations. By "real" I here mean actual cities, whose situation can be ascertained at a certain latitude and on a certain longitude on a globe of the world. Often readers will have acquired vicarious knowledge of such places through other literary texts, or films, or television. In most instances the description of these conspicuous cities tends to be more cursory that that of more recondite spots. Balzac, for example, always devotes far more attention to the specification of provincial settings than to those in Paris, where he is content to sketch the atmosphere and social level of a particular area.

By virtue of their very familiarity, the names of eminent places act as a cipher of an order of existence anterior to the fiction. Merely to invoke such names is, therefore, one expression of the "magic" that Welty attributes to them. The site of the fictive action in *Middlemarch* is instantly endowed with a degree of credibility through its relationship to a named place such as London, whose authenticity is widely accepted. So these famous names have a twofold function: their presence alone carries the suggestion of veracity, while the acknowledgment of their real existence provides a backcloth onto which the fictional realm can be mounted. Ultimately, these readily recognizable names may be compared to a kind of anchor, which grounds the created universe of the fiction in a knowable dimension of actuality. Like the historical allusions, they form a code to which readers are able to relate, and whose ulterior message is a corroboration of the realist novel's aspiration to truthfulness.

Other, lesser known place names have generally been taken as exerting the same legitimizing impulse. On closer scrutiny, however, not only do some of the fallacies inherent in such an interpretation become apparent, but, more interestingly, so too do the games that the text plays with readers through the widespread recourse to names. Those that fall into this second category would include Saumur (in Balzac's *Eugénie Grandet*), Rouen (in Flaubert's *Madame Bovary*), Leeds and Avignon (in *Middlemarch*), Travemünde (in Thomas Mann's *Buddenbrooks*), Albany, Calais, San Remo, Turin, and Ancona (in James' *The Portrait of a Lady*), and Topeka (in his *The Bostonians*). None of these is so prominent as to be immediately located by readers, most of whom would indeed experience some discomfort if asked to mark them on a map. And the exegesis contained within the text may be unilluminating or partial. To tell readers that Saumur is in Tourraine, as the Balzacian narrator does at the opening of *Eugénie Grandet*, is not helpful to readers unacquainted with either. Nor, curiously, is the venerable riding school mentioned, with which the name of Saumur is associated for French natives. But this omission becomes comprehensible as soon as readers come to realize that the presentation of Saumur is by no means a guidebook account, geared to accuracy. The riding school is not introduced because it has no relevance to the plot. The description is an overture to the narrative so that the emphasis, in this tale of greed and domination, must be on the economic and political factors that determine life in this small provincial town.

Places such as Saumur, Leeds, or Topeka are no less real than London, Paris, or New York insofar as they too have a geographic existence. But the efficacy of these names as shorthand warrants of veracity is severely undercut by a combination of factors. Foremost among them is the limitation of readers' horizon: How much prior knowledge can readers be expected to bring to the construction of the text? Everything depends on the individual reader's educational level and the happenstance of where one was born as well as where one has traveled. These variables, though unpredictable, cannot be totally ignored. The problem of geographical remoteness is compounded nowadays by that of the intervening historical distance, which will be discussed in the next chapter. The hazardousness of recognition as a methodology in dealing with names becomes fully apparent when Saumur, Leeds, or Topeka is substituted for London, Paris, or New York. So the contention, put forward in connection with the pension Vauquer in Balzac's *Le Père Goriot*: "Anyone who has lived in a boarding-house will recognize the atmosphere"[13] represents the worst possible approach in its surrender to subjectivity. Even the term "boarding-house" may denote something other to an American than to a European, and certainly "atmosphere" is open to multiple interpretations. Ultimately, however, this pragmatic objection is overridden by the more fundamental theoretical one, namely: that to assess the impact of a text by reference to an anterior reality misdirects the lens of the reader.

The real but less well known names are the supreme illustration of the slippages inherent to place names. Readers unfamiliar with regional or provincial names will harbor genuine doubts as to whether they are actual or invented. In so doing they will become aware of the continual interchange between reality and fiction. At best the names may be taken as real through an act of supposition devolving from trust in the integrity of the narratorial voice.

This view contravenes that of Philippe Hamon, who envisages names as appropriating a function similar to that of "*citations:*" "ils assurent des points d'ancrage, rétablissant la performation (garants-*auctores*) de l'énoncé référentiel en embrayant le texte sur un extra-texte valorisé"[14] ("they assure points of anchorage, re-establish the performance (*authorially*-warranted) of the referential enunciation by imbricating the text in a validated extraneous text"). Underlying this argument is Hamon's concept of the documentary as the "discours de l'autre" ("discourse of the other"), to be naturalized into the narrative by diverse procedures. Proper names are seen as "des entités sémantiques stables, qu'il ne s'agit d'ailleurs pas de comprendre que de reconnaître comme noms propres"[15] ("stable semantic entities which are not so much to be understood as to be recognized as proper names"). This is an alluring but dangerous path that rests on cultural hypotheses about implied readers. Yet there are readers to whom Paris means a small town in Texas or in Missouri as well as the capital of France. Admittedly, they are exceptions, who stand out, perhaps as a joke, against consensual opinion.[16] Nonetheless, Hamon's assertions jump a step by not confronting the precariousness of positing recognition. As a critical approach recognition can all too quickly lead into the quagmire of readers' subjectivity.

Once the fluidity of the lines of demarcation between fact and fiction has been conceded, the difficulty of reading place names and of appreciating the games being played with them (and with us as readers) increases incrementally. At some point all readers, however knowledgeable and well-traveled they may be, reach and cross the threshold of uncertainty. To take a simple example: Yonville-L'Abbaye in *Madame Bovary* is, according to the narrator's account, eight miles from Rouen between the Abbeville and the Rouen roads on the borders of Normandy, Picardy, and the Ile-de-France, just off the new Abbeville-Amiens highway.[17] So far, so good, particularly to anyone who has driven through Northern France. Not only is the location very specific; the narrator's tone is that of factual reportage, as in travel writing. But these fairly well-known names (Normandy, Amiens, Rouen) soon give way to ones that very few readers are likely to have heard outside the confines of the novel: Bray, Boissière, Leux, Argueil, Saint-Jean (73), Doudeville (266), Longueville, Saint-Victoire (13), Quincampoix (261), Vissonville (32), Goderville, Normanville, Cany (28), Thibouville (58), Barneville near Aumale, Bas-Diauville (119), Buchy (139), etc. This sample suffices to make my point. What are readers to do with such names? Ought they to get a very large-scale map of the area? Are they victims of their ignorance? The only thing beyond dispute is the palpable decline in readers' sense of assurance in regard to the factuality of the text, and hence a heightened awareness of their dependence on the narrator and the discourse. Parallel instances occur with Gottfried Keller's Seldwyla (in the cycle *Die Leute von Seldwyla [The People of Seldwyla]*), Elizabeth Gaskell's Cranford in the novel of that name, and Thomas Hardy's Casterbridge, all of which sound quite possible place names. So do Donchéry, Briancourt, Marancourt, Vrignes-aux-Bois, Doudy, Sarignan, Rubécourt, Pouru-aux-Bois, Francheval, Villers-Cernay, and Saint-Monges in Zola's *La Débâcle*. But, as Michael Riffaterre has shown,[18] our reading is not significantly affected by his impish substitution of names from the local telephone book: Geaume, Hagetmau, Montfort, Ondes-aux-Bois, Momuy, Cambrans, Coudures, Pontes-les-Forges, Mugron, Oeyreluy, La Chapelle, and Saint-Criqu!

Riffaterre's amusing little controlled experiment lends strong support to the postulate that readers' apprehension of place names derives not from their geographic expertise but from their competence as readers. As Riffaterre insists, the explanation of the literary phenomenon lies in the relation between text and reader, not between either text and author, or text and reality. "If," he maintains, "there is any difference between texts like Rabelais's and the Surrealists and those by Balzac and Zola, it is that the former openly proclaim that they are verbal calisthenics, while the latter conceal the fact."[19] Taking this view to its logical con-

clusion, he asserts that *"the referent has no pertinence to the analysis.*
No advantage can be gained by comparing literary expression to reality
or by evaluating a work of literature in terms of such a comparison."[20]
Therefore, he adds: "A description can be false without striking us as
wrong or improbable, for the representation does not refer to reality but,
instead, replaces it."[21] To bear out Riffaterre's argument, we may take a
reader of *Eugénie Grandet* who happens to know Saumur and is dis-
mayed by the lack of any mention of the riding school; he/she is in fact
handicapped in the formation of the mental image evoked by the text by
the intrusion of material extraneous and alien to the text.

Extreme though Riffaterre's position may seem at first glance, it is
far more productive than its opposite which relies on subjective appeals
to readers' knowledge of boarding-houses, etc. Steering somewhere between the two is Benjamin Harshav's theory of the dual fields of reference
in fiction. The attractiveness of Harshav's model lies precisely in the possibility it offers of admitting the input of both external and textual information. With greater subtlety than Riffaterre, Harshav concedes the "dou-
ble-layered nature of literary reference."[22] "External fields of reference"
are defined as those

> outside of a given text: the real world in time and space, history, a phi-
> losophy, ideologies, views of human nature, other texts. A literary text
> may either refer directly to or invoke referents from such External
> Fields of Reference. This category includes not only such obvious exter-
> nal referents as names of places and streets, historical events and dates
> or actual historical figures, but also various statements about human na-
> ture, society, technology, national character, psychology, religion, etc.
> (243).

Complementary to these are the "Internal Fields of Reference:"

> a whole network of interrelated referents of various kinds: characters,
> events, situations, ideas, dialogues, etc. The language of the text contrib-
> utes to the establishment of this Internal Field and refers to it at the
> same time. (230).

Thus a fiction may have a referential grounding (and a realist fiction certainly will), within and upon which it builds its own internal universe.

In the interlacement of these two fields, names have a very special
role as the favored vehicles of transition. Because of their frequently indeterminate status, they may be part of either or both fields of reference.
The analysis of the image of Paris in three narratives in chapter 2 shows

how a real, external name may be assimilated into a fiction and transformed in a variety of ways. The Paris of Gervaise in *L'Assommoir* differs
from that of Rastignac in *Le Père Goriot* and from that of Malte in *Malte
Laurids Brigge*, yet they share a common external frame of reference to
the capital city of France. In these instances the translation from external
to internal field of reference occurs without any spatial displacement,
merely by the move into the consciousness of the protagonist. Often,
however, the transfer involves also a physical shift from one place to another, which coincides with the crossing from fact into fiction.

To return now to the case of Yonville-L'Abbaye in *Madame Bovary:*
it is introduced in a quasi-guidebook discourse which informs readers of
its location, the quality of its soil, its agricultural products, and its climate.
But its pretentiously high-flown hyphenated name, which suggests the romantic spot of Emma's desires, is promptly subverted by the parenthetical aside that it is called after an old abbey, of which not even ruins remain. The conflict of codes between the expository and the ironic opens
up an aperture of doubt that throws the existential status of Yonville into
question. Such a deliberately ambivalent image, similar to the *sfumato*
technique in painting,[23] leaves the reader undecided as to the ontological
standing of the setting, suspended between the potentially real and the
fictive. The description of the one-street town is

> far from innocent: it is neither a neutral background description to help
> situate the couple in their new milieu nor a description of their point of
> view as they arrive in the new place — either one of which would have
> been in keeping with narrative logic and economy. Instead, we are pre-
> sented with a highly selective, evaluative description of the town and its
> surrounding countryside — not an impartial, panoramic view from lofty
> heights, but a biased view from an ironic distance. This ironic mode is
> communicated through the almost exclusive focus on the negative as-
> pects of the place, backed up by a series of derogatory and disparaging
> analogies. This excess of information through the steady focus on neg-
> ative details puts us on our guard.[24]

Not only are readers put on their guard by the narrator's obvious bias
toward the negative in the description of Yonville; they are also alerted to
its essentially **literary** texture, in which all the details are calculated to
create a certain impression. It is as much the mood of Yonville that is
evoked as its physical appearance. The symbolism is quite transparent in
the positioning of the somewhat dilapidated church on one side of the
street, and opposite it, near the market square and the townhall, the striking and colorful storefront of the Homais pharmacy. While tradition is de-
clining, modern science (or pseudo-science) is in the ascendant here. The

short main street leads nowhere but to the cemetery. Even before Emma has set foot in Yonville, this description forecloses her life there, and hints that her only exit will be into death.

In the creation of Yonville, the internal field of reference, produced by the narrator's survey of the town, is predominant. The place takes on an autonomous existence as an active agent in the story of Emma's life. It does so by virtue of the internal textual signals, not by reference to any extraneous reality. That Yonville-L'Abbaye may have been modelled on the small Norman town of Rye is wholly irrelevant. The linguistic elaborations in themselves (i.e., -ville-L'Abbaye) are strong indicators of the imaginative transfiguration that has intervened between the real place and its fictive outcome. In mounting Yonville-L'Abbaye into the landscape of Normandy, Flaubert has related the scene of the action to an external field of reference, which in turn yields to the internal field established through the ironic and symbolic description of the town.

A parallel process can be observed in *Middlemarch*, into whose genesis George Eliot's notebooks, the so-called *Quarry*,[25] give illuminating insight. Middlemarch is situated in the north east corner of Loamshire, which is an invented British county, and which therefore betokens the fictitiousness of the location. The names, too, Middle-march and Loamshire, carry clear symbolic overtones. To flesh out this internal field of reference, George Eliot, in the second part of the *Quarry* (45), drew a schematic map on which the exact distances are specified in miles between Middlemarch and the protagonists' abodes, Tipton, Lowick, and Freshitt. At the same time, like Yonville-L'Abbaye, Middlemarch is related to London, Paris, Rome, Lausanne, Lyons, Avignon, Leeds, and Manchester, which represent the external field of reference, onto which the fictive scene is grafted. Again like Yonville, Middlemarch has a putative prototype in George Eliot's native Coventry, but this fact is immaterial to the understanding of the novel. Unlike Flaubert, George Eliot offers virtually no physical picture of Middlemarch, preferring such indirect means as the widespread recourse to gossip to elicit the mentality of the place. In the final analysis, Middlemarch assumes actuality in readers' minds as the force shaping the lives of all the main characters through the pressures it exerts on them by its unwritten laws. Its vitality, as well as its plausibility for readers, rests not on topographical data, but on its ethical and social import as a complex system of values. Though coexistent and continuous temporally and geographically with the contemporary circumstances in which it is embedded, Middlemarch, like Yonville-L'Abbaye and the unnamed place in *Buddenbrooks*, is essentially a verbal product of the text.

These examples illustrate the primacy of textual and reading strategies over recognition in the construction of names. The physical existence of a named place is in the last resort of very little import. What the fiction demands of its readers is not extensive geographic erudition, but acts of belief and pretense stimulated by an alertness to the signals emitted by the text itself. In this context it is illuminating to go back to that most far-fetched name, Xanadu. By dint of ingenious research, John Livingstone Lowes discovered its origins in Coleridge's reading of *Purchas His Pilgrimage* by Samuel Purchas and of *Purchas His Pilgrimes*, in which the travels of Marco Polo were included.[26] In the first edition of *Purchas His Pilgrimage* of 1613, the name takes the form of "Xaindu," while in the second of 1617, which is more likely what Coleridge saw because Wordsworth owned a copy, it appears as "Xamdu." These cacophonous versions were transformed by Coleridge into the euphonious and rhythmically pleasing "Xanadu." Readers do not need to know anything about the Purchas volumes, nor about Marco Polo, much less about the exploration of the summer capital of Kubla Khan. They must instead allow themselves to respond imaginatively to the spell cast by the magic of the outré and exciting name that beckons into a visionary realm of the wondrous.

"Xanadu" also reveals the difficulties encountered in reading fiction in dissociating "real references" from "pretended acts of referring." That distinction has been put forward by John R. Searle, who argues that not necessarily all references in a work of fiction are "pretended acts of referring."[27] Geographic place names might be presumed to fall into the latter category; London, Paris, or New York would fit this paradigm. But more often, as I have shown, readers experience doubts as to the existential status of the places named, and are unable to decide on the proportion of reality or pretense contained in the reference. The situation is particularly vexed in realist fiction because it purports to be wholly true to reality, and therefore deliberately sets out to subvert the kind of differentiation attempted by Searle. A much more workable hypothesis is that put forward by Barbara Herrnstein Smith, who points out that a " 'saying' " that has "no original sayer ... appears uncontaminated by ordinary human error or bias, and thus 'oracular.' "[28] Herrnstein Smith's " 'oracular,' " though clothed in the language of scholarliness, is another way of expressing Welty's insight into the "magic" of names.

That magic may stem from an acoustic, onomatopoeic appeal, as in Xanadu or Yonville-L'Abbaye, or it may be provoked by a metaphorical, symbolizing suggestivity, as in Middlemarch, Lowick, and Freshitt. Generally, however, neither the sound nor the possible meanings are decisive in the spell cast by names. Their primary function in realist narrative is to maintain the continuity between reality and the fiction. It is, of course, a pretended continuity, but this in no way diminishes its force. The fiction presents itself as an extension of the actual world, in a parallel co-existence with it. To envisage the fiction in this light as not necessarily a mimetic replica, but rather a possible continuance of reality obviates several of the problems that have beset the question of realism. With the displacement of mimesis in favor of textual strategies as the mainspring of realist writing, reading, as a corollary, is converted from an exercise in recognition and memory into one of competence at linguistic analysis. Names are constructed not by triggering reality keys, but by a process of cognitive mapping in readers' minds according to a schema projected by the text. And accuracy as a criterion for assessing the effectiveness of descriptions of place must yield to poetic validity in the economy of the fiction.

The invocation of place names is an equivocal tactic whose impact on readers is more contradictory than has generally been assumed. On the one hand, names, especially those of world renown, can impart an "air of truth" by appearing to anchor the fiction in reality. On the other hand, however, they represent a major bridge for the readers' crossing of the boundaries between reality and fiction that results eventually in wholehearted belief in the fiction. In this respect names also facilitate that casting of the anchor to reality in the surrender to the fiction as a substitute reality. The landscape of actuality hovering on the margins of the fiction is superseded by a powerful landscape of consciousness within its parameters as the internal field of reference comes to supplant the external one.

The essential lesson of the game of the name is the fluidity and porosity of all categories. The real and the fictive are reciprocally permeable. For this reason, the antithetical polarities traditional in criticism of realism, such as Marianne Moore's "real" and "imaginary,"[29] George Levine's "truth" and "lying,"[30] and Hayden White's "empirical" and "conceptual,"[31] are inappropriate and misleading. Only be re-adjusting the sights in their lens and willingly but consciously participating in realism's performative pretense can readers begin to understand its games.

9

Not So Long Ago: Historical Allusion in Realist Fiction

My title refers to a phrase familiar to all of us since childhood: 'Long ago and far away.' As listeners and fledgling readers we learn to respond to that stock turn with pleasurable excitement as an invitation to enter a world of fiction. 'Long ago and far away' ushers us through the gates of ivory into a realm of romance and fantasy. It does so by underscoring remoteness from the present. It is worth noting that the parallel formulae: 'once upon a time,' 'il y a longtemps,' 'es war einmal' also concentrate on the temporal element to create readers' horizon of expectation. The distancing from the here and now is a central convention of romance to project readers into an alternative universe. 'Long ago and far away' functions as an overt signal to readers of the narrative's intention and of its mode, and we immediately recognize it as such because we have been culturally conditioned to these conventions of storytelling. If we grow up to be literary critics, we may apply to 'long ago and far away' a term coined by Bakhtin and call it a "chronotope,"[1] an intersection of time and place where the fictive action can develop.

But, as Eudora Welty has so eloquently argued:

> there are only four words, of all the millions we've hatched, that a novel rules out: 'Once upon a time.' They make a story a fairy tale by the simple sweep of the remove — by abolishing the present and the place where we are instead of conveying them to us.[2]

"Fiction," Welty continues, whereby she obviously means realist fiction, "is properly at work on the here and now, or the past made here and now; for in novels *we* have to be there."[3] This makes the task of realist fiction considerably more complicated than that of romance, which creates a timeless time and an unplacable place merely through the invocation of

133

stock semiotic phrases. As a mode of narration, realism endeavors, however, to do the opposite to romance: to make readers believe that the action takes place in a credible and close present. At first glance this may seem a less difficult task to achieve, but on reflection its innate problematics become increasingly troubling. Whereas 'long ago and far away' is an enveloping formula that leaves everything to readers' imagination, the here and now has to be evoked in its individual specificity so as to persuade readers that they are indeed "there." Moreover, instead of admitting, as 'long ago and far away' does, that the story is just that: a story, a make-believe, the realist novel sponsors, on the contrary, the myth of its authenticity.

Its self-image, as summarized in the subtitle to Shakespeare's *Henry VIII* which Balzac introduces near the beginning of *Le Père Goriot: "All is true,"*[4] has already been discussed in chapter seven. The aim of the sundry assertions about truth, and faithfulness, and mirrors, cited there, is to affirm the proximity of realist fiction to a contemporary actuality close to hand. One of the major distinctions between romance and realist fiction resides precisely in this dichotomy: that romance is drawn to the distant, some nebulous merry old England or eerie old Germany or enchanting old France, exotic islands or splendid castles: in short, the 'long ago and far away,' while the realist novel centers its interest on the here and now of ordinary, even humble existences lived out in a modest, nearly present environment.

How then is this preferred time setting not so long ago presented in realist fiction? An interesting answer to this question is given in George Eliot's *Daniel Deronda.* One of its minor characters, Anna Gascoigne, has an older brother, Rex, who has been crossed in love, and who proposes to go to " 'the colonies' "[5] as an escape. Young Anna wants to go with him, thinking: "I should have done with going out, and gloves, and crinoline, and having to talk when I am taken to dinner — and all that!"[6] Here the narrator intervenes, and this is the key passage:

> I like to mark the time and connect the course of individual lives with the historic stream, for all classes of thinkers. This was the period when the broadening of gauge in crinolines seemed to demand an enlargment of churches, ballrooms, and vehicles. But Anna Gascoigne's figure would only allow the size of skirt manufactured for young ladies of fourteen.[7]

Apart from the pleasure afforded by its irony and humor, this is a crystalline statement of the way the realist novelist envisaged the temporal contextualization of the action: "I like to mark the time, and connect the course of individual lives with the historic stream."

Daniel Deronda appeared in 1876, but the events of the plot take
place a good ten years earlier. Gwendolen's imperviousness to the momentous happenings of her day is underscored as a means to convey the
limitations of her mentality. Again, this is narratorial comment:

> Could there be a slenderer, more insignificant thread in human history
> than this consciousness of a girl busy with her small inferences of the
> way in which she could make her life pleasant?—in a time, too, when
> ideas were with fresh vigour making armies of themselves, and the uni-
> versal kinship was declaring itself fiercely: when women on the other
> side of the world would not mourn for their husbands and sons who died
> bravely in a common cause, and men stinted of bread on our side of the
> world heard of that willing loss and were patient: a time when the soul
> of man was waking to pulses which had for centuries been beating in
> him unheard, until their new sun made a life of terror or of joy.[8]

As Barbara Hardy points out in her introduction to the novel,[9] the references here are "topical": what Gwendolen is unaware of is the suffering
caused by the American Civil War and the consequent unemployment and
famine among the Lancashire textile workers in 1862–3, when the Northern blockade of the Southern ports stopped the export of raw cotton for
processing in the British mills. Slavery, poverty, and even freedom are
concepts foreign to the mind of this young English Victorian woman, eager only "to make her life pleasant" by marrying as comfortably as she
can. Gwendolen's spectacular failure to achieve that goal stems from her
misjudgment of her future husband, which is another manifestation of the
overall narrowness of her horizon and her obliviousness to human nature
and experience. Her lens is limited in its peripheral vision so that she can
see only what is immediately before her.

The temporal disposition of *Daniel Deronda* is typical of the usage
current in the nineteenth century European realist novel. In their theoretical enouncements writers liked to place considerable emphasis on the
fact that it was the commonplace occurrences of everyday life that were
to be portrayed—in contrast to the exotic 'long ago and far away' favored
by the romantics. In practice, however, the notion of the contemporaneous is not to be taken quite literally, for a certain remove often intervenes between the time of the action and that of writing. Because dates
are almost invariably mentioned with great precision at or near the outset, it is easy enough to determine the extent of that interval. Nearly all of
Balzac's novels are set several years back from the time of writing, and
range even further into the past to give the economic, political, and social
background to the figures and happenings. *Eugénie Grandet*, published
in 1833, starts its action in November 1819 and moves forward some ten

years but also reaches back to 1789 and the economic turmoil in the aftermath of the French Revolution to explain Grandet's rise to fame and fortune. Similarly, *Illusions perdues* (1837; *Lost Illusions*) unfolds between 1819 and 1830, although it also looks as far back as 1793 for the evolution of printing. *César Birotteau* (1837) begins when César is forty in 1816, yet goes back to 1792 for his pre-history. Eliot's *Middlemarch*, which came out in 1872, takes place forty years previously between the end of September 1829 and the end of May 1832 during the campaign for the First Reform Bill. Her *Adam Bede* (1859) is sited "Sixty years ago—it is a long time, so no wonder things have changed."[10] Zola's *L'Assommoir*, which dates from 1877, spans the nineteen years from 1850 to 1869 in Gervaise's life, from the moment she comes to Paris until her death. The greatest interspace occurs in Thomas Mann's *Buddenbrooks*, whose date of publication is 1901, but whose time of action extends over the forty years from 1835 to 1875, the period leading up to the unification of Germany under Bismarck.

In many realist novels a precise date for the action is included. Generally this appears right near the beginning when at least a decade, sometimes a month, and occasionally a specific day is named. Many of Balzac's novels follow this pattern: *Le Père Goriot* (1835) refers on its first page to 1819 as "l'époque à laquelle ce drame commence" ("the time when this drama begins"); *La Cousine Bette* (1846) starts with the words: "Vers le milieu du mois de juillet de l'année 1838" ("Toward the middle of July in the year 1838"), while the action of *Illusions perdues* (1837) is located "En 1821, dans les premiers jours de mai"[11] ("In 1821, in the early days of May"). This habit of overt time markers is continued by other novelists: the second chapter of *Pickwick Papers* (1837) locates its happenings exactly "on the morning of the thirteenth of May, one thousand eight hundred and twenty seven." The initial phrase of Flaubert's *L'Education sentimentale* (1869; *Sentimental Education*) is a categoric date: "Le 15 septembre 1840" ("On the fifteenth of September 1840), just as George Eliot's *Felix Holt* (1866) begins with: "On the 1st of September, in the memorable year 1832, some one was expected at Transome Court." The first paragraph of Henry James' *The Europeans* (1878) denotes "a certain 12th of May, upwards of thirty years since" as the time of the events portrayed.

Such dates function, as Käthe Hamburger has pointed out, as "a fictive Now": "it is not a Then in the directly or indirectly experienced past of the reader or the author, for this past is not a part of the experience of fiction."[12] According to Hamburger, the "here and now, i.e., presentified"[13] is created not by the insertion of the date itself but by the choice of narrative tense. The present tense, which Philippe Hamon has appropriately described as "le présent d'attestation"[14] ("the attesting present") is the crucial factor in evoking the now in which the narrator is telling the story and into which the reader is being asked to enter. The switch to the present tense for the beginning of the action reinforces the exact dating not only to place the fiction temporally but also to foster the illusion of its actuality.

The examples I have adduced illustrate both how the realist novel sets about the task of creating its internal timeframe, and support the argument that even at the point of its first publication, it was not, strictly speaking, about contemporaneous happenings. But the political and social conditions, which form the frame for the fictive action, were still sufficiently close to the minds of readers of that period to be readily retrievable. They were certainly within the boundaries of human memory and oral reminiscence in the same way as the Vietnam era or the Second World War still remain present in collective memory today. So normally the narrator assumes that readers will have a certain familiarity with the situations alluded to, although varying amounts of explanatory commentary may also be included.

While such an assumption of familiarity was justified for the vast majority of nineteenth century readers because of their relative closeness to the events in question, that is hardly the case nowadays. What is the position of readers of today, distanced by over a hundred years from the settings of the nineteenth century novel? What then was barely gone by has, through the passage of time, become a far more remote past, retrievable no longer by memory or word-of-mouth report, but solely through the annals of history—or the words of the text. How does this fundamental shift of perspective affect our reading of these novels? What narrative strategies are instrumental in informing readers of the temporal parameters of the fiction? What are the differing means whereby the timeframe of the novel is created? And how do readers of today manage to grasp and process the data contained in the text?

Two main lines of approach are possible. Interestingly, though they are so divergent as to be virtually antithetical, they are both not only valid but even mutually compatible. The one is to treat the texts as having acquired *de facto* the status of historical novels, period pieces that may be used as adjuncts to social history. The other, more literary perception is to regard the temporal markers as a kind of code, or, to put it another way, as one of the sustaining conventions of realist fiction, which readers recognize as such without having to master the particularities of the actual historical circumstances. I will briefly outline the first, more obvious approach before going on to elaborate the second, more provocative one.

To read nineteenth fiction as history has become quite common. Attempts have been made, often very successfully, to reconstruct the Paris of Balzac or Zola, the Lübeck of Thomas Mann's *Buddenbrooks*, the Chicago of Dreiser's *Sister Carrie*.[15] Even more important, with the increasing interest on the part of many historians in the lives of ordinary people, the nineteenth century realist novel has come to be seen as a valuable repository of information about such matters as family relationships and women's experiences. Obviously, any discerning historian will evaluate such evidence with due caution, mindful always of the underlying fact that fiction is indeed fiction, and that its aims differ from those of biography or history. Nevertheless, despite this reservation, the nineteenth century realist novel yields significant insight into social customs at various levels on the class spectrum. For instance, women's working conditions are vividly shown in many of these texts: the formation and role of the governess in *Jane Eyre, Villette*, and *Agnes Grey*, the vicissitudes of a servant's employment in George Moore's *Esther Waters*, the business of laundering in Zola's *L'Assommoir*, the occupation of dressmaker in Elizabeth Gaskell's *Mary Barton*, and the pursuit of prostitution in Zola's *Nana* and the Goncourt brothers' *Germinie Lacerteux*. To read through the lens of the historian is, literally, an act of retrieval in which the novel is cast into the role of a primary document, a nearly contemporaneous eye-witness account of places, customs, and predicaments, as they appeared to one particular observer. It is to confirm Balzac's grandiose vision of the novelist as "the secretary"[16] to the nineteenth century, recording for posterity a present that has since become a past, yet that remains vivid for ever through the images evoked by the text. The undesirable corollary to such a perception of the realist novel stems from its tendency to reduce the fiction to mere material by disregarding its aesthetic configuration.

The aesthetic configuration, on the other hand, is central to the alternative mode of reading the past in nineteenth century realist fiction. The act of retrieval here has an entirely different thrust: instead of envisaging the historical allusions as reflections of a once existent actuality, it seeks for recognition of their representative status as signals of contextuality. This is a predominantly literary mode of apprehension because it focuses on the overall tactics of the discourse and their impact on readers rather than on the details of specific happenings, or even the truthfulness of the account. The fiction appropriates historical materials, assimilating them into its fictive fabric. The narrative thus draws on temporal elements as a scaffold, a means not only of ordering its own time but also of placing itself on the time-scale of historicity. Areas of overlap between historic and fictive time are partnered by points of disjuncture as the historiography within the text stands at the crossroads between functionality and performance.[17] Such a conception envisages the novelist not primarily as a historian, as Balzac would have it, but rather as a creative writer who chooses to appropriate the historical into the service of the fiction. Such an order of priorities does not impugn the veracity of the historical moment, as presented in the text. On the contrary, historical facts are brought into the fiction precisely to buttress its semblance of truth. The introduction of the historical dimension into realist fiction is clearly intended as a warranty of authenticity, but it fulfills this purpose by more oblique means than is generally thought.

In order to clarify these theoretical assertions, I propose now to explore several concrete examples which show the diverse ways of introducing historical allusions into a fictional text. At one end of the spectrum is Balzac, whose narrator functions openly as a chronicler, expounding the geographic location and the social and economic background to the plot before it gets under way. So *Eugénie Grandet* has a packed thirty-page overture, which tends to exasperate most readers eager to hear her story. The voice of the narrator, plainly addressing postulated readers in the second person ("vous" — "you"), first describes in highly evocative detail the street, the house, and the town where the Grandets live. From this present time of the narrative he moves thirty years into the past to 1789 to trace old Grandet's rise to fortune and eminence during the tempestuous post-Revolutionary years. The various financial transactions and speculations by which he made his money over the years are explained with the utmost precision in a series of figures, which may not mean much to readers today, but which nonetheless convey a clear idea of Grandet's shrewd and inventive business acumen. What makes his career so fascinating is its immediate connection to the economic and political vicissitudes of France during and just after the Napoleonic period. We are told exactly where Grandet stood financially and socially in 1789, what steps he took in 1793, 1806, 1811, 1816, and 1817 in order to arrive at his present, i.e., 1819 wealth and power in the little town of Saumur. He is a product of his time who has cleverly been able to turn the rapid shifts in government from Consulate to Empire to Restoration to his own advantage. The sale of clergy property put him on the path to prosperity, and he has used his position as mayor to build roads which further his business interests by providing easier access to his vineyards.

Readers who are not trained historians of the French Revolution, which is to say most of us, are bewildered by this onslaught of economic data, and very likely tempted to skip a few pages, merely registering that Grandet is very rich, and that he has become so by rather devious manipulations. Such a hasty skimming of the text at this point is a pity because the account of Grandet's ascent is given for good reason. It is far more than a reflection of Balzac's own passionate involvement with money matters, or even than an expression of his chosen role as chronicler of the

nineteenth century, revealing its hidden mainsprings. In the transformation of French society through the emergence of a more powerful bourgeoisie to replace the weakened aristocracy, the redistribution of capital
is a central factor. Grandet, with his millions made in the wine trade, his
authority as mayor of Saumur, and his prestige as a holder of the Legion
of Honor, is evidently one of this new breed. From this perspective already, Grandet's background is important to the novel, as well as to my
argument. The knowledge readers are given of him serves to ground the
text in a historical context.

Beyond that, however, the plausibility of the created story of Eugénie
is enhanced through its roots in her father's career and its embedment in
the historical situation. The credibility evinced by the outer historical setting, whose accuracy is open to substantiation, is extended to the fictitious areas of the text, which readers of course know to be invented, but
whose capacity to convince is sustained by the high truth quotient of the
frame. The possibles of realist fiction derive much of their force from the
deliberate ways in which they are related to the actuals of history. The
belief that readers are prepared to invest in Grandet's life history, because it coincides with facts ascertainable from other sources, such as
documents of the period, is, as it were, transferred onto the fictitious life-
story of Eugénie. Without merely playing on words, story can here be
seen as partaking of history and as growing out of it, seeking through that
conjunction to accredit itself as truth and to command readers' trust. The
specifics of Grandet's finances, tedious though they may be in themselves, produce something tantamount to Barthes' "effet de réel"[18] ("the
effect of the real"), the impression through the accumulation of particu-
lars that the text is indeed a representation of reality. So does Balzac's
evident attachment to worn, old, shabby objects, which have had adventures and thus possess a historical past correlative to that of their own-
ers.[19] What is so curious about Balzac's practice in *Eugénie Grandet* and
elsewhere is that once the historical frame is in place, he more or less for-
gets it as soon as he launches into the plot. The progress of fictional time
is noted with care (ten years in *Eugénie Grandet*), but there are no further extraneous historical markers. The world of the fiction becomes sufficient unto itself.

Balzac's practice differs from that prevailing in most other nineteenth century realist novels, where there is a continuing dialogic interchange between history and fiction as the characters not only comment
on the events of the day but become involved in them, and find their lives
directly affected by them. So the protagonists themselves, rather than the
narrating voice, become the source of historical intelligence. The historicity retains the same function as in Balzac, providing a larger enframing

dimension for the fiction and a link to a reality external and prior to the narrative. Yet at the same time it is subsumed into the fabric of the fiction. Such use of historical allusion can well be illustrated in George Eliot's *Middlemarch*, Zola's *L'Assommoir*, and, in a separate chapter, in Thomas Mann's *Buddenbrooks*. All of them draw on history to help to establish the validity of the fictional realm, though they do so in somewhat different ways and through diverse lenses.

Middlemarch, published in 1872, has its action take place between 30 September 1829 and the end of May 1832. A date, 1829, is specified only once in the novel in chapter 15;[20] nevertheless, the historical undercurrent is strong and extremely important. Eliot's notebooks, the so-called *Quarry for "Middlemarch,"*[21] reveal the care with which she collected her data. The first part of the *Quarry* is devoted largely to medical matters, such as the then current views on delirium tremens (35–6), the spread of cholera (36), the distinction between typhus and typhoid fevers (29), microscopic discovery and cell theory (25), and the organization and remuneration of the profession as recorded in *The Lancet* of 1830 (21–5). A section records political dates too (33–4). Though fragmentary, the information is remarkably specific. The second part of the *Quarry* begins by mapping the dates of the major happenings of the fiction. Eliot's veritable passion for exactitude is shown in her listing of the dates of university examinations at Oxford and Cambridge (44) in order to fix when Fred Vincy could have taken his degree. In the outline (46–51), a month is assigned to each of the novel's eight parts. The main dates of political events 1830–33 are listed (43–4 and 55–6), and these are related to the "Private dates," i.e., the principal events in the lives of the protagonists such as births, marriages, and deaths (45–6). The *Quarry* therefore affords a unique and fascinating glimpse of the process of mounting the fictive onto the actual.

Middlemarch portrays an England in a state of transition on several levels. Politically, the death of George IV, to which indirect reference is made, and the campaign for the First Reform Bill, which was passed on 7 June 1832, i.e., shortly after the fictional timespan, mark the passage from one era to the next. Socially, the transitions are adumbrated in the mention of the Catholic Question early on, in the evidence of some increasing mobility between the classes in the marriages that are, despite opposition, contracted, and above all in Lydgate's endeavors to modernize the system of medical care, which fail because of the entrenched conservatism and suspiciousness of the leading citizens of Middlemarch. Economically, a rural artisan mode of production is on the verge of industrialization: there is some talk about machine-breaking as a problem of the day, and lengthy discussion of the impact of the railroad line to be cut near the town. The progress of the Reform Bill acts both as a guiding thread in its physical incidents and as a structural metaphor to symbolize the efforts of individuals to evolve or reform themselves.

So the mythopoeic as well as the factual aspects of historicity are brought into play. In the opening words to the Prelude, readers are invited to ponder on the processes of history, and to view the happenings of the fiction through the lens of history as well as of myth:

> Who that cares much to know the history of man, and how the mysteri-
> ous mixture behaves under the varying experiments of time, has not
> dwelt, at least briefly, on the life of Saint Theresa . . . ?[22]

This is one of the few direct invocations of history by the narrating voice. Eliot's predominant procedure is, as Jerome Beaty has aptly described it, "history by indirection,"[23] whereby significant events and trends are adduced piecemeal and almost casually in contrast to the tactics of the Balzacian narrator, who stands up at the beginning to recite a cohesive account of the characters' past in relation to their time.

Eliot's method, though it makes greater demands on the reader, is more subtle. History becomes central to the plot insofar as it represents the limitations encountered by the protagonists, and as they experience this obstruction of their desires, we as readers come to have a live sense of the time and place. Middlemarch itself, with all its gossip and web of personal and family connections, is the incarnation of a mentality, one that resists progress and thwarts daring. Mr. Brooke, who favors the Reform Bill, is not elected to parliament. Dorothea is not able to carry out her benevolent schemes for cottages, her dream of social improvements for the poor, nor is she ever recognized as an intellectual equal of men. "Young ladies," she is told, "don't understand political economy"[24] and "women were expected to have weak opinions."[25] Lydgate's advanced plans for an isolation hospital for such contagious diseases as cholera, derived from his partly European training, arouse so much hostility and distrust of his judgment as a doctor that he has to leave Middlemarch for lack of patients and income. In all these instances, historical situations are immanent to the text, present in dim silhouette by allusion, yet decisively active in the unfolding of the plot as they determine the lives of the protagonists. Through this very circumspect, calculated infusion of historical matter into the scenario of Middlemarch, the macrocosm of the world beyond the microcosm of this small provincial town is adumbrated. This gives the place both a wider universality and a heightened air of reality as the frontiers of fact and fiction become blurred within the novel. The response of fictitious characters to actual happenings or dilemmas of their

time is a fine practical instance of that technique of montage characteristic of realist fiction, whereby the fictive story is mounted into a knowable context, which serves by metonymic implication as a warrant for its
authenticity.

There are similarities but also some cardinal differences between
Middlemarch and *L'Assommoir.* Like George Eliot, Zola practices "history by indirection," weaving allusions to current concerns into the characters' conversation. However, he also resembles Balzac in conceiving
the novelist as a social historian. The subtitle of the cycle of twenty novels, of which *L'Assommoir* is the seventh, is "Histoire naturelle et sociale
d'une famille sous le Second Empire" ("Natural and Social History of a
Family under the Second Empire"). This provides explicitly the temporal
parameters in the dates of the Second Empire (1852 – 70) as well as the
writer's avowed intention to proceed as an analytical annalist of the period. The action of *L'Assommoir,* which was published in 1877, takes
place between 1850 and 1869, and is punctuated by references to events
of the day, as in *Middlemarch.* But while the main characters in Eliot's
novel are educated middle to upper class, those in *L'Assommoir* are
working class struggling to survive in the slums of Paris. Their perspective is affected by their lowly position in society. Although they speak
about voting in elections, about Bonaparte, the head of state, and about
revolutions and republics, they have no immediate stake in these political
developments. They are much rather the recipients, the victims of circumstances, watching passively on the margins as changes are enacted
that will shape their lives too. Historicity enters into the fiction as a de-
terminant of human lives, but on a less conscious and intellectual level
than in *Middlemarch.* The fact that many of the political discussions are
held while the characters are drunk both accounts for and denotes their
lack of understanding. The historical markers also become more scant in
the latter part of the novel; as the family declines into more abject poverty
and alcoholism, they are increasingly preoccupied with mere day-to-day
existence, intent on their own pressing problems with food and heating
to the exclusion of larger issues.

As in *Middlemarch,* the women never voice any political views or
have any say in discussions. In contrast to this absence, however, a more
domestic aspect of history is registered largely through the eyes of the
main female figure, Gervaise. The time-span of *L'Assommoir* coincides
with the architectural transformation of Paris by Baron Haussmann into
a modern, designed city with avenues fanning out from the Arc de
Triomphe. As Gervaise wanders through the streets of the area where she
lives, she sees the reconstruction in progress with the demolition of the
old hovels and their replacement with what seem to her like monuments:

houses with six storeys, their facades sculptured like churches, with bright windows hung with curtains, all exhaling an aura of prosperity. She feels disturbed and threatened by this splendor, dislodged from her familiar district, which is being gentrified beyond her means. Like the men with politics, she does not understand the causes or the significance of what she sees; hers is a gut reaction from her angle of vision. But for readers these allusions to the rebuilding of Paris are a clever way of referring to a known project of that time, and so again of locating the fictive characters and happenings in an actual setting.

The same strategies occur in Thomas Mann's *Buddenbrooks*. The social level is closer to that of *Middlemarch*, perhaps even somewhat higher, for the Buddenbrooks are patricians, deeply involved in the government of the North German Hanseatic city where they have lived for generations. The historical panorama emerges, as in *Middlemarch*, through the experiences and conversations of the characters, not through recital by a narrator. Also as in *Middlemarch*, the problems of the time are assimilated into the fiction through their effect on the protagonists. The fiction absorbs fact, and uses historicity to project and confirm its own truthfulness in readers' minds.

This interplay of fact and fiction as it occurs in *Middlemarch*, *L'Assommoir*, and *Buddenbrooks* represents the dominant pattern in the nineteenth century realist novel. They stand toward the center of the spectrum of approaches to the task of evoking the 'not so long ago.' At one end of that spectrum is Balzac, whose narrator, as it were, stands up before the class of readers to give them instructive information. In the middle and in the majority are those writers such as George Eliot, Zola, and Thomas Mann, who cunningly fuse history and fiction, making readers cognizant of the historical situation vicariously through the protagonists' experience. An extreme variant on this is Henry James, who is at the opposite pole to Balzac in providing readers with virtually no data, and letting everything transpire from the interaction of the characters.

This method is apparent in *The Bostonians*. The paramount historical fact underlying *The Bostonians* is the Civil War, over twenty years past at the time of its publication in 1886, and a good ten years anterior to the fictive action. Although the internal passage of time is carefully followed, the year is left open as 187–, and even that is not mentioned until page 129,[26] contrary to the customary practices of realist fiction. On the other hand, there are multiple overt references to the war as a recent, traumatic event that has fundamentally affected every one of the main characters. The war and the toll it has taken in lives and economic ruination in the South are a constant presence throughout the novel.

It is reiterated too in the plot, in the confrontation between the Southerner, Basil Ransom, who has come North to start up as a lawyer, and the Northern establishment incarnated in his Bostonian cousin, Olive Chancellor. In the opening scenes, Basil spends much time waiting: the Southerner being manipulated by wily Northerners. The tensions between North and South are compounded by the parallel antagonism between men and women in the early phases of the feminist struggle for women's suffrage. In the rivalry between Basil and Olive for the affection of Verena Tarrant, a segment of political history is enacted through the plot of the novel. The historical situation has a motivational and explanatory function. One of the novel's great climaxes comes in the episode when Verena shows Basil round Harvard and takes him into Memorial Hall, which commemorates "the sons of the University who fell in the long Civil War" and which makes the Southerner forget "the whole question of sides and parties" in a reverie of remembrance that "arched over friends as well as enemies, the victims of defeat as well as the sons of triumph."[27] In this scene it becomes very clear how historical fact, that is, the existence of Memorial Hall at Harvard and its public meaning are incorporated into the fiction to serve its purposes, in this case to reveal the Southerner's changing understanding of the Civil War and the North. Since power is conceived in *The Bostonians* as the ability to establish one's own sense of time and one's own version of history, this episode marks, structurally, a pivotal turning point in the middle of the novel. Equally important, Basil's response to the tablets inscribed with the names of the dead consummates the interface of fact and fiction.

The narrator in *The Bostonians* makes historical allusions on the patent assumption of readers' familiarity with the Civil War. At the time of publication that was undoubtedly justified, and probably even a hundred years later most readers command a sufficient outline of American history to construct the plot without difficulty, grasping the implications of the conflict between the North and the South. The Jamesian narrator always postulates readers as erudite and globe trotting as he is himself, whereas Balzac conceives readers didactically as in need of instruction.

The contrast between Balzac's and James' methods of alluding to historical circumstances raises a fundamental issue: the varying presumptions of readers' knowledge. "We are more easily prey to referential illusion," Inge Crosman Wimmers asserts, "when the work we are reading abounds in historical or geographic detail, evoking a whole era or milieu."[28] Drawing on Umberto Eco's theories of semiotics, she points to the cultural connotations of words and particularly of names such as "Napoleon." For informed readers such connotations are indeed vital clues emanating from the text and liable to trigger a chain of associations, which can be brought to bear on the process of reading, turning it in part into a system of recognitions. But what of readers who do not, or perhaps not yet, command such an extensive range of cultural connotations? Are they automatically excluded, by the sin of ignorance, from the pleasures of reading realist fiction? This possibility is not merely elitist in its snobbish arrogance, but wholly erroneous, as anyone knows who has watched American undergraduates reading European realist fiction and vice versa.

It is perfectly feasible to read *Middlemarch* without much knowledge of British constitutional law or the advance of industrialization, and the same holds true for *L'Assommoir* in regard to the politics of the Second Empire in France and the reconstruction of Paris by Baron Haussmann, and of *Buddenbrooks* in relation to the Austro-Prussian war of 1865, the North German Confederation of 1867, and the steps towards the unification of Germany under Bismarck in 1870. Rare indeed would be the reader conversant with the Preston weavers' strike of 1853, which forms the core of Dickens' *Hard Times*, or the 1884 strike of miners at Anzin in Northern France in Zola's *Germinal*, or the British Chartist movement of the early 1840s, in which John Barton in Elizabeth Gaskell's *Mary Barton* takes part as a delegate in the march from Manchester to London to present a petition to parliament. In none of these instances are readers at all likely to be well informed of the factual basis of the narrative, yet in every case the plot remains readily intelligible. In other words, it is not by virtue of our expertise as historians but rather through our competence as readers that we are enabled to grasp the historical strands of these novels. The intelligent exercise of the accepted strategies of reading supersedes the necessity for proficiency in history.

If this argument holds, as I firmly believe it does, we have to ask how readers' quasi automatic retrieval of the past occurs. What is the inherent process? Unless we are consciously reading as social historians, the extent of our knowledge (or ignorance) of the historical data ultimately matters very little. Readers do not need to have the various dates and developments at their fingertips because they do not construct the text by direct reference to an external chronological format. Within the economy of the fictive realm the historical allusions function as a code that represents past happenings. Once the dimension of historicity is conceived in this way as essentially a code denoting a past time, it becomes apparent that rigorous knowledge of its intricacies is not a prerequisite for reading. Indeed, the annotations and footnotes, however illuminating they may be informationally, tend to interfere with our capacity to organize the narrative because they intrude materials extraneous to the realm of the fiction in which we are engrossed.

To acknowledge historicity as a code accounts for readers' capacity to retrieve the past directly from the promptings of the text without prior or additional instruction. As a recognizable code, the historical substratum in realist fiction fulfills in many respects a function parallel to the 'Long ago and far away' of romance. Just as that formulaic phrase signals entry into a sphere of fantasy, dream, and desire, remote from the here and now, the historical allusions in realist fiction give access, through the gates of horn, to a fictive universe that purports to offer a true and faithful image of an actuality of not so long ago. The interweaving of historical allusions into the texture of the fiction invites readers to pretend to believe in the truthfulness of the narrative. It is, therefore, a manipulation of readers by verbal means, again like 'long ago and far away' dependent on cultural programming: in this instance, our tendency to associate history with fact, and fact with truth. The process in realist fiction turns out in the last resort to be not so different from that in romance, although the tactics are more intricate, comprising a detour via history.

When reading becomes a matter of recognizing in the historical allusions a code associated with truthtelling, and accepting it as a cipher for trustworthiness, it is in effect a form of inventiveness and invention. As Clayton T. Koelb has maintained: "The inventions of reading are no less inventions of history."[29] Such a statement follows in the wake of Hayden White's radical reassessment of the reciprocal relationship of history and fiction. White subverts the longstanding, conventional view, represented by E. M. Forster, who saw the novel as "bounded by two chains of mountains, neither of which rises very abruptly — the opposing ranges of Poetry and of History."[30] This cozy dichotomization is vigorously refuted by White, who conceives the writing of history as an act of reconstructive narration akin to that of fiction. This has special repercussions for realist fiction:

> In my view, the whole discussion of the nature of 'realism' in literature flounders in the failure to assess critically what a genuinely 'historical' conception of 'reality' consists of. The usual tactic is to set the 'historical' over against the 'mythical,' as if the former were genuinely *empirical* and the latter were nothing but *conceptual*, and then to locate the realm of the 'fictive' between the two poles. Literature is then viewed as being more or less *realistic*, depending upon the ratio of empirical to conceptual elements contained within it.[31]

White is quite right in lambasting the old, polarized conceptualization of realism. The insistence nowadays must be on the porosity between history and fiction. The boundary is open[32] in both directions: the role of fictionalization is conceded in the writing of history, just as the input of historicity is prominent in the creation of the fictive universe. In realist fiction those boundaries are constantly crossed in the close interface between the strands of historicity and fictionality. In most realist novels the two are so intimately intertwined as to be virtually inseparable. Lives, and plots, are dependent on circumstances.

Historicity is thus the most potent prop of realist fiction. The word 'prop' is used here in both its senses: as a support, and as a stage decor. Historical allusion sustains the realist novel's claim that *"All is true,"* while at the same time contributing to the evocation of a credible setting not so long ago. As an actuality of the recent past becomes the present of the narrative, an "air of reality"[33] is lent to the fiction. When history merges into fiction, fiction legitimizes itself as history.

10

Rereading *Buddenbrooks*

"Ein Bild hanseatischen Lebens aus dem neunzehnten Jahrhundert"[1]
("a picture of Hanseatic life from the nineteenth century"): Thomas
Mann's familiar description of his novel has been widely taken as a cue
for the reading of *Buddenbrooks*. "Von Jugenderinnerungen," he adds,
"lebt der ganze Roman, der unter meinen Büchern zu Lübeck die unmit-
telbarsten stofflichen Beziehungen besitzt" (377; "The entire novel lives off
memories of my youth, and has, of all my works, the most direct material
connections to Lübeck"). While deeming it both in his lecture "Lübeck als
geistige Lebensform" ("Lübeck as a Spiritual Way of Life") and in the introduction "Zu einem Kapitel aus *Buddenbrooks*" ("To a Chapter from
Buddenbrooks"), written more than twenty years later, as "ein nach Form
und Inhalt sehr deutsches Buch" (383; "a very German book in both form
and content"), he counters that assertion by also pointing to its strong
"Hang zum Europäischen und zum literarischen Kosmopolitismus"[2]
("tendency to the European and to literary cosmopolitanism") which distances it from the genre of *Heimatkunst* (regional art) and turns it into
"ein Stück Seelengeschichte des europäischen Bürgertums überhaupt"[3]
("a piece of the history of the soul of the European bourgeoisie").

This series of much quoted statements by Mann himself about his
novel has formed the basis for readings that privilege its autobiographical
and contextual aspects over its textual configuration. Critics have de-
lighted in expounding on the novel's origins in Mann's own early experiences and their precipitate in the work. Henry Hatfield, who regards *Buddenbrooks* as "profoundly autobiographical," espies many personal
equivalences in a plot in which he sees Mann taking "the decay of his own
family as a subject."[4] Mann's careful supplementation of his personal
memories through enquiries to family and friends about business practices, menus and recipes, the circumstances of his aunt's marriage, the peculiarities of the Munich dialect, etc. is well known, and the use he made

of this documentation has frequently been discussed.[5] Dozens of articles
have related the Buddenbrooks' family customs to the lifestyle typical of
their class, time, and place.[6] Indeed, *Buddenbrooks* was so close to recognizable models as to have been considered a *roman à clef;* the author's
uncle, Friedrich Mann, inserted an announcement in the *Lübecker An-
zeiger* of 28 October 1913 to disclaim any resemblance between himself
and Christian. Ample evidence exists, therefore, to justify the customary
referential approach.

Mann's comments also encourage the tendency to view *Buddenbrooks* as a sociological novel: "ein als Familien-Saga verkleideter
Gesellschaftsroman"[7] ("a social novel disguised as a family saga") is his
phrase. Hugh Ridley has recently called it "a civic chronicle, a history of
the city of Lübeck across nearly one hundred years."[8] The title itself, the
family name without the definite article, has an immediate dual effect, as
T. J. Reed[9] points out: the single word suggests not only the family's omnipresence, its power to fill and dominate the narrative, but also adumbrates a community within which the name is one to conjure with. As an
explanatory framework to the lives of the Buddenbrooks, the novel records the city's social institutions, ceremonies, and hierarchy. Pictorial
techniques, sated with detail, are interwoven into the scenic method to
render the concrete manifestations of this distinctive culture. The opening chapter with its lengthy and loving evocation of atmosphere as the
new house is consecrated is a fine example of the material specificity
characteristic of *Buddenbrooks.* An economic dimension is created that
proves central to the plot dynamics in an environment where hard money
values play an increasing role. No wonder that the novel has provoked a
number of Marxist readings such as Lukács' reflections on the search for
the bourgeois[10] and Pierre-Paul Sagave's analysis of class consciousness
and capitalist practices.[11] Mann concentrates on sociohistorical issues
rather than merely providing local color, yet his portrayal of the waning
of a complex social ethos is a subsidiary, though integral part of the novel's major theme. Social criticism remains by and large muted except in
the depiction of Hanno's school day, where a satirical tendentiousness
comes into evidence.

As "ein Bild hanseatischen Lebens aus dem neunzehnten Jahrhundert" ("a picture of Hanseatic life from the nineteenth century") *Buddenbrooks* is the nearest approximation among Mann's works—and perhaps
in the entire canon of German literature—to fulfilling the traditional realist aim of rendering a recognizable reality. It represents, to cite Reed
again, "a sustained attempt to grasp the totality of a place, a historical
span, a group of people, and an ethos."[12] Despite Mann's own somewhat
curious claim that *Buddenbrooks* is "für Deutschland der vielleicht erste

und einzige naturalistische Roman"[13] ("perhaps the first and only naturalist novel in Germany"), the three foremost present British critics on
Mann, Reed, Ridley, and Swales, are unanimous in envisaging the novel as
firmly embedded in the conventions of nineteenth century realism.[14] It
could be seen as marking the point where German realism finally over-
comes the ambivalences characteristic of it throughout the nineteenth
century to merge into the European mainstream.[15]

   To read *Buddenbrooks* in the traditional manner as an essentially
realist novel portraying a particular place at a particular time is, therefore, fully warranted. Given the wealth of the data to support such an approach, it would patently be absurd to try to abstract *Buddenbrooks* from
its roots in a past actuality, and to reread it in some new fangled fashion
by foisting onto it an extravagant post-structuralist reading that would
conceive the novel purely as an amalgam of verbal, narrational, and com-
municative strategies wholly divorced from any anterior reality. Nevertheless, it is arguable that criticism of *Buddenbrooks* has been unduly
slanted in one direction. Precisely because of the obviousness of its sociohistorical grounding in the author's experiences and environment, the
novel has been the object of readings which have underscored its referential facets, and consequently have not paid sufficient attention to its
aesthetic configuration.

   To be fair, the majority of critics of *Buddenbrooks* have been models
of tact and prudence. Far from subscribing to Balzac's superlative pronouncement that in realist fiction "*All is true,*"[16] they have been mindful
of the complexities of the interplay between the real and the fictive, and,
above all, of the importance of the writer's imagination in shaping the aesthetic artifact and welding its diverse elements. The extraordinary skill
with which the factual has been assimilated into the fictive plot has been
given recognition. As Ridley so aptly puts it: "If, as a child of his class and
of his literary age, Mann was interested in documentary material, it was
as grist to an artistic intention, not as providing the shaping principle of
the work itself."[17] The more closely the exact relationship of the text to
the model is examined, the greater the discrepancies that come to light.
Haskell Block, in his *Naturalistic Triptych: The Fictive and the Real in
Zola, Mann, and Dreiser,* reaches the following conclusion: "Because of
Mann's bold imaginative approach to his materials, his novel will not support a literal and thorough-going identification of the members of his family with their fictional analogues."[18] Considerations of discretion may, of
course, have played some part in, for example, the many infringements of
chronology noted by Block. The cumulative effect of such dislocations
should be to prompt some hesitation about pushing the referential reading too far. But, in the last resort, the only convincing plea for a rereading

of *Buddenbrooks* as an aesthetic artifact must be based on its ontological standing as a fiction, and on the fundamental dubiousness of taking any fiction, however realistic, literally as a mirror of actuality.

Mann himself addresses this issue in "Bilse und Ich." Admittedly, it is a polemical piece, originally published in the feuilleton section of the *Münchener Neuesten Nachrichten*, and designed as a riposte to the charges of defamation brought against him after the publication of *Buddenbrooks*. Mann calls it "ein sehr persönliches Dokument" ("a very personal document") and makes no bones about its "defensiv-polemischer Charakter" ("defensive and polemical character").[19] Yet after the dust first raised by his anger has settled, he goes on to an illuminating and hitherto largely neglected discussion of the status of representation in art, and specifically the connections of *Buddenbrooks* to Lübeck. Without denying the input of "Heimatserinnerungen verschiedener Art"[20] ("various kinds of memories of my home"), Mann emphasizes throughout the artist's creative act in transforming and animating the underlying reality into a work of art. His comments concerning his physical distance from the locale of the novel at the time of writing[21] are less compelling than his theroretical observations, although they are reiterated in "Lübeck als geistige Lebensform" when Mann maintains that "dessen örtlich-stoffliches Teil ihn im Grunde wenig begeisterte"[22] ("its material-spatial dimension basically interested him little"). In both "Bilse und Ich" and "Lübeck als geistige Lebensform," Mann projects a concept of art as "Traum" ("dream") and "Vorstellung" ("representation"),[23] devolving neither purely from the artist's memory nor from his ability to invent, but essentially from his capacity for "Beseelung" ("animation"):

> Die Beseelung ... da ist es, das schöne Wort. Es ist nicht die Gabe der Erfindung, — die der Beseelung ist es, welche den Dichter macht. Und ob es nun eine übernommene Mär oder ein Stück lebendiger Wirklichkeit mit seinem Odem und Wesen erfüllt, die Beseelung, die Durchdringung und Erfüllung des Stoffes mit dem, was des Dichters ist, macht den Stoff zu seinem Eigentum, auf das, seiner innersten Meinung nach, niemand die Hand legen darf. Daß dies zu Konflikten mit der achtbaren Wirklichkeit führen kann und muß, welche sehr auf sich hält und sich keineswegs durch Beseelung kompromittieren zu lassen wünsche, — das liegt auf der Hand. Aber die Wirklichkeit überschätzt dabei den Grad, in welchem sie für den Dichter, der sie sich aneignet, überhaupt noch Wirklichkeit bleibt — besonders in dem Falle, daß Zeit und Raum ihn von ihr trennen.[24]

The tone is here perhaps somewhat strident because Mann is on the defensive/aggressive. Nonetheless, the passage is highly suggestive in delineating the possibility of an alternative approach to the reading of *Buddenbrooks*. Moreover, Mann carries his argument much further in the later half of "Bilse und Ich," espousing a position that could be described as positively anti-representational. He identifies the artist's motivation as a "benennder Trieb" ("urge to name") and refers to him as "der wahre Liebhaber des Wortes"[25] ("the true lover of the word"). Ironically waxing autobiographical again, he recalls a telling incident from his childhood when he had drawn a small figure: " 'Wer soll es sein?' — 'Niemand soll es sein!' schrie ich und weinte beinahe. 'Es ist ein Mann, wie du siehst, eine Zeichnung, die ich gemacht, bestehend aus Umrissen' "[26] (" 'Who is that?' — 'It isn't anyone!' I shouted and nearly cried. 'It's a man, as you can see, a drawing I have done, consisting of lines' "). This claim for the autonomy of the aesthetic artifact independent of its origins in reality is then in turn applied to the image of Lübeck in *Buddenbrooks*:

> Was hatte das wirkliche Lübeck von heute mit meinem in dreijähriger Arbeit erbautem Werk zu tun? Dummheit . . . Wenn ich aus einer Sache einen Satz gemacht habe — was hat die Sache noch mit dem Satz zu tun?[27]

This dissociation of object and word has an almost post-modernist ring to it. Although "Bilse und Ich" has to be taken with some reserve because of its combative intent, it deserves to be more heeded in the reading of *Buddenbrooks* than it has been in the past. Its outspoken championship of the textual acts as a necessary corrective to the preponderance of contextualization.

It is something of a surprise to realize how contradictory Mann's assertions about *Buddenbrooks* are, when collated in this way. His statements are temporally quite far apart, "Bilse und Ich" dating from 1906, "Lübeck als geistige Lebensform" from 1926, and "Zu einem Kapitel aus *Buddenbrooks*" from 1947. All three are occasional pieces. If the first was triggered by indignation, the latter two are unquestionably tinged with a retrospective sentimentality as Thomas Mann returns to address his native city as an honored Nobel Prize laureate, and as he contemplates the inclusion of a chapter from his novel in an anthology of Western literature (shades of Aschenbach!). Yet far from being an impediment, this very dissonance can be a stimulus for a richer rereading of *Buddenbrooks:* one that acknowledges but at the same time transcends the mimetic to show how the text both grows out of its context and beyond it to develop its own meanings within the framework of the plot by verbal and narrational strategies.

The narrative plunges in *medias res* with a fragment of dialogue, which leads to a brief sketch of the speakers and others in the room. The time, the year 1835, and the styles of clothing, an indication of social standing, are described considerably before the locale. It is almost three pages into the narration before the "Landschaftszimmer" ("landscape room"), the subsequent scene of many of the crucial happenings in the Buddenbrooks family, is mentioned, and even then the exposé is relatively scant. Mann's preference is for the vignette, the rapid though exact sketch of a room, often inserted as an interlude in a dramatic verbal exchange. It as if readers were asked to suspend listening just long enough to look round and assess the arena of the action.

Reference to the context of this arena occurs in *Buddenbrooks*, as in most realist fiction, in two major domains: the historical and the geographic. Together they coalesce into what Bakhtin calls the "chronotope,"[28] that intersection of time and place where the fictive action can begin to make its own internal reality. The procedure is similar to that of cinematographic montage as a created realm is grafted onto the known one, and comes gradually to supersede it. *Buddenbrooks* allows us to trace this process with particular clarity, and so to observe the interaction of the referential and the textual in a realist novel.

The historical context is sketched with great deftness to form a verifiable external frame of reference for the fictive action.[29] The time span of *Buddenbrooks* extends from 1835 – 1875; exact temporal indicators, such as dates, occur at or near the beginning of each section, and are generously interspersed elsewhere. Each of the first three generations is shown in response to the events of the day. Old Johann has doubts about the July Monarchy of 1830, while his son, Jean, favors Louis-Philippe. Morten Schwarzkopf's views, too, have been decisively shaped by the upheavals of 1848. During the turbulence of that year, the peace of the household is rudely disturbed by the maid's open insurrection. That little domestic scene is a vivid instance of Mann's ability to integrate the macrocosm of history into the microcosm of the fiction as the "neue Geist der Empörung" ("the new spirit of rebellion")[30] penetrates even into the Buddenbrooks' dining room. The Austro-Prussian war of 1870 also makes incursions on the Buddenbrooks both physically and financially: Prussian officers are billetted for a while in the Buddenbrook residences, and the following year the firm suffers big losses in the post-war reorganization.

As political and economic happenings impinge on the Buddenbrooks' lives, the boundaries between the actual and the fictive are thrown open. The historical is interwoven into the fictitious in an extraordinarily adept and quite unobtrusive manner: for example, the part played by street lighting in quelling the 1848 riots, and, later, Thomas' progressive advocacy of gas lighting. The coverage of problematical sociohistorical issues, such as the formation of the North German Customs Union and the development of railway communications amounts to much more than local color; the history of Lübeck is subsumed into the plot as the factors shaping its fortune simultaneously affect those of the Buddenbrooks. The eclipse of the old-style patricians and the concomitant empowerment of a vigorous new capitalist bourgeoisie is a fundamental aspect of the change traced in the novel.

It is tempting to cast these historical allusions as an anchor mooring the fictional world of the Buddenbrooks to an ascertainable extraneous dimension; this is certainly the way in which the historical allusions have generally been interpreted. There is, however, a strong counter argument to such a claim, and its crux resides in the problem of readers' knowledge. Many readers of today, specially non-Europeans, have too little acquaintance with nineteenth century German history to enable them to use historical data as a test of authenticity. But this does not invalidate the effectiveness of the historical scaffold in the practice of reading. For historicity is not *per se* a warranty of the veracity of the fiction; it merely lends what James called "an air of reality."[31] Readers construct not so much by direct reference to the specifics of a chronological format as by recognizing a code. The code of historicity is one of the central conventions of realism. Its force as a narrative convention resides in its aptitude for persuading readers to accept the verisimilitude of the fiction. Just as 'long ago and far away' is the culturally conditioned marker of the entrance into the realm of romance, so a historical subtext, as in *Buddenbrooks*, serves to prompt readers into belief in the actuality of the fiction.

Geographic reference works in rather a parallel way. In *Buddenbrooks*, the key name, Lübeck, is conspicuous by its absence, although many of its streets and landmarks such as the Fischergrube, the Beckergrube, the Königsstrasse, the Burgtor, the Jerusalemsfeld, and the Marienkirche are freely cited. It is, however, mistaken to assert that the novel "gibt dem Leser mit der Erwähnung der bekannten Marienkirche einen Hinweis auf den Handlungsort Lübeck"[32] ("gives the reader with the mention of the well known Church of Mary an indication of the scene of the action, Lübeck"). This is, again, as with the historical allusions, to assume automatic reader recognition without realizing that to those unfamiliar with Lübeck the references do not carry immediate — or, indeed, any — signification, unless accompanied by explanatory notes. The names of neighboring places, including Hamburg, Travemünde, Rostock, and the railway junction at Wismar provide corroborating evidence of location, though once more only to those knowledgeable enough. Even to geographically uninformed readers, however, the Northern setting is made explicit through reiterated mention of the food, the climate, and the mentality. Local color is given in the smells of water, fish, and oil from the harbor, and the silhouettes of the ships engaged in the grain trade. The Hanseatic stamp is imparted to this setting by the Buddenbrooks' involvement in the city governance, by the meeting of the city elders to confer about the handling of the 1848 riots, and by the circumstances of Thomas' election to the senate. But these references will have meaning exclusively to those readers cognizant of German history. More readily comprehensible is the tension between North and South in the episode of Tony's second marriage, where it forms the central motivational axis.

Language plays an equally important part in evoking and creating place for the reader. Mann writes eloquently in "Lübeck als geistige Lebensform" of the "Heimatlaut" ("sound of home") as conjuring up "den Geist der Landschaft"[33] ("the spirit of the landscape"). So in *Buddenbrooks* he often resorts to the phonographic to convey at times the peculiarities of individual speech, as in the case of Sesemi Weichbrodt, but more frequently to capture the regional. The "Plattdeutsch" ("Low German") of the "Wasserkante" ("Water's Edge," i.e., the North German coast) exposes readers to an immediate encounter with the provincial. The mixture, in the novel's opening words, of the homely dialect with the aristocratic French of polite conversation, illustrates at once the Buddenbrooks' roots in their native environment and their reaching out for a refined cosmopolitanism. Speech also functions as a performative enactment of place in Munich. Indeed, throughout, linguistic variations serve as regional and social indicators to site speakers both geographically and along the class spectrum.

The lively drama of the dialogic scenes makes a stronger impression on readers than Mann's descriptive passages, which are on the whole perfunctory and schematic, specially as far as land- and streetscapes go. Travemünde, for instance, is given short shrift with a few nondescript adjectives: the sea is "blau" ("blue") and "friedlich" ("peaceful"), the lighthouse "rund" ("round") and "gelb" ("yellow"): "sie übersahen eine Weile Bucht und Bollwerk ... " (120; "they looked for a while over the bay and the rampart"). That is a crucial device among Mann's narrational strategies. The transfer of the perceiving lens from narrator to protagonist forms one of the main bridges from referentiality to textuality in the realist novel. The outcome of this manipulation of viewpoint is to make readers share the protagonists' angle of vision and their experience. So we catch the first glimpse of Travemünde from the carriage with Tom and Tony; we see what they see. The actuality of the scene hinges not on our knowledge of Travemünde, but on their credibility as characters, and therefore ultimately on the potency of Mann's rhetoric.

The presentation of Travemünde offers a good example of the way textuality interfaces with referentiality in *Buddenbrooks*. Travemünde is part of an existent reality: it is an actual town that can be found at a certain latitude and on a certain longitude on a map of Germany. But its referential charge is fairly weak since it is not a well-known place such as London, Paris, or Boston, immediately recognizable as actual. It may strike a non-European as possibly fictitious. However, for the reading of *Buddenbrooks*, that proves immaterial because Travemünde comes less to denote a physical spot than to connote a state of relaxed happiness. It is a resort town with a park, a band, a beach, a small harbor, and a lighthouse, but beyond and above that, it is a place of the mind, an alternative mode of life to the enclosed austerity of Lübeck. The open vistas of the beach and the unrestricted space of the sea suggest freedom for the individual to expand at will in a way that is not possible in the narrow streets of the home city. Travemünde is endowed with this signification within the fiction as the action develops with repeated visits there. For Tony it is the unforgettable scene of her early and only love for Morten Schwarzkopf, while for Hanno it is a blessed release from the tyranny of school, a haven of dreamy *dolce far niente*. So Travemünde becomes a symbolical cipher for a paradise of ease denied to the Buddenbrooks except for brief, tantalizing spells. It continues to play the same role later in the novel when Thomas, suffering from increasing nervous exhaustion, is packed off there by his doctor in order to relax a little.

On this metaphoric plane, reader recognition is wholly independent of geographic referentiality. It is through the fictive context and its associations, i.e., textually, that Travemünde assumes its meaning. The text has fashioned its own internal field of reference,[34] which does not exclude the outer frame of reference, but which complements and transcends it. The reading of Travemünde in *Buddenbrooks* throws into question one of the claims commonly made for realism, namely that: "Als literarische Richtung appelliert der Realismus in erster Linie nicht an die ästhetische Kompetenz des Rezipienten, sondern an seine Alltagserfahrung"[35] ("As a literary tendency realism appeals not to the recipient's aesthetic competence, but to his/her everyday experience"). To read realist fiction requires the same degree of aesthetic competence as any other genre and not necessarily more extraneous information.

Like Travemünde, the Lübeck of *Buddenbrooks* is the mind's own place. It may well be in order to enhance its intangible presence as a "geistige Lebensform" ("spiritual way of life") that Mann limited external description, which is surprisingly sparse in this novel, certainly compared to the dense proliferation of detail characteristic of Balzac or Zola. The sense of place emanates primarily from the protagonists' own consciousness of it as a moral factor, indeed almost as an ethical category. It becomes a propelling force within the fictional world as it shapes their lives, through either their rebellion or their submission. Tony acquiesces by marrying Grünlich contrary to her inclinations for the sake of fulfilling her obligations to "die Familie und die Firma" (107; "the family and the firm"). Thomas, the doubter and waverer, intent on getting by by keeping up appearances, makes a characteristic compromise by giving up the girl in the flowershop, Anna, and marrying Gerda. Though financially and socially a brilliant match, it also indicates his attraction to the aesthetic and the exotic. Christian attempts to resolve the difficulty by absence, spending his life in England, South America, Hamburg, anywhere other than his hometown. And finally Hanno contracts out by fleeing into the artistic pleasures of musical improvisation. The burden of expectation weighs heavily on every one of the Buddenbrooks; each responds to its presence, reckoning with its demands in the daily round as well as in major decisions.

Through its commanding role in determining the characters' conduct, place is internalized as a mindset. The interiorization of the action becomes increasingly evident as the novel progresses, and is reflected in the growing proportion of free indirect speech and interior monlogue. This has been noted by several critics, and most often interpreted historically as denoting the crossing of the threshold from the nineteenth century narrative techniques of Fontane to the more modern exploration of the hidden recesses of the soul.[36] But it has an import other than this historical one. The insight that H. Meili Steele presents into Henry James' *The Golden Bowl* is apposite to *Buddenbrooks:* "The characters' generation of their own text is part of the novel's effacement of the differences between life and art, between factual or realistic discourse and imaginative and metaphoric discourse."[37] It is the introverted, subjective reality of the characters that finds cogent expression in *Buddenbrooks* and that, in its moral and social ramifications, makes so lasting an impression on readers. The place of the fiction comes to authenticate itself through its internal field of reference, through the power it wields over the protagonists in the dynamics of the plot much more than through any extraneous allusion. That is why readers who have never been to Lübeck, who do not even know whether it is an actual or an invented location, have no trouble in reading and believing *Buddenbrooks.*

Our willingness to believe in the world of the fiction is fostered by certain verbal and narrational strategies. Mann does not have recourse to the more obvious tactics of the "engaging narrator";[38] he refrains from overt comment, allowing only his irony to betray his presence. Yet despite this discretion, he seduces readers to enter the realm of the fiction. He does so in part through his preference throughout for third-person constructions: "Man saß im Landschaftszimmer" (12; "One[39] sat in the landscape room"); "Man sitzt bei Tisch, man ist beim Obste angelangt" (69; "One sits at the dinner table, one has got to the fruit course"); "Man hatte mit dem Kaffeetrinken heute ungemein lange gewartet, und man saß lange beieinander" (124; "One had lingered unusually long over coffee today, and sat together for a while"); "Man saß in dem großen Kinderzimmer im zweiten Stockwerk" (519; "One was sitting in the big nursery on the second floor"). There are literally dozens of similar examples. This is not a mere mannerism; it has the effect of drawing readers into the action. That reiterated, open-ended "man" is an important device for situating readers among the circle of participants, thereby attenuating the distinction between the world of the fiction, where *they* sit, and the world in which we read. That "man" makes the two co-extensive; we, too, sit and eat and drink in the fictive realm as we join the Buddenbrooks' communal activities. We, in the guise of "man," are present at all the celebrations; we inspect the new house, learn its layout, and enter the dining room along with the guests, to whom we are assimilated. Through the grammatical disposition, the narrator coaxes readers into complicity with the world being evoked.

This complicity is also encouraged by the role of eavesdropper into which readers are cast. Like that hotbed of gossip, Middlemarch, this Northern harbor city is full of talkers and listeners, whom readers overhear. There are many different sorts of talk: the celebratory rhetoric at the opening dinner and at the firm's centenary; the leisurely chatter of the Travemünde summer community; the snippets of speculation among the crowd awaiting the outcome of the Senate elections; the informal conversations with the barber who spreads word on his morning rounds. Our familiarity with this world is further enhanced by the patterns of recurrence in both characters and scenes. *Buddenbrooks* is peopled by a large cast of scrupulously delineated, sporadically reappearing subsidiary characters such as Ida Jungmann, Sesemi Weichbrodt, pastor Pringsheim, Sigismund Gosch, Dr. Grabow and his successor, Dr. Langhals. In addition, there are the members of those first families, the Hagenströms, the Möllendorpfs, the Kistenmakers, the Krögers, the Döhlmanns, whose names are dropped with an almost obsessive insistence to reveal the unremitting awareness of class, wealth, and social standing as a central feature of this environment. The dynastic continuities reinforce the substantiality of this fictive world as each figure is deliberately related to his antecedents and associates. A cyclical return is conveyed by the weekly and seasonal rituals: the Thursday evening family gatherings, the Bible-reading circle, the big dinners, Christmas, summer at the seaside, deaths and funerals, all with their distinctive smells and sounds. The rhythm of recurrence is underscored too by the constancy of the scene, the "Landschaftszimmer," where many of the social occasions are set. Linguistically, the technique of the leitmotif acts as another mode of repetition. What is remarkable about *Buddenbrooks* is the density and richness of texture that results cumulatively from these various kinds of reiteration. As this web of connections knits into a consensual social fabric, the internal field of reference comes to predominate. Readers construe the text from the information on the printed page, not from acquaintance with an anterior reality.

The best example of the double face of this novel is the Buddenbrook house. From one perspective it represents the supreme instance of referentiality: that typically North German gable house, which decorates the cover of the German paperback edition, is known to be based on the house where Mann's aunt used to live. Its exterior is described more in *Tonio Kröger* than in *Buddenbrooks*, where the emphasis is on interiors for their semiotic significance. The "Landschaftszimmer" signals the Buddenbrooks' class, prosperity, and taste. In its orderliness, in its light but muted colors, in its idyllic and rather artificially pretty iconography as in its self-conscious harmoniousness, its somewhat old-fashioned elegance, and its controlled spaced, it conjures up an image of the world as the Buddenbrooks would wish it to be. The whole room bespeaks a sense of restraint guided by security, an ease within a known and mastered universe. Nature is here filtered, tempered, and tamed in the same way as each of the Buddenbrooks will be expected to check his or her passions for the sake of maintaining the order established in the family. Later, in consonance with the decline already setting in, the rear of the house is allowed to fall into disrepair; the cats running wild in the former billiard room are an invasion of primal animal indifference into what was the civilized, carefully tended play-area of serious men of affairs. The dilapidation of the house behind its still impressive facade parallels Thomas' nervous exhaustion masked by his exaggerated personal grooming and meticulous clothing. His own new house carries patrician distinction to extravagant lengths; fully a quarter of its living space is occupied by the music room, while the bedroom is connected to an ample bath and dressing room. On the other hand, it is entirely lacking in office premises. It represents, in Tony's eyes, "die Macht, den Glanz und Triumph der Buddenbrooks" (427; "the might, the splendor, the triumph of the Buddenbrooks"), but it also embodies in its design the turn away from commerce to aesthetics.

In all these instances the house functions as an objective correlative of its inhabitants' situation. It is invested with symbolic significations within the fiction, and assumes meanings for readers independent of its origins in external time and place, as a construct derived from the text. The persuasive power of the rhetoric is demonstrated by what happened subsequently: the house on the Mengstrasse turned into a tourist attraction, cited in Lübeck publicity material as the Buddenbrook house. The fiction, through its symbolizing transfiguration of an actual antecedent, spawns a mythology that fuses the referential with the textual and takes on a quasi-autonomous existence.

The mythology created by the novel itself blends into another one pre-existent to it and absorbed into its very core. Characterized by Mann as consisting of "recht unlübeckische geistige Erlebnisse"[40] ("very non-Lübeckian experiences") this ancillary mythology is woven out of the nineteenth century speculative tradition, of which Wagner, Nietzsche, and Schopenhauer are the chief exponents. Mann repeatedly testified to their impact on him,[41] although the extent and timing of Schopenhauer's influence remains controversial.[42] The implications of Wagner's music and the potential for radically opposed interpretations are openly debated in *Buddenbrooks.* Thomas' forceful encounter with Schopenhauer parallels Mann's own response to *Die Welt als Wille und Vorstellung (The World as Will and Representation)*, as he records it in his *Lebensabriß (Sketch of My Life)*.[43] These are the novel's guiding spirits, decisive in determining both its plot and its timbre. The imminence of this specific ideology serves not only to site *Buddenbrooks* in relation to the intellectual and artistic currents of its period, but also to provide readers with a cultural frame of reference. For Wagner, Nietzsche, and Schopenhauer occupy a curious intermediary position between fact and text insofar as they possess a spiritual existence extraneous to the realm of the fiction, yet no concrete reality. Their assimilation into the novel enables readers to discern an intertextual chain of ideas, and so to construct the text in the context of an extrafictional, though intangible order. For this reason they play a vital role in *Buddenbrooks* as buttresses and glosses on its subtitle, "Verfall einer Familie" ("Decline of a Family"). This suggestive subtitle offers readers a cogent way of organizing the events of the novel from a symbolic angle, which complements and eventually supersedes the referential.

Buddenbrooks therefore invites a dualistic approach that fuses its referential self-image as "ein Bild hanseatischen Lebens aus dem neunzehnten Jahrhundert" ("a picture of Hanseatic life from the nineteenth century") with its symbolical representation of that material in the "Verfall einer Familie." Its dyadic mode of narration demands a parallel two-pronged reading which recognizes the stratagems whereby the text produces its own internal meanings, while allowing the possibility of reference. In the stories of Hanno's friend, Kai, an internal model for reading *Buddenbrooks* is adumbrated: they "gewannen an Interesse dadurch, daß sie nicht gänzlich in der Luft standen, sondern von der Wirklichkeit

ausgingen und diese in ein seltsames und geheimnisvolles Licht rückten"
(520; "gained in interest by not floating purely in the air, but by originating
in actuality and illuminating it with a strange and mysterious light"). It is
through the aesthetic configuration of the text that the actuality, which
was its starting-point, is transformed into a fictive entity, which assumes
an existence independent of its origins and universal in its appeal. *Buddenbrooks* is indeed, as Mann claimed, both a very German book and a
European and World book, whose fictive evocation of a once existent "actuality" puts it into a light that is "strange and mysterious" for those who
partook of it, but also still vivid and palpable for readers far away in time
and place.

Notes

In Lieu of a Theory

1. C. S. Lewis, *An Experiment in Criticism*. Cambridge: Cambridge Univ. Press, 1961, 141.

2. For a concise statement of Iser's position see "Interaction between Text and Reader." In *The Reader in the Text*. Ed. Susan R. Suleiman and Inge Crosman. Princeton, N.J.: Princeton Univ. Press, 1980, 106–119.

3. Norman Holland, *Five Readers Reading*. New Haven and London: Yale Univ. Press, 1975, 1–5. The blatant sexism apparent in the notation of the only female's attractiveness is disturbing.

4. Holland, *op. cit.*, 13.

5. David Bleich, *Subjective Criticism*. Baltimore and London: The Johns Hopkins Univ. Press, 1978, 98.

6. The difference should, however, be noted here between the use of the phrase "reader response" predominant among most Anglo-American critics, for whom it turns essentially on subjectivity, and that of Wolfgang Iser, who envisages it more as the cognitive process that I outline.

Goethe's *Italienische Reise*

1. Attributed to Dr. Johnson in James Boswell, *Life of Johnson*. Oxford: Clarendon Press, 1934, III, 36.

2. William E. Stewart, *Die Reisebeschreibung und ihre Theorie im Deutschland des 18. Jahrhunderts*. Bonn: Bouvier, 1978, 1

3. See Charles L. Batten, *Pleasurable Instruction. Form and Convention in Eighteenth Century Travel Literature*. Berkeley and London: Univ. of California Press, 1978.

4. See *inter al.* Ludwig Hirzel, *Göthe's "Italienische Reise."* Basel: Schweighauerische Verlagsbuchhandlung, 1871; Carl Meyer, *Goethe und seine italienische Reise*. Hamburg: Richter, 1886; Melitta Gerhard, "Die Redaktion der *Italien-*

ischen Reise im Lichte von Goethes autobiographischem Gesamtwerk,"
Jahrbuch des Freien Deutschen Hochstifts (1930), rpt. in *Leben im Gesetz.* Bern:
Francke, 1966, 34–51; Emil Staiger, *Goethe.* Zurich: Atlantis, 1956, II, 7–56.

5. The best analysis of German travel writing as literature is in an unpublished dissertation: Manfred Link, "Der Reisebericht als literarische Kunstform von Goethe bis Heine." Diss. Cologne, 1963.

6. For detailed itineraries and the impact of Addison's route see William Edward Mead, *The Grand Tour in the Eighteenth Century.* Boston and New York: Houghton Mifflin, 1914, especially pp. 272–81.

7. See Percy G. Adams, *Travel Literature and the Evolution of the Novel.* Lexington, KY.: Univ. of Kentucky Press, 1983).

8. *Journal of English and German Philology* 48 (1949) 445–68.

9. *Viaggio per l'Italia* was not published until 1932 (Rome: Reale Accademia d'Italia) under the editorship of Arturo Farinelli. A partial German version appeared under the title *Goethes Vater reist in Italien.* Ed. Erwin Koppen. Trs. Carl Nagel (Mainz: Kupferberg, c. 1972), and a complete new one, *Reise durch Italien im Jahre 1740.* and commented on by Albert Meier (Munich: dtv. 2179, 1986).

10. Rpt. in *Werke.* Ed. Jürgen Jahn. Berlin and Weimar: Aufbau, 1973, I, 3–199.

11. Wilhelm Heinse, *Briefe deutscher Gelehrter.* Ed. Wilhelm Körte. Zurich, 1906, II.

12. Johann Joachim Winckelmann *Werke.* Ed. Joseph Eiselein. Donaueschingen: im Verlag deutscher Classiker, 1825–29, X and XI.

13. Johann Wolfgang von Goethe, *Werke.* Weimar: Böhlau, 1887, section IV, I, 241. All subsequent references are to this edition.

14. For earlier accounts of Sicily see Camillo von Klenze, *The Interpretation of Italy during the last Two Centuries: A Contribution to the study of Goethe's "Italienische Reise."* Chicago: Univ. of Chicago Press, 1907, 59–64.

15. François Auguste René de Chateaubriand, *Oeuvres complètes.* Paris: Ladvocat, 1827, VII, 237. All subsequent references are to this edition.

16. Tobias George Smollett, *Travels Through France and Italy.* Ed. Frank Felsenstein. London and New York: Oxford Univ. Press, 1919. 210. All subsequent references are to this edition.

17. William Hazlitt, *Notes of a Journey Through France and Italy. Complete Works of William Hazlitt.* Ed. P. P. Howe. London and Toronto: Dent, 1932, X, 85. All subsequent references are to this edition.

18. First you see in its totality a very luscious landscape, and you say: "That's fine"; but when you come to look at the objects in detail, enchantment overtakes you. Meadows whose greenness surpasses English turf in freshness and softness

meld into fields of maize, rice, and grain; these in turn are crowned with vineyards, terrassed on poles to form garlands over the harvest; and all this is interspersed with mulberry and walnut trees, elms, willows, poplars, and watered by rivers and canals.

19. I saw the illuminations and the fireworks heralding the next day's great ceremony to the prince of the Apostles: while I was supposed to be admiring a light placed high above the Vatican, I was looking at the effect of the moon on the Tiber, on these Roman houses, on those ruins hanging everywhere.

20. Stendhal, *Oeuvres complètes*. Ed. George Eudes. Paris: Larive, 1951, IV, 41–41.

21. The squares are very crowded on market days, fruits and vegetables in superabundance, garlic and onions to heart's delight. Anyway, they shout, jest, and sing the whole day, wriggle and romp, jubilate and laugh incessantly. The mild air, the reasonable food lets them live at ease. All who can are out in the open air. At night the singing and racketing start in earnest. The song about Marlborough is heard on every street, then a guitar, a violin. They practice imitating all the birds on pipes. The strangest burst forth everywhere. Such an exuberant sense of existence is bestowed even on the poor by a mild climate, and the shadow of the people seems itself worthy of honor.

22. Emil Staiger, *Goethe*. Zurich: Atlantis, 2nd. rev. ed., 1958 (1956), II, 28.

23. For an amphitheater like this is really made in such a way as to enable the people to be impressed with themselves, to have the best of themselves.
If anything worth seeing happens on flat land, and everyone flocks to see it, those at the back endeavor by all means to raise themselves above those at the front: they stand on benches, roll up barrels, drive up in carts, put planks across each other, occupy a neighboring hill, and quickly a crater is formed.

24. *Werke*, section III, I, 219. 10 November 1786.

25. *Werke*, section III, I, 219.

"Paris Change!"

1. Paris is changing! but nothing in its melancholy
   Has altered! new edifices, scaffolds, blocks
   Old areas, everything becomes to me an allegory
   And my cherished memories are heavier than rocks.

2. See Pierre Citron, *La Poésie de Paris dans la littérature française de Rousseau à Baudelaire*. Paris: Editions de minuit, 1961, 2 vols.; George B. Raser, *Guide to Balzac's Paris*. Choisy-le-Roi: Imp. de France, 1964; Robert Minder, *Paris in der neueren französischen Literatur 1770 – 1890*. Wiesbaden: Steiner, 1965; Stefan Max, *Les Métamorphoses de la grande ville dans les "Rougon-*

Macquart." Paris: Nizet, 1966; Nathan Kranowski, *Paris dans les romans de Zola.*
Paris: Presses universitaires, 1968; Marie-Claire Bancquart, *Images littéraires de
Paris 'fin-de-siècle.'* Paris: aux éditions de la différence, 1979; Hans-Joachim Lotz,
"L'image iréelle, bizarre et mythique de Paris chez Balzac et Baudelaire," in *Paris
au XIXè siècle.* Lyons: Presses universitaires, 1984, 93 – 106. For a more general
overview see Burton Pike, *The Image of the City in Modern Literature.* Prince-
ton, N.J.: Princeton Univ. Press, 1981; also *Unreal City: Urban Experience in
Modern European Literature.* Ed. Edward Timms and David Kelley. Manchester:
Manchester Univ. Press, 1985, especially Peter Collier, "Nineteenth Century Paris:
Vision and Nightmare," 24 – 44.

3. See A. K. Chandra, "The Young Man from the Provinces," *Comparative
Literature* 33 (1981) 321 – 41.

4. Honoré de Balzac, *La Comédie humaine.* Ed. Marcel Bouteron. Paris:
Gallimard, 1956, II, 939. All subsequent references are to this edition.

5. Emile Zola, *Les Rougon-Macquart.* Ed. Henri Mittérand. Paris: Gallimard,
1961, II, 449 – 50. All subsequent references are to this edition.

6. The still, with its weirdly shaped receptacles and endless coils of piping,
looked dour and forbidding; no steam was coming out of it; hardly an inner
breathing or a subterranean rumble was audible; it was like some black midnight
deed being done in broad daylight by a morose, powerful, and mute worker.

7. The house seemed all the more colossal because it rose between two low,
rickety hovels clinging to either side of it; and, foursquare, like a roughly cast
block of cement, decaying and flaking away in the rain, it thrust the silhouette of its
vast cube with its unplastered wall the color of mud up into the pale sky above the
neighboring rooftops; of an interminable nudity, like the walls of prisons, where
rows of toothing-stones seemed to lurk in wait like decrepit jaws snapping in the
void.

8. It was onto this sidewalk, into this heat as in a furnace, that she was being
thrown all alone with the little ones; and she cast her eyes to the right and to the
left up and down the outer boulevards, stopping at both ends, seized by a dull terror, as if her life, from now on, was to be played out here between a slaughterhouse
and a hospital.

9. Citron in *La Poésie de Paris* traces "fournaise" to Vigny's poem, *Paris,*
(I, 274), and cites its recurrence in Hugo, Lamartine, Alexandre Dumas, Banville,
and Michelet *inter alia* (II, 422).

10. Rainer Maria Rilke, *Die Aufzeichnungen des Malte Laurids Brigge.*
Wiesbaden: Insel Verlag, 1951, 7. All subsequent references are to this edition.

11. Maurice Blanchot, "Rilke et l'exigence de la mort," *L'Espace littéraire.*
Paris: Gallimard, 1968, 151.

12. So it became clear to me that I was never a real reader. In my childhood
reading struck me as a calling, which one would assume, sometime later, when all

callings came, one after the other. I had, truth to tell, no definite conception, when this could be. I relied on the belief that one would notice when life somehow turned round and came only from without, as earlier it had from within.

13. Judith Ryan, "Hypothetisches Erzählen: Zur Funktion von Phantasie und Einbildung in Rilkes *Malte Laurids Brigge.*" *Jahrbuch der deutschen Schillergesellschaft*, 1971, 341–74; rpt. in *Materialien zu Rainer Maria Rilke, "Die Aufzeichnungen des Malte Laurids Brigge."* Ed. Hartmut Englehardt. Frankfurt: Suhrkamp, 1974, 244–79. Reference is to this reprint, 265.

Reading "Nasty" Great Books

1. J. Hillis Miller, *The Ethics of Reading.* New York: Columbia Univ. Press, 1987, 1.

2. Miller, *The Ethics of Reading*, 2.

3. Miller, *The Ethics of Reading*, 9.

4. Matthew Arnold, "Count Leo Tolstoy," *The Works of Matthew Arnold.* London: Macmillan, 1903, IV, 203.

5. Thomas Mann, *Meistererzählungen.* Zurich: Manesse, 1945, 194. All subsequent references are to this edition.

6. Gustave Flaubert, *Madame Bovary.* Ed. Edouard Maynial. Paris: Garnier, 1947, 122. All subsequent references are to this edition.

7. Wayne C. Booth, *The Company We Keep. An Ethics of Fiction.* Berkeley and London: Univ. of California Press, 1988, 174.

8. Gustave Flaubert, *Correspondance. Oeuvres complètes.* Paris: Conard, 1926–27, XIV, 164.

9. See Lilian R. Furst, "The Role of Food in *Madame Bovary."* *Orbis Litterarum* 34 (1979), 53–65.

10. Booth, *The Company We Keep*, 174.

11. T. J. Reed, *Thomas Mann: The Uses of Tradition.* Oxford: Clarendon Press, 1974, 164ff.

12. Reed, *Thomas Mann*, 167.

13. Reed, *Thomas Mann*, 162–63.

14. John Porter Houston, *Fictional Technique in France, 1802–1927.* Baton Rouge, LA.: Louisiana State Univ. Press, 1972, 66ff.

15. André Gide, *L'Immoraliste.* Paris: Mercure de France, 1902, 184.

Assert and Resistance in *Die Marquise von O—* and *Der Tod in Venedig*

1. Heinrich von Kleist, *Sämliche Werke und Briefe*. Ed. Helmut Sembdner. 2nd. rev. ed. Munich: Hanser, 1961, II, 101. All subsequent references are to this edition.

2. Thomas Mann, *Meistererzählungen*. Zurich: Manesse, 1945, 245. All subsequent references are to this edition.

3. In M-, a major city in northern Italy, the widowed Marquise of O-, a lady of impeccable reputation and mother of several well brought-up children, announced in the newspapers, that she had, without her knowledge, come into a certain condition, that the father of the child, which she was about to bear, should come forward, and that she was resolved, out of consideration for her family, to marry him.

4. She was dragged into the inner courtyard, where she was just about to sink to the ground under the most shameful assaults when a Russian officer appeared, alerted by the lady's piercing screams, and scattered the dogs lusting for their prey with furious blows of his sword. To the marquise he seemed an angel sent from heaven. He smashed the hilt of his sword into the face of the last of the murderous brutes, who still had his arms round her slender waist, so that he reeled back with blood gushing from his mouth, offered the lady his arm with a courteous French address, and led her, speechless from her ordeal, into the other wing of the palace, which was untouched by the fire, and where she sank down totally unconscious. Here—when shortly thereafter her servants appeared, he made arrangements to call a doctor, assured her, as he put his hat back on, that she would soon recover, and returned to the fighting.

5. Dorrit Cohn, "Kleist's *Marquise von O—: The Problem of Knowledge.*" *Monatshefte* 67:2 (1975) 133.

6. Erika Swales, "The Beleaguered Citadel: A Study of Kleist's *Die Marquise von O—. Deutsche Vierteljahresschrift* 51 (1977) 129–47.

7. Cohn, *op. cit.*, 132.

8. Cohn, *op. cit.*, 139–40.

9. With astonishment Aschenbach noticed that the youth was of a perfect beauty. His face, pale and of a graceful reserve, surrounded by honey-colored curls, with its straight nose, its winning mouth, its expression of pure and divine serenity, was reminiscent of Greek sculptures of the noblest period, and yet with all this chaste perfection of form it possessed a uniquely personal charm such as the viewer never recalled seeing in either nature or art.

10. When at about the age of thirty-five he fell ill in Vienna, a shrewd observer made this comment about him at a social gathering: "You see, Aschenbach has

always lived only like this"—and the speaker clenched the fingers of his left hand into a tight fist—; "never like this"—and he let his open hand dangle comfortably from the back of the chair.

11. The best English translation is by David Luke and Nigel Reeves, *The Marquise of O— and Other Stories*. (New York: Penguin Books, 1978). But even their version: "that she would presumably not expect him to explain the facts of life to her" (86), while correct in meaning, wholly misses the intertextual allusion to Kant, and consequently reduces the metaphysical "causes of things" to the merely physical "facts of life."

Through Multiple Lenses: Ironics in Kleist's *Die Marquise von O—*

1. Heinrich von Kleist, *Sämtliche Werke und Briefe*. Ed. Helmut Sembdner. 2nd. rev. ed. Munich: Hanser, 1961, II, 127. All subsequent references are to this edition.

2. Erika Swales, "The Beleaguered Citadel: A Study of Kleist's *Die Marquise von O—*." *Deutsche Vierteljahresschrift* 51 (1977), 129.

3. Michael Moehring, *Witz und Ironie in der Prosa Heinrich von Kleists*. Munich: Fink, 1971, 153.

4. A common German circumlocution for pregnancy at that period.

5. See Dorrit Cohn, "Kleist's *Die Marquise von O—*: The Problem of Knowledge." *Monatshefte* 67 (1975), and Swales, *op. cit.*

6. Moehring *Witz und Ironie*, 239.

7. H. W. Fowler, *A Dictionary of English Usage*. London: Oxford Univ. Press, 1965, 305–306.

8. That he could not describe the pleasure and the pain that had been conjoined in this image; that he had finally after his recovery returned to the army; that there, too, he had experienced the most violent agitation.

9. Moehring in *Witz und Ironie* reads Kleist's prose sociologically as an ironic satirization of the speech patterns of the aristocracy.

10. Wolfgang Kayser, "Kleist als Erzähler." *German Life and Letters* 8 (1954 –5), 19–29; rpt. in *Die Vortragsreise. Studien zur Literatur.* Bern: Francke, 1958, 169–83; and in *Heinrich von Kleist. Aufsätze und Essays.* Ed. Walter Müller-Seidel. Darmstadt: Wissenschaftliche Buchgesellschaft, 1967, 230–43. All references are to this most recent reprint; 233.

11. Kayser, *op. cit.* 233.

12. Kayser, *op. cit.*, 236.

13. "The Impossible Object: The Feminine, The Narrative (Laclos' *Liaisons dangereuses* and Kleist's *Marquise von O—*)." *Modern Language Notes* 91 (1976), 1320.

14. "Unwißentlich" is the word Luther used in translating the story of the Virgin's impregnation by the Holy Ghost in *Luke* I, 34.

15. Her mother, by contrast and in secret opposition to her husband, has always hoped for a re-marriage of her daughter (117), and is, therefore, ultimately supportive of her alliance with the count.

16. That evening she cooked for him all the strengthening and calming foods she could find in the kitchen, prepared and warmed his bed in order to put him there as soon as he appeared at his daughter's side.

17. Cohn, *op. cit.*, 130–33.

18. "The Style of Kleist." *Diacritics* 9, iv (1979) 47–61.

19. Klaus Müller-Salget, "Das Prinzip der Doppeldeutigkeit in Kleists Erzählungen." *Zeitschrift für deutsche Philologie* 92 (1973) 191.

20. Friedrich Schlegel, "Lyceumsfragment" 48. *Kritische Ausgabe*. Ed. Hans Eichner. Munich, Paderborn, Vienna: Ferdinand Schöningh, 1967. II, 153.

21. A borrowing of the term Friedrich Schlegel used to describe romantic poetry. See Friedrich Schlegel, "Athenäumfragment" 116, *op. cit.*, II, 182.

Reading Kleist and Kafka

1. rpt. in Jürgen Born, "Kafka und seine Kritiker (1912–1924). Ein Überblick." in *Kafka-Symposium*, 2nd. rev. ed. Berlin: Wagenbach, 1966, 140.

2. Beda Allemann, "Kleist und Kafka." in *Franz Kafka. Themen und Probleme*. Ed. Claude David. Gottingen: Vandenhoeck & Ruprecht, 1980, 153. It is a recurrent experience in Kafka as well as Kleist seminars that sooner or later a particularly gifted student asks to speak and poses the question: could not something similar be found in Kleist (or Kafka, as the case may be).

3. See, for example, Wolfgang Jahn, *Kafkas Roman "Der Verschollene."* Stuttgart: Metzler, 1965, 79–83; Hartmut Binder, *Motiv und Gestaltung bei Franz Kafka*. Bonn: Bouvier, 1966, 279–86; Bernhard Blume, "Kleist und Goethe." *Monatshefte* 33 (1946) 94; Wilhelm Emrich, "Kleist und die moderne Literatur," in *Heinrich von Kleist*. Ed. Walter Müller-Seidel. Berlin: Schmidt, 1966, 23 ff. Günter Blöcker has gone so far as to maintain that there is hardly a work about Kleist nowadays that does not allude to Kafka; see his *Heinrich von Kleist oder das absolute Ich*. Berlin: Argon, 1960, 12.

4. Franz Kafka, *Briefe an Felice*. Ed. Erich Heller and Jürgen Born. Frankfurt: Fischer, 1967, 291.

5. *Tagebücher 1910–1923.* New York: Schocken, 1949, 43.

6. *Briefe 1902–1924.* Frankfurt: Fischer, 1958, 87.

7. *Briefe an Felice,* 460.

8. Helmut Lamprecht, "Mühe und Kunst des Anfangs. Ein Versuch über Kleist und Kafka." *Neue Deutsche Hefte* 66, 1960, 939.

9. Heinz Politzer, "Franz Kafkas vollendeter Roman: Zur Typologie seiner Briefe an Felice," in *Das Nachleben der deutschen Romantik.* Ed. Wolfgang Paulsen. Heidelberg: Lothar Stiehm, 1969, 205.

10. Jörg Dittkrist, *Vergleichende Untersuchungen zu Heinrich von Kleist und Franz Kafka.* Diss. Cologne, 1971, 28–56.

11. Mark Harman, *Literary Echoes: Heinrich von Kleist and Franz Kafka.* Diss, Yale, 1980.

12. J. M. Lindsay, "Kohlhaas and K: Two Men in Search of Justice." *German Life and Letters* 13 (1959–60), 190. The same topic is pursued by Eric Mason in "Justice and the Obsessed Character in *Michael Kohlhaas, Der Prozess,* and *L'Etranger,*" *Seminar* 2:2 (1966), 21–33. More extensive and elaborate thematic comparisons are a prominent part of several later studies of the filiation between Kleist and Kafka. F. G. Peters, in *Kleist and Kafka,* Oxford German Studies 1 (1966), surveys a series of thematic conjunctions: between *Der Findling* and *Das Urteil* in the motifs of father and son, of accusation and revenge; between *Die Marquise von O—* and *Die Verwandlung* in the bodily transformation and in the reactions of both the family and the protagonist; between *Michael Kohlhaas* and *Das Schloß* in the concentration on the nature of authority and the attempts to contact authority. The final part of Peters' monograph is devoted to three major themes: rejection, love and sex, confused and ambivalent feelings, which recur throughout the narratives of both Kleist and Kafka. While Peters' orientation is primarily psychoanalytical, John Martin Grandin's paradigm is existential. In *Kafka's Prussian Advocate* (Columbia, S.C.: Camden House, 1987), he moves from theme to type, emphasizing similarities without taking differences into consideration.

13. Lamprecht, *op. cit.,* 935–40.

14. David F. Smith, *Gesture as a Device in Kleist's "Michael Kohlhaas" and Kafka's "Der Prozess,"* Stanford Studies in German, 11. Frankfurt: Peter Lang, 1970, and Dittkrist, *op. cit.*

15. Harman, *op. cit.,* especially chapter 3, "Theatrical Style," 58–105.

16. Jahn, *op. cit.,* 79–83.

17. Hermann Pongs, "Kleist und Kafka." *Welt und Wort* 11 (1952) 380.

18. Binder, *op. cit.,* 279–86.

19. Binder, *op. cit.,* 155.

20. Wolfgang Kayser, "Kleist als Erzähler." *German Life and Letters* 8 (1954–55) 19; rpt. in *Heinrich von Kleist: Aufsätze und Essays.* Ed. Walter Müller-Seidel. Darmstadt: Wissenschaftliche Buchgesellschaft, 1967, 230. All subsequent references are to this reprint.

21. Emil Staiger, "Heinrich von Kleist, *Das Bettelweib von Locarno:* Zum Problem des dramatischen Stils." *Meisterwerke deutscher Sprache aus dem neunzehnten Jahrhundert.* Zurich: Atlantis, 1963, 103; rpt. in *Heinrich von Kleist.* Ed. Walter Müller-Seidel, 116. All subsequent references are to this edition.

22. Heinrich von Kleist, *Sämtliche Werke und Briefe.* Ed. Helmut Sembdner. 2nd. rev. ed. Munich: Hanser, 1961, II, 196. All subsequent references are to this edition.

23. *Erzählungen und kleine Prosa. Gesammelte Schriften.* Ed. Max Brod. New York: Schocken, 1946,I,53. All subsequent references are to this edition.

24. Staiger, *op. cit.,* 17.

25. This incident, which caused an extraordinary stir, frightened off a number of buyers to the marquis' extreme vexation; with the result that, as a rumor of a midnight ghost in the room spread, strangely and incomprehensibly, among his own servants, the marquis, in order to scotch it in a decisive manner, resolved to investigate the matter himself the following night.

26. There was otherwise no need to do so, for he saw his father constantly at business, they took their mid-day meal together at an eating-house, in the evening, it is true, each one did as he pleased, yet generally they then sat for a while in their common sitting room, each with his newspaper, unless George, as happened most often, went out with friends or more recently visited his bride.

27. In the foothills of the Alps, near Locarno in Northern Italy, there used to stand an old castle belonging to a marquis, which can now, when one comes from the St. Gotthard, be seen lying in ruins; a castle with high-ceilinged, spacious rooms, in one of which the mistress of the house one day, having taken pity on an old sick woman, who had turned up begging at the door, had allowed her to lie down on the floor on some straw which was spread under her.

28. The marquis, who, on his return from hunting, by chance entered the room, where he was used to keeping his gun, unwillingly ordered the woman to get up from the corner where she lay, and to remove herself to behind the stove.

29. *op. cit.,* 214.

30. *The Marquise of O— and Other Stories.* Trs. Martin Greenberg. New York: Ungar, 1960, 187.

31. The woman, as she arose, slipped with her crutch on the polished floor and sustained a dangerous injury to her back: with the result that she did manage to stand up with indescribable difficulty and to cross the room from one side to the

other, as had been prescribed to her, and then collapsed behind the stove amid moans and groans and passed away.

32. Blöcker, *op. cit.*, 20.

33. to this day his whitened bones, gathered together by the local people, lie in that corner of the room from which he had ordered the beggarwoman of Locarno to arise.

34. Dieter Hasselblatt, *Zauber und Logik. Eine Kafka-Studie.* Cologne: Verlag Wissenschaft und Politik, 1964, 80.

35. For these reasons one could not, supposing one wished to maintain the epistolary connection, impart any real news to him, such as might frankly be told to even the most distant acquaintance.

36. Translated by Willa and Edwin Muir as "all the same." Franz Kafka, *The Complete Stories.* Ed. Nahum M. Glatzer. New York: Schocken Books, 1971, 88.

37. The image comes from Kayser, *op. cit.*, 232.

38. Albert Camus, "L'espoir et l'absurde dans l'oeuvre de Kafka." In *Le Mythe de Sisyphe.* Paris: Gallimard, 1942, 171.

39. Stanley Corngold, *Franz Kafka: The Necessity of Form.* Ithaca and London: Cornell Univ. Press, 1988, 28.

Realism and its "Code of Accreditation"

1. *Prétexte: Roland Barthes.* Paris: Union générale d'éditions, 1978, 77 – 8, *sic.* Every narration is thus subject to this alternative: to set its rhetorical orientation by underlining that "this is only a story" (this one then having no other reality than to mediate between its source and its receivers . . .); or, on the other hand, to give itself the means (by verisimilitude, realism (prodecures of accreditation) to efface itself as narration.

2. Barthes, *op. cit.*, 84. In light of the problem of codes of accreditation realism ought to be reinterpreted, for, paradoxically, what is normally called realism is a literary genre that rejects the code of accreditation. In Balzac and in Flaubert there is no accreditation, and in a way that is what is realistic.

3. The concept of realism has undergone major revision in the past two decades. Older views tended to be formulaic and bipolar, centered on the opposition between such pairs as idealism and realism, subjectivity and objectivity, symbolism and referentiality. An amendment of this schema is attempted in Richard Brinkmann's *Wirklichkeit und Ilusion* (Tubingen: Niemeyer, 1957) in its distinction between outer realism with its aspiration to a slice of life and inner, psychological realism, which aims to capture the realities of the mind. The decisive im-

petus for a fundamental reassessment emanates from E. H. Gombrich's *Art and Illusion* (Princeton: Princeton Univ. Press, 1960) through its insistence that works of art are "not a faithful record of a visual experience but the faithful construction of a relational model" (90). Recent criticism has sought to analyze the means used to produce an alternative fictional world parallel to an external reality but only appearing to be dependent on it, while actually creating its own internal frame of reference. See *inter alia* J. Hillis Miller, "The Fiction of Realism: *Sketches by Boz, Oliver Twist*, and Cruickshank's Illustrations" in *Dickens Centennial Essays*. Ed. Ada Nisbet and Blake Nevius. Berkeley: Univ. of California Press, 1971, 85 – 153; J. P. Stern, *On Realism*. London and Boston: Routledge & Kegan Paul, 1973; *The Monster in the Mirror*. Ed. D. A. Williams. London: Oxford Univ. Press, 1978; and Elizabeth D. Ermarth, *Realism and Consensus in the English Novel*. Princeton: Princeton Univ. Press, 1983. The previous polarization has been replaced by a recognition of the coexistence of opposites, the dual allegiance to art and to life, the interplay between literal and figurative language, the metonymic and the metaphoric; in short, the inherent tensions between referentiality and textuality.

4. Honoré de Balzac, *La Comédie humaine*. Ed. Marcel Bouteron. Paris: Gallimard, 1956, II, 848. All subsequent references are to this edition.

5. Charles Dickens, *Our Mutual Friend*. New York: New American Library, 1980, 24.

6. George Eliot, *Adam Bede*. Edinburgh and London: William Blackwood & Sons, 1896, 171.

7. Emile Zola, "Le naturalisme au théâtre," *Le Roman expérimental*. Paris: Fasquelle, 1913, 111. Zola repeats the formula with the substitution of "création" for "nature" in *Mes Haines*. Paris: François Bernouard, 1928, 230.

8. In underscoring specificity as a distinguishing characteristic of the emergent realist novel, Ian Watt in *The Rise of the Novel* (1957; Berkeley: Univ. of California Press, 1974) contrasts "neo-classical generality and realist particularity" (17), and points out that "the characters of the novel can only be individualised if they are set in a background of a particularised time and place." (21)

9. Eliot, *Adam Bede*, 151.

10. Watt, *op. cit.*, 13.

11. Roland Barthes, "To Write: An Intransitive Verb?" in *The Language of Criticism and the Sciences of Man: The Structuralist Controversy*. Ed. Richard Macksey and Eugene Donato. Baltimore: The Johns Hopkins Univ. Press, 1970.

12. Roland Barthes, "L'effet de réel." *Communications* 11 (1968), 84–9. "The Reality Effect." Trs. R. Carter. In *French Literary Theory Today. A Reader*. Ed. Tzvetan Todorov. Cambridge and New York: Cambridge Univ. Press, 1982, 11 – 17.

13. Michel Butor, "Recherches sur la technique du roman." *Répertoire II.* Paris: Editions de minuit, 1964, 89.

14. Kendall L. Walton, "Appreciating Fictions: Suspending Disbelief or Pretending Belief?" *Dispositio* 5 (1983), 2.

15. Kendall L. Walton, "How Remote are Fictional Worlds from the Real World?" *Journal of Aesthetics and Art Criticism* 37 (1978), 20.

16. Walton, ibid., 13.

17. Kendall L. Walton, "Points of View in Narrative and Deceptive Representation." *Nous* 10 (1976), 49. Italics are Walton's.

18. The example is Walton's in "How Remote are Fictional Worlds from the Real World?" *loc. cit.*, 17.

19. Alexis Meinong, "The Theory of Objects." *Realism and the Background of Phenomenology.* Ed. Roderick Chisholm. Glencoe. IL.: The Free Press, 1960, 76 – 117. Originally published in *Untersuchungen zur Gegenstandstheorie und Psychologie.* Leipzig, 1904.

20. Cf. Peter Van Inwagen, "Creatures of Fiction." *American Philosophical Quarterly* 14 (1977), 305.

21. Baltimore and London: Johns Hopkins Univ. Press, 1973.

22. Walton, "How Remote are Fictional Worlds from the Real World?" *loc. cit.* 12.

23. Walton, "Appreciating Fictions: Suspending Disbelief or Pretending Belief ?" *loc. cit.*, 6–7.

24. *Prétexte: Roland Barthes*, 84.

25. See R. W. Chapman, "The Chronology of *Pride and Prejudice.*" *The Novels of Jane Austen.* Ed. R. W. Chapman. 3rd. ed. London: Oxford Univ. Press, 1933, II, 400–407.

26. Jane Austen, *Letters to Her Sister Cassandra and Others.* Ed. R. W. Chapman. London: Oxford Univ. Press, 1955, 132.

27. Gabriel Zoran, "Toward a Theory of Space in Narrative." *Poetics Today* 5:2 (1984) 309–310.

28. *The Role of Place in Literature.* Syracuse: Syracuse Univ. Press, 1985.

29. George Eliot, *Middlemarch.* Harmondsworth: Penguin, 1965, 65. All subsequent references are to this edition.

30. Eliot, *Middlemarch*, 47.

31. Eliot, *Middlemarch*, 51.

32. See Benjamin Harshav (Hrushovski), "Fictionality and Fields of Reference." *Poetics Today* 5:2 (1984), 227–51.

33. The connection between "the levels of reality in literature" and the need to distinguish between the author and the narrator is cogently argued by Italo Calvino in "I livelli della realtà." *Una pietra sopra.* Torino: Einaudi, 1980, 310–23.

34. Elizabeth Gaskell, *Mary Barton.* London: Dent (1911), 1971, 13.

35. Balzac, *op. cit.,* II, 53.

36. Balzac, *op. cit.,* III, 1029.

37. Balzac, *op. cit.,* III, 1127. In certain towns in the provinces there are houses whose aspect gives rise to a sense of melancholy equal to that inspired by the gloomiest cloisters, the most forlorn heaths, or the most desolated ruins.

38. Balzac, *op. cit.,* III, 1044.

39. Balzac, *op. cit.,* III, 1198.

40. Balzac, *op. cit.,* III, 1198.

41. Balzac, *op. cit.,* III, 1035 and 1044.

42. Walter J. Ong, S.J. argues for the implicit supposition that "The Writer's Audience Is Always A Fiction" (*PMLA* 90 [1975], 9–21) by pointing to the "unpublished directives for readers" (12) in the opening passage of Hemingway's *A Farewell to Arms.* See also Jane S. Smith, "The Reader as Part of the Fiction: *Middlemarch.*" *Texas Studies in Literature and Language* 19 (1977), 188–233.

43. For further documentation and development of this hypothesis see "Rereading *Buddenbrooks.*"

44. Robyn R. Warhol in "Toward a Theory of the Engaging Narrator" (*PMLA* 101 [1986], 81–88) draws a useful distinction between 'distancing' and 'engaging' narrators. The latter, whom she finds mainly in women writers, engage a reader response of recognition and identification by "earnest interventions" which encourage readers to see the ways in which the fictions "accurately mirror and concretely affect the real world" (817). Her argument is tendentious both in its focus on gender differentiation since male novelists use the same technique, and in its acceptance of the novel as a mirror. However, the concept of the 'engaging' narrator is an important one, especially in relation to realist narration.

The Game of the Name

1. An earlier brief version of this paper was presented at the meeting of the International Comparative Literature Association in Munich in August 1988.

2. "Place in Fiction." *South Atlantic Quarterly* 55 (January 1956) 59.

3. Henry James, *The Art of Fiction*. New York: Scribner's 1934, 8.

4. Welty, *op. cit.*, 60. Italics are hers.

5. *The Rise of the Novel*. Berkeley and London: Univ. of California Press, 1957, 17–18.

6. Welty, *op. cit.*, 62.

7. M. M. Bakhtin, *The Dialogic Imagination*. Trs. Caryl Emerson and Michael Holquist. Austin: Univ. of Texas Press, 1981, 84.

8. *Communications* 11 (1968) 84–89. Trs. R. Carter, "The Reality Effect." In *French Literary Theory Today*. Ed. Tzvetan Todorov. New York: Cambridge Univ. Press, 1982, 11–18.

9. Philippe Hamon, *Introduction à l'analyse du descriptif*. Paris: Hachette, 1981, 53.

10. *The Art of the Novel*, 35.

11. Welty, *op. cit.*, 59.

12. Alexander Gelley, "Setting and a Sense of World in the Novel." *Yale Review* 62 (Winter 1973) 193.

13. George E. Downing, "A Famous Boarding-House." In *Studies in Balzac's Realism*. Ed. Preston Dargan and W. L. Crain. Chicago: Univ. of Chicago Press, 1932, 141.

14 "Un discours contraint." *Poétique* 16 (1973) 426. Italics are Hamon's.

15. Hamon, ibid., 426.

16. Cf. Elizabeth Deeds Ermarth, *Realism and Consensus in the English Novel*. Princeton, N.J.: Princeton Univ. Press, 1983.

17. Gustave Flaubert, *Madame Bovary*. Ed. Edouard Maynial. Paris: Garnier, 1947. All subsequent references are to this edition.

18. "Explaining Literary Phenomena," *Text Production*. New York: Columbia Univ. Press, 1983, 23–24.

19. Ibid., 24.

20. Ibid., 25. Italics are Riffaterre's.

21. Ibid., 22.

22. Benjamin Harshav (Hrushovski), "Fictionality and Fields of Reference." *Poetics Today* 5:2 (1984) 243.

23. Cf. E. H. Gombrich, *Art and Illusion*. Princeton, N.J.: Princeton Univ. Press, 1982, 221.

24. Inge Crosman Wimmers, *Poetics of Reading: Approaches to the Novel.* Princeton, N.J.: Princeton Univ. Press, 1988, 80–81.

25. *Quarry for "Middlemarch."* Ed. Anna Theresa Kitchel. Berkeley and Los Angeles: Univ. of California Press, and London: Cambridge Univ. Press, 1950.

26. John Livingston Lowes, *The Road to Xanadu.* Boston and New York: Houghton Mifflin, 1927, 360ff.

27. "The Logical Status of Fictional Discourse." *New Literary History* 6 (1975) 332.

28. *On the Margins of Discourse.* Chicago: The University of Chicago Press, 1978, 72.

29. "Poetry." In *The Complete Poems.* New York: Macmillan/Viking, 1981 (1967) 267.

30. "Realism, or, In Praise of Lying: Some Nineteenth Century Novels." *College English* 31 (1970) 355–365.

31. *Metahistory.* Baltimore and London: The Johns Hopkins Univ. Press, 1973.

Not So Long Ago: Historical Allusion in Realist Fiction

1. M. M. Bakhtin, *The Dialogic Imagination.* Trs. Caryl Emerson and Michael Holquist. Austin, TX.: Univ. of Texas Press, 1981, 84.

2. Eudora Welty, "Place in Fiction." *South Atlantic Quarterly* 55 (1956) 58.

3. Welty, *op. cit.,* 58; italics are hers.

4. Honoré de Balzac, *La Comédie humaine.* Ed. Marcel Bouteron. Paris: Gallimard, 1956, II, 848.

5. George Eliot, *Daniel Deronda.* Harmondsworth: Penguin, 1967, 121.

6. Eliot, *Daniel Deronda,* 121.

7. Eliot, *Daniel Deronda,* 121–22.

8. Eliot, *Daniel Deronda,* 159–60.

9. Hardy in Eliot, *Daniel Deronda,* 22.

10. George Eliot, *Adam Bede.* New York: Dutton, 1966, 171.

11. Honoré de Balzac, *Illusions perdues.* Paris: Garnier Flammarion, 1966, 58.

12. Käthe Hamburger, *The Logic of Literature*. Trs. Marilyn J. Rese. Bloomington: Indiana Univ. Press, 1973, 110–111.

13. Hamburger, *op. cit.*, 96.

14. Philippe Hamon, *Introduction à l'analyse du descriptif.* Paris: Hachette, 1981, 66.

15. See note 2 of "Paris Change!: Perception and Narration," and note 6 of "Rereading *Buddenbrooks.*" Also, Haskell M. Block, *Naturalistic Triptych: The Real and the Fictive in Zola, Mann, and Dreiser.* New York: Random House, 1970.

16. Honoré de Balzac, "Avant propos" to *La Comédie humaine.* I, 7. "La Société française allait être l'historien, je ne devais être que le secrétaire."

17. See Robert Weimann, "History, Appropriation, and the Uses of Representation in Modern Narrative." In *The Aims of Representation: Subject/Text/History.* Ed. Murray Krieger. New York: Columbia Univ. Press, 1987, 181–5.

18. Roland Barthes, "L'effet de réel." *Communications* 11 (1968) 84–9. "The Reality Effect" in *French Literary Theory Today. A Reader.* Ed. Tzvetan Todorov. Trs. R. Carter. Cambridge and New York: Cambridge Univ. Press, 1982, 11–17.

19. See Michel Butor, "Philosophie d'ameublement." *Répertoire II. Etudes et conférences 1959–63.* Paris: Editions de minuit, 1964, 54.

20. Eliot, *Middlemarch,* 177.

21. *Quarry for "Middlemarch."* Ed. Anna Theresa Kitchel. Berkeley: Univ. of California Press and London: Cambridge Univ. Press, 1938.

22. Eliot, *Middlemarch,* 25.

23. Jerome Beaty, "History by Indirection: The Era of Reform in *Middlemarch.*" *Victorian Studies* 1 (1957–8), 173–9. Reprinted in *Middlemarch.* Ed. Bert G. Hornback. New York: Norton, 1977, 700–706.

24. Eliot, *Middlemarch,* 39.

25. Eliot, *Middlemarch,* 31.

26. Henry James, *The Bostonians.* New York: New American Library, 1980.

27. James, *The Bostonians,* 198.

28. Inge Crosman Wimmers, *Poetics of Reading. Approaches to the Novel.* Princeton, N.J.: Princeton Univ. Press, 1988, 33–4.

29. Clayton T. Koelb, *Inventions of Reading. Rhetoric and the Literary Imagination.* Ithaca and London: Cornell Univ. Press, 1988, xi.

30. E. M. Forster, *Aspects of the Novel.* New York: Harcourt, Brace & World, 1927, 6.

31. Hayden White, *Metahistory*. Baltimore and London: The Johns Hopkins Univ. Press, 1973, 3, footnote.

32. See Suzanne Gearhart, *The Open Boundary. A Critical Approach to the French Enlightenment*. Princeton, N.J.: Princeton Univ. Press, 1984.

33. Henry James, "The Art of Fiction." In *The Portable Henry James*. Ed. M. D. Zabel. New York: Vintage, 1968, 399.

Rereading *Buddenbrooks*

1. "Lübeck als geistige Lebensform." *Gesammelte Werke*. Frankfurt: Fischer, 1974, XI, 383. All subsequent references are to this edition, abbreviated to *GW.*

2. "Zu einem Kapitel aus *Buddenbrooks.*" *GW* XI, 554.

3. "Lübeck als geistige Lebensform." *GW* XI, 383.

4. Henry Hatfield, *Thomas Mann*. London: Peter Owen, 1952, 34–5.

5. Cf. T. J. Reed, *Thomas Mann: The Uses of Tradition*. Oxford: Clarendon Press, 1974, 38–40; and Haskell M. Block, *Naturalistic Triptych: The Real and the Fictive in Zola, Mann, and Dreiser.* New York: Random House, 1970, 32–53.

6. Cf. Section "Lübeck" in *Die Literatur über Thomas Mann: Eine Bibliographie 1891–1968*. Ed. Harry Matter. Berlin: Aufbau, 1972, 338–44; and *Buddenbrooks-Handbuch*. Ed. Ken Moulden and Gero von Wilpert. Stuttgart: Alfred Körner, 1988, 11–40.

7. *GW,* XI, 554.

8. Hugh Ridley, *Mann: Buddenbrooks*. Cambridge: Cambridge Univ. Press, 1987, 24.

9. Reed, *op. cit.*, 51.

10. George Lukács, "Auf der Suche nach dem Bürger," *Thomas Mann*. Berlin: Aufbau, 1949, 9–48.

11. Pierre-Paul Sagave, "Zur Geschichtlichkeit von Thomas Manns Jugendroman: Bürgerliches Klassenbewußtsein und kapitalistische Praxis in *Buddenbrooks*" in *Literaturwissenschaft und Geschichtsphilosophie. Festschrift für Wilhelm Emrich*. Berlin: 1975, 436–52.

12. Reed, *op. cit.*, 38.

13. *GW* XII, 89. See also my essay "Thomas Mann's *Buddenbrooks:* 'the first and only naturalist novel in Germany'?" in *The European Naturalist Novel.* Ed. Brian Nelson. Berg European Studies series, 1991.

14. See Reed, *op. cit.*, 37; Ridley, *op. cit.*, 84; Martin Swales, *Thomas Mann: A Study*. Totowa, N.J.: Rowman & Littlefield, 1980, 17.

15. See J. M. Ritchie, "The Ambivalence of 'Realism' in German Literature 1830–1880," *Orbis Litterarum* 15, 1961, 200–217.

16. Honoré de Balzac, *La Comédie humaine*. Ed. Marcel Bouteron. Paris; Gallimard, 1956, II, 848.

17. Ridley, *op. cit.*, 23.

18. Block, *op. ict.*, 37.

19. *GW* X, 10.

20. *GW* X, 11.

21. "Als ich *Buddenbrooks* zu schreiben begann, saß ich in Rom, Via Torre Argentino, trenta quattro, drei Stiegen hoch. Meine Vaterstadt hatte nicht viel Realität für mich." (*GW* X, 15. "When I began to write *Buddenbrooks*, I was in Rome, three floors up at 34 Via Torre Argentino. My home city did not have much reality for me.")

22. *GW* IX, 379.

23. *GW* X, 22.

24. *GW* X, 15. Animation ... that's it, the beautiful word. It is not the gift of invention, but that of animation that makes the poet. And whether it fills a traditional tale or a piece of live reality with its breath and being, animation, the penetration and filling of the material with what is the poet's, turns that material into his possession, which may, according to his conviction, be touched by no one. That this can and must lead to conflicts with respectable reality, which has a high opinion of itself and wishes in no way to be compromised by animation — that is obvious. But reality overestimates the degree to which it remains reality at all to the poet who has appropriated it — particularly if time and space separate him from it.

25. *GW* X, 21.

26. *GW* X, 17–18.

27. *GW* X, 15–16. What did the real Lübeck of today have to do with the work I had created in three years' work? Nonsense ... If I have made a sentence out of something — what does the thing still have to do with the sentence?

28. M. M. Bakhtin, *The Dialogic Imagination*. Trs. Caryl Emerson and Michael Holquist. Austin, TX: Univ. of Texas Press, 1981, 84.

29. For a fine overview of the historical situation see Ridley, *op. cit.*, 10–19.

30. *Buddenbrooks*, *GW* I, 178. All subsequent references are to this edition.

31. Henry James, "The Art of Fiction." In *The Portable Henry James*. Ed. M. D. Zabel. New York: Viking, 1968, 399.

32. Jochen Vogt, *Thomas Mann: "Buddenbrooks."* Munich: Fink, 1983, 17.

33. *GW* XI, 390.

34. Cf. Benjamin Harshav (Hrushovski), "Fictionality and Fields of Reference." *Poetics Today* 5:2 (1984) 227–51.

35. Klaus-Detlef Müller, "Realismus als Provokation" in *Bürgerlicher Realismus*. Ed. Klaus-Detlef Müller. Königstein/Ts., 20.

36. Cf. Reed, *op. cit.*, 56; Ridley, *op. cit.*, 32; Swales, *op. cit.*, 35.

37. H. Meili Steele, *Realism and the Drama of Reference.* University Park and London: Penn State Univ. Press, 1988, 88.

38. Robyn R. Warhol, "Toward A Theory of the Engaging Narrator." *PMLA* 101,5 (1986), 811–818.

39. There is no satisfactory equivalent in English for the impersonal construction of the German *man* or the French *on*. Translators would normally opt for *they*, but that misses the openness to include *us*, the readers, implied in the German. In order to capture the effect, I have decided on a literal rendering.

40. *GW* XI, 379.

41. As late as 1947 Mann maintained that: "Der junge Verfasser von *Buddenbrooks* hatte die Psychologie des Verfalls von Nietzsche gelernt" (*GW*, XI, 556; "The young author of *Buddenbrooks* had learned the psychology of decadence from Nietzsche"). He dwelt repeatedly on the directly formative effect of Wagner, comparing the expansion of *Buddenbrooks* from a short story about Hanno into a long novel to the development of Wagner's conception of *Siegfrieds Tod* into the "leitmotivistisch-durchwobene Tetralogie" ("leitmotivistically interwoven tetralogy") of the *Ring* cycle (*GW*, XI, 381). He identifies the musical component of *Buddenbrooks* as an essentially Germanic quality, and singles out the leitmotif as *"das Wagnerische" ("the Wagnerian")* in a letter of 26 November 1901 to Otto Grautoff (*Briefe an Otto Grautoff 1894 – 1901 and Ida Boy-Ed 1903 – 1928.* Ed. Peter de Mendelssohn. Frankfurt: Fischer, 1975, 140; italics are Mann's).

42. He did not read *Die Welt als Wille und Vorstellung* until rather an advanced stage in the composition of *Buddenbrooks*, probably autumn 1899. This fact undermines Erich Heller's contention (in *The Ironic German*. London: Secker & Warburg, 1958, 27–67) that the entire intellectual plot of the novel derives from Schopenhauer, and represents a brilliant exegetic commentary on a canonical text. A more judicious assessment is presented by Reed (*op. cit.*, 80–84), and a wholly adversarial one by Helmut Koopmann ("Thomas Mann und Schopenhauer," in *Thomas Mann und die Tradition*. Ed. Peter Pütz, Frankfurt: Athenäum, 1971, 180–200), who sees no evidence of great enthusiasm for Schopenhauer on Mann's part at any time.

43. *GW* XI, 111.

Index